The Charmed Garden
by
Diane Morgan

First published by Findhorn Press 2004

ISBN 1 84409 034 5

British Library Cataloguing-in-Publication Data.
A catalogue record for this book is available from
the British Library.

Edited by Lynn Barton
Cover by Thierry Bogliolo
Internal design by Karin Bogliolo
Cover photograph by Digital Vision

Printed and bound by WS Bookwell, Finland

Published by
Findhorn Press
305a The Park, Findhorn
Forres IV36 3TE
Scotland, UK
tel 01309 690582
fax 01309 690036
e-mail: info@findhornpress.com
www.findhornpress.com

Table of Contents

The Garden as a Magical Place

"In nature's infinite book of secrecy
A little I can read."
—*Shakespeare, Julius Caesar*

In the beginning was the garden. It is the archetype of our desire, the source of delight, the abode of beauty, and the place of power. It is also, as we all know, the seat of temptation. The garden is embedded deep in our cultural psyche. In Greek myth, Hercules wrested Hera's golden apples from the walled Garden of the Hesperides at the ends of the earth. The nymph Calypso used her magical garden and its secret herbs to keep Odysseus and his crew in thrall for a year. The agony of Christ began in the Garden of Gethsemane. In alchemy, the garden represents the secret spiritual domain that can be attained only through great struggle and enormous sacrifice. In the ancient Chinese tradition, every stone, plant, and leaf of the garden is a manifestation of divinity. And out of all spots in creation, it was in a garden that the God of the Bible chose to walk in the cool of the evening.

What is more mysterious than the secret curled within a seed? What more magical than the slow unfolding of a rose? The garden holds the key to many secrets – even the secrets of life and death. Plants contain not only powerful healing attributes, but also some of the most deadly toxins known. Very often, these two properties co-exist within the same plant.

And while flowers are undeniably associated with the feminine aspect of nature, it would not be wise to confuse the potent magic of the plant kingdom with a frilly, pseudo-femininity that existed only in the pop culture of the 1950s. The true feminine power of plants is more akin to the ancient Mother Goddesses, the divine aspects of sexuality, and the fierce, terrible beauty of Indian deities such as Durga.

Plants have an elemental wisdom unknown to the kingdom of animals. From sun and earth and air and water, from these simple things, rise towering oaks and delicate violets, deadly nightshade and healthful herbs. They do not need to draw blood or kill each other for sustenance. (And although there are a few parasitic plants, most dwell peaceably together.) They use their lethal powers, usually against predatory insects or herbivores, only in self-defense. And more. The power of earth, the fire of sun, the spirit of air, and the lifeblood of water are the bones, flesh, breath, and blood of the mystic, the poet, the philosopher, and the scientist and the true sources of all magic.

All gardens are magical places. They occupy the threshold realm between the wild and the civilized, between human beings and nature. Their ambiguous character, half wilderness, half paradise, fills them with mystery.

The Renaissance magician and philosopher Paracelsus taught us that magic reveals the true nature of the inner person, as well as the organization of his outward body. "What is below is like that which is above, and what is above is like that below." It was Paracelsus who developed the Doctrine of Signatures, which maintains that the physical aspects of a plant gives clues to its healing or magical properties. "Nature," said Emerson, "always wears the colors of the spirit."

Magic teaches the knowledge of the visible and the invisible. Science sees objectivity in nature, a disjunction between the world and the spirit (insofar as the scientist acknowledges the spirit at all). Magic knows the resonance between them. This wisdom is as true of the garden as it is of the human person. Those who delve (a word drawn from gardening) into magic and healing stand in awe of even the narrowest plot of earth, the smallest seed. They know they are looking into the heart of mystery. The same spell that binds the universe and tilts the earth controls the breaking of a bud, the dropping of a leaf. The gardener is one who participates in this sacred cycle of birth, growth, change, death, and rebirth. Into her hands the riddle of life whispers its secrets. As Emerson wrote in his journal, "See how carefully she covers up the skeleton. The eye shall not see it, the sun shall not shine on it, she weaves muscle and tendon and flesh and skin and down and hair and beautiful colors of day over it, forces death down under ground, and makes haste to cover it with leaves and vines and wipes carefully out every trace by new creation."

Concerning Magic

Although this is not a book on magic per se, I'd like to consider briefly what magic is. In the first place, magic has nothing to do with rabbits and hats. It is the very opposite of show business, for the best magic takes place in secret. It is a holy enterprise that honors life and beauty. The greatest magic-makers, the most ardent gardeners, are also shamans, persons who are spiritually connected to the Otherworld that permeates our own. "Heaven and earth and I are of the same root," wrote Zen Master Sojo (384–414). "The ten thousand things and I are of one substance."

Does magic "work"? No – not if you mean "work" to replace the hard work of responsible living and caring and striving. But if you mean by "work" a way to open up to us a spiritual dimension, to reveal the connection between the things we see and the things we can't, it is the only thing that does works.

Because this book is devoted to botanical magic in its spiritual aspect, I do not give out recipes for medical use, dyes, brewing, cookery, or potions, although I mention that specific plants have such uses. Unless you are a trained herbalist, it is dangerous to use plants for self-medication or to treat others. (And cooking is not my forte!) Many of the flowers and herbs listed here can be dangerous, even deadly, if ingested. It is because of their power that they need to be handled carefully.

Magic is a complex art that depends as much on methods as on materials. This book can touch only on the surface of these deeper matters. The art of magical incantation and spells is a specialty in itself. I urge readers to study the magical arts of spells and incantations from a qualified mentor. The power of a spell does not emanate from the syllables that compose it, though it is shaped by them – the power comes from the mind and spirit of the practitioner. This power must be honed, protected, and purified for any spell to rise above gibberish and reach the level of magic.

So what is a herb? At one time, the word referred to any grassy or leafy plant. Over time, however, the meaning has adjusted. Today an herb is considered to be any plant with culinary, medicinal or magical qualities. This expands the traditional definition of herbs far beyond rosemary and thyme: it includes many trees and even some "ornamentals".

The Three "P's" of Herbal Magic

Three interrelated elements inform all ritually correct herbal magic. I call them the three "P's":

Purpose: Good magic requires pure purpose. Magic done with an ill intention falls back threefold on the maker. To insure your purpose is good requires a careful examination of your own nature and mind. This is a spiritual principle.

Plant: Each plant has its own set of magical properties. Choosing the wrong plant for magical rites, while probably not dangerous, is a waste of time. This principle requires a deep commitment to learning the ways of plants, both natural and magical. This is an intellectual principle.

Preparation: Preparation refers to both the plant and the gardener. Not only must the soil and the plants themselves be carefully prepared, but so must the gardener. The "when" "where" and "how" of planting is a physical principle.

Preparation, of course, is also an essential part of successful spell-casting. For example, those doing love spells are well advised to dress all in white linen, or white with purple vestments, to loosen their hair and to make sure there are no knots of any kind in the hair or clothing. All workers in magic must be scrupulously and ritually clean at the time of making magic. A ritual bath and proper anointing with oil must be done. Certain foods, especially fish, must be avoided. Most important, the magic-maker must have faith in the efficacy of the rites

Universal Principles

In addition, there are a few universal principles of magic.

Things are not as they appear.
Everything is capable of transformation.
Magical operations necessarily transform their practitioner.
Magical rites express secrets from our collective past.
Magical rites, by focusing attention, can help change the future.

Magic is not a mechanical operation. "Add 4 grams of X and 3 liters of Y, boil for 12 minutes" are directions for cooks and chemists. Magicians must take into account intangibles like intention, care, love, and hope. They must have faith, not just expectations. The physicist Heisenberg taught us that observing particles changes them. Magicians know that performing magic changes the magician. Whether the change is for good or ill depends upon the magic used and the purpose for which it is employed.

Magical Ceremonies

Most magical rites fall under one of the following headings:

> **Purifications, Consecrations, and Blessings**
> **Banishments and Exorcisms**
> **Protection**
> **Divination**
> **Wish-Magic, including rites for love, fertility, health,**
> **prosperity, success, or victory.**

These categories are pretty much self-explanatory, but the performance of them is not. Success in magical undertakings depends upon following the principles previously outlined. But it also depends upon a body of knowledge, some widely available in various books on Wicca and similar subjects, some obtained from working with a mentor, some based on personal experience or revelation. Effective magic is a delicate balancing act between tradition and personal experience. The creative practitioner learns when to adhere to a long-established magical heritage and when to add, alter, omit, or create anew. And, since you live in these times there are many, many choices for you to make. Unlike your ancestors, you are not bound to live your life in one tradition only. Celtic, Neo-Pagan, Norse, Teutonic, Eastern, Native American, and many other traditions have a rich treasure of rites and wisdom. They don't come easily, and each is a long path. Read deeply, explore, and then make your choice – or, as many people do, select from each what seems appropriate for you. That's why this book is merely a guide, a hint at fabulous possibilities that only you can attain. and it's the same when working with the plants themselves. Each plant has its own set of growing conditions, its own response to light and earth and wind and water. But plants too are adaptable. With your creative care and with study and experience, you can grow a wider variety of herbs than you may have ever imagined.

Sorcery and Exorcism

I have not included in this book so-called "black magic", as it is a contradiction in terms and a logical impossibility. Magic aimed at harming others is not magic but sorcery. To my mind sorcery is a product of an evil imagination, to give it space helps realize its evil ends. Exorcisms are particularly difficult. It is no accident that the Church restricts the performance of exorcisms to highly qualified people and only permits them when all possible medical and psychological conditions have been ruled out. *Never* attempt an exorcism alone; they can be extremely dangerous not only to the patient but to the practitioner. *Never* attempt an exorcism without informed permission of the patient or those responsible for his care. *Never* do anything that might conceivably cause the patient physical or psychological harm.

Magic is spiritual, not physical. I have read of spells designed to make physical changes in things – for example, a set of magical chants to get rid of groundhogs and moles. Magic may banish ghosts; moles, groundhogs and rabbits are a different matter. While there is certainly no harm in trying such things, it is unlikely, at least in my experience, that they will succeed. The magical doctrine of correspondences teaches us that, for spiritual trouble, seek a spiritual solution. For physical problems, find a physical cure. And while it's true that many problems in the material world have their roots in spiritual malaise, rabbit invasion isn't one of them. If you look at things from the cosmic point of view, you will see at once that rabbits, whose right to existence is as divinely granted as your own, may view your garden as the divine feast. As you become more and more attuned to the ways of earth, you may discover that the unending challenge of thwarting rabbits, groundhogs, and moles without hurting them, while keeping your own sense of humor and balance, requires every bit of your magical abilities. That's half the fun.

Evil Spirits

Frequently in this book we mention "evil spirits." While this is a term that most people today understand in a symbolic way, it wasn't always so.

It should go without saying that any pact, either literal or figurative, with such spirits leads to no good end. They are corruptive in this life and destructive of the world to come. This is true whether the demons are in the Otherworld or in your heart.

Fairies and Elves

Fairies are a much-misunderstood class of beings. Most people think of these "little folk" as rather frivolous pink or green sprites, imaginary beings who spend their days singing and dancing in the woods and playing tricks on people. The truth is darker. Fairies are what remain of the great gods and goddesses, who have fled to the dimmest forests and outskirts of civilization until they are called again into full being by those who need them.

Elves don't frequent gardens as frequently as fairies, but they can be drawn by a few plants – notably elms. If anything, elves are more dangerous than fairies. Elves are generally divided into two camps, the Light Elves, who tend to be beneficent and the Dark Elves, who aren't. Light elves are shape-shifting, insubstantial creatures. They are very seldom seen. You're more likely to encounter Dark Elves, perhaps even in your cellar or attic. The most common variety of elf, however, is Dusky Elf, who partakes of the attributes of both. Some people claim that elves and fairies are practically indistinguishable. I leave that for you to decide. But I wouldn't turn my back on any of them for long.

Botanical and Magical Information for the New Magical Gardener

Plant Names and Classification

Because we don't live as close to the earth as we once did, some of the terminology and basic facts about plants can be a little baffling. However it's important for all gardeners to become acquainted with the basic language of plants and their keepers (that's us!)

One of the most stubborn and knotty problems in gardening concerns names. The wise gardener should never buy plants based on the common name alone, since many different plants may go by the same common name. For example, in the US the name Rose of Sharon refers to a *hibiscus*, but in the UK it refers to a member of the *hypericum* family. The *hibiscus* and the *hypericum* are two totally unrelated plants. There are also two kinds of hemlock, one a stately evergreen and the other the deadly herb used to kill Socrates. Conversely, one plant may have several common names. Bachelor's button is also known as the cornflower. The bay laurel is sometimes called a bay tree and sometimes a laurel. (In culinary usage the term "bay" is always used.)

On the other hand, the scientific, botanical name for each species is unique and permanent. (At least sort of. Every once in a while, somebody decides that "mistakes were made" and there's a change, which no one likes. The most awful examples were when Brontosaurus became Apaosaurus and the Baltimore oriole became the Eastern oriole. Everyone was furious.)

The scientific name is also important because it gives the gardener an idea about which family the plant belongs to. Experienced gardeners quickly grow used to using scientific names, and ultimately find it quite easy. We still employ the naming system devised by the Swedish botanist Carl Linnaeus in the eighteenth century. In his binomial system, the scientific name for each plant contains two words.

The first word is the *genus* name and begins with a capital letter. The second word is the *species* name. There may sometimes follow the name of a subspecies, geographical subtype, variety, form, or cultivar. (The differences between *form, cultivar, variety, subtype,* and *subspecies* are pretty technical and need not concern us here.) Many of our common garden species are cultivars descended from a wild plant, but selected for beauty, habit, or long bloom. The genus includes all the species of a certain type of plant; the plural of the word is genera (that's Latin for you) and several *genera* are grouped together in a *family*.

Family names usually end is *-aceae*, so the family *Rosaceae* includes all member of the rose family and *Liliaceae* includes all members of the lily family. Of course, when you run into something like *Campanulaceae*, you may have to guess. When the family name is not part of the common name of the plant, you usually have to look it up in a garden book.

In magical work, as opposed to herbology, it is not always necessary to possess precisely the same species or cultivar mentioned in the text you are working with. Plants of the same group or *genus* often have similar magical properties. Even in cases where a cultivar may not possess the same pharmacological properties as the original (wild) plant, the magical qualities remain. That's why it's magic.

Plants are broadly divided into vascular and nonvascular types. The vascular plants comprise most of our well-known garden plants. They grow in more variety and become much larger than the nonvascular plants, which include such humble plants as algae, lichens, and moss.

Plants are also classified as annuals, biennials, and perennials. Annual plants germinate, flower, produce seeds, and die, all in one season. Biennials germinate during the first season, then flower, produce seeds, and die during the second season. Perennials live for an indefinite period; some last for decades – and peonies will probably outlive you! Perennials tend to be slower growing than the others. The advantage of annuals is that they have a very long bloom season – usually all summer.

The Magical Frame of Mind

While magical gardeners do many of the same things that ordinary gardeners do, they do them with a different purpose. To this end, always approach your garden in a magical frame of mind. Most of the time, you should be alone, unless you have a partner in magic who is sympathetic to your aims. Wear your most comfortable gardening clothes. Carrying a talisman or amulet of the herbs you are working with helps to empower the herb's growth. You should be silent while gardening, except when talking, singing, and enchanting your plants. When working an enchantment use all the powers available to you. Learn the songs and spells of your magical tradition. Always remember: You must enchant your garden before it can enchant you!

Your Plants and the Four Ancient Elements of Earth, Water, Fire, and Air

Climate Zones (Air Element)

In Section V, the Encyclopedia of Magical Plants, I sometimes refer to climate zone, which indicates the plant's cold (and in some cases heat) hardiness. In the United States, climate zones are numbered from 1 (most northerly) to 10 (most southerly). The British climate corresponds primarily to zone 8, but areas around the coast of the UK are in the equivalent of zone 9, and the Highlands of Scotland are in the equivalent of zone 7. The most important factor for both US and UK gardeners, however, is to ascertain when the first and last frost occurs in your area; that's what makes the most difference. In the United States, the zones are determined by the average number of frost-free days per year and the minimum winter temperature. The zone you live in can give you a ballpark figure about what plants you can and cannot grow. However, the proximity you live to the edge of a zone, the altitude of the garden (and which way it faces) can all make a big difference in what your true climate zone is.

The climate affects the quality of the soil too. Cold wet climates tend to produce a lot of decayed, enriching material into the soil. In hot, dry climates, however, the material is leached out of the soil faster than it can be replaced. This is why, contrary to what you might expect, many tropical regions have very poor soil: every available nutrient is taken up by the forest. Altitude makes a huge difference as well, with mountainous regions often a full zone or more colder than their valley neighbors.

Air considerations also include exposure to wind, extreme heat, and frost. Gardens subject to strong prevailing winds are the most challenging, although you can erect windbreaks of evergreen shrubs or trees that may help. The best windbreaks are *not* solid fences, by the way; such barriers can create a really damaging airflow pattern. Figuring out the prevailing wind pattern can be tricky, as it is apt to be different in the summer than in the winter. For magical purposes, plants should be harvested when no winds are blowing, if possible. But the magician can make good use of winds when working her magic. If the magic is to be sent afar, perform it when the wind in blowing in the correct direction. Remember that a North Wind comes from the north and so blows south, and so on.

Everyone knows the Four Winds; what is less well known is that in western magical tradition you can be more specific. You have not only Subsolanus (Due East Wind), but also Eurus (Southeast Wind) and Caecias (Northeast Wind); Boaeas (Due West), Corus (Northwest), and Aquilo (Northeast); Auster (Due South), Notus (Southeast), and Affricus (Southwest); Favonius (Due West), Zephyus (Southwest), and Circius (Northwest). Knowing and invoking the winds by name is a powerful aid to magic.

Climate not only controls where plants can or cannot naturally grow, it also affects blooming times. The blooming times listed for the plants in this book are approximate and may vary from climate zone to climate zone. Blooming time is also strongly affected by the number of sunlight hours available to the plant. If you aren't sure of when the daffodils generally bloom in your area, ask an experienced local gardener or nursery-person.

It may seem odd, but air also belongs in the soil. A solid, packed, airless soil gives no breathing room to plants. Keep your garden soil turned and loose by regular hoeing!

Light Requirements (Fire Element)

Most plants thrive best under full sunlight (fire element), some prefer partial shade, while a few need deep shade (a full canopy of leaves above them). Morning and evening light have different qualities, as do spring and autumn light. In **Section III Designing the Charmed Garden**, I'll suggest how you can create the right light environment for your plants by judicious pruning and siting your plants to make the most (or least) of what you have. However, you can make everything easy on yourself by selecting the most suitable plants in the first place. The plant encyclopedia in this book will help guide your decision. Luckily, the same magic can often be found in plants with differing light reqirements.

Soil Quality and Type (Earth Element)

Soil is, of course, the basis of the garden, and the single most important thing you can do as a gardener is to prepare the soil well for planting. There's a quick test to tell how good your soil is: take a look at it. Rich soils are lush with vegetation. Poor soils are comparatively barren. While poor soils can be amended, the basic type of your soil needs to be carefully assessed. And soils can pretty much be categorized first as acid or alkaline, and second as sandy, loamy, silty, or clayey. Clay soil is heavy and sticky when wet, and hard as rock when dry. Sandy soil warms up a lot faster in the spring, making it ideal for those early fruits like strawberries. Silty soil is a very fine soil (with particles usually less than $^1/_{20}$ of a millimeter in diameter); it can be improved with the addition of organic matter, or even perhaps a bit of sand.

The pH, or acid/alkaline scale goes from 0 to 14. Soil below 7 is regarded as acid and soil above 7 as alkaline. Seven itself is neutral. As a general rule cold, hilly, damp regions are more acid while warm, flat dry areas are more alkaline. And most acidic soil is sandy. Alkaline soil tends to be more clayey, chalky, or rocky. One easy way to decide what your soil is like is to check the kinds of plants that grow naturally around your property. A good wildflower book will identify your weeds and indicate the type of soil they prefer to grow on. If you want to go more high-tech, you can buy a soil test kit or contact a commercial soil testing service. Most garden plants like a soil somewhere between 4.5 and 8.5. To make soil more acid, add sand, leaf mold, gypsum, and pine needles. To make it more alkaline, add, wood ash, eggshells, dolomite, bonemeal, or limestone.

Most plants prefer a slightly acid, porous, crumbly soil that is obtained by a pretty equal mix of sand, clay, and organic matter. This type of soil is called *loam*, and as rule makes the best kind of soil for a garden. Soil that is heavily compacted tends to hold water, and that's enough to kill many perennials over the winter. While you're inside toasty warm, enjoying Yuletide – your poor plants are out there drowning.

However, it's hard to generalize about the "best" soil; clay, for example, has a bad reputation, but it actually holds nutrients very well. If sufficiently broken up and enriched with loam, it can make an excellent garden soil. And sandy soil, while easy to dig, is terribly poor in nutrients. One very quick way to test the quality of the soil is its color. Dark soil is usually full of nutrients; a pale, yellowish soil is likely to be poor.

Never forget the role of the humble earthworm in improving soil quality. While worms may not correspond to anyone's idea of beauty, they possess a down-to-earth magic (sorry for the pun) that can't be ignored. Earthworms change nutrients into a dissolvable form that can easily be taken up by plants. They aerate the soil with their tunneling and they also improve the compost pile. Once worms get going, they are hard to stop. An acre of soil can easily contain 1000 pounds of worms. (To get the most magical power from your earthworms, invoke the blessing of Crom Cruaich, the Celtic god of worms, upon them.)

As important as the soil itself is what lies beneath it. If you have hardpan (rocklike, compressed soil), your garden is in trouble, since the plant roots may not be able to penetrate the material. The same is true if the subsoil is rocky, or if the water table is too close to the surface drowning many plants.

To improve the soil, you must double-dig. This means digging down and loosening the subsoil, then adding rich, decaying organic matter to the topsoil. It's ideal to do this work in the autumn, so the soil can mature over the winter.

In addition to these practical measures, magical methods include digging in some ground up mistletoe into the earth. This is an empowering rite that upgrades the magical quality of the plants it produces.

Another old tradition is to bury some hair (your own hair combings or even some from the family dog will suffice). Some say the tradition is supported by the fact that hair has important nutrients not readily available from other sources. (Hair is indeed full of nutrients, although how available they are for plant use is hard to say. Hair certainly doesn't decompose very fast!) The real purpose of planting the hair is magical; it infuses the earth with elements from the human and animal world. It is not necessary that the hair be from your own family, but I think it works better that way.

Moisture Requirement (Water Element)

All plants need water, and some need a lot. (As a rule annuals require more water than perennials.) If you live in a low-moisture area, plant things that don't require much. Some plants thrive in a damp climate; others rejoice in drier conditions. A simple, usually reliable way to spot water-saving plants is to look for those with tiny or succulent (fleshy) leaves. "Silvery" plants with a coating of silky hairs are also usually thrifty with water. The same is true for plants with long roots. Plants with larger leaves often require more water (and more shade).

Many plants don't care for wet soils, although irises and a few others prefer it. Most plants should be watered when the soil one inch beneath the plant is dry. (You can insert a toothpick to test it. If the toothpick comes out clean, get out the watering can.)

Remember that all plants, even desert ones, need at least some water. So even if you live in a dry area and wish (wisely) to choose plants that can withstand a drought, don't expect that they will thrive if permanently derived of this most precious ingredient. It is especially critical to keep new plants well watered, until they can put down their deep roots. You might like to employ a drip-irrigation system that goes directly to the roots and that can be automated to water the plants even while you are away. When watering, it's important to water thoroughly. If you water only the surface of the ground, the roots will curl upward trying to get the water; this is worse than no watering at all, since it makes the roots weak. If the soil is dry an inch or two beneath the surface, it's time to water again. It is best to water during a waxing moon, if you have a choice. Whenever possible water early in the morning to allow the foliage to dry out in the sunshine of the day. This will reduce the chance of fungal disease, which thrives in wet, dark conditions. Plants generally prefer a water temperature of about 70°F (21°C). (Of course, most of the time you will have no control over this, as there is little you can do about the temperature of the rain.)

Sometimes, it's hard to figure what an "average" amount of water is – but one simple rule-of-thumb: consider an inch a week is average. If you get more than that naturally, you have a damper climate, less, a dryer one. Of course, soil matters too. A sandy soil that drains quickly will be dryer with an inch a week than a moisture-retentive soil. If you dig down 3–4 inches and find the soil is moist (not wet or dry) most of the time, you can consider your soil average.

Sowing and Planting Tips

Old magical tradition declares that one should be naked while sowing and planting. Presumably, this is to put oneself in a suitable state of nature; others suggest that nakedness is a form of supplication to the gods. A somewhat more cynical interpretation of the ancient injunction is that if it's too cold to be outside naked, it's too cold to sow or plant anything. This is a matter for individual interpretation. The sixth day of the month is considered an auspicious day for sowing and planting, if the moon is right.

If you live adjacent to a wild area, please do not sow or plant aggressive foreign imports that then escape your garden and take over the native flora. It can spell ecological disaster. When possible plant native or naturalized species, since bees and hummingbirds can cross-pollinate varieties and reduce diversity.

Sow your seeds generously. They don't cost much. Not only will many fail to sprout (Nature's prodigality in this respect is legend), but it is also important to sow extra for the birds and other animals who may visit your garden. An immemorial rhyme declares:

> *One for the rook, one for the crow,*
> *One to die and one to grow.*

Use a good organic mulch to protect the plant, suppress weeds, save precious gardening time, reduce water evaporation, and add nutrients to the soil. The bigger the plant, the more deeply you should mulch. Many different types of mulch exist. Choose one right for your plants, soil type, and climatic conditions. Grass clippings make a handsome, inexpensive mulch and really smother those weeds. (I have nothing against non-magical weeds, philosophically speaking, They just need to stay out of my garden.) You can also use leaf mold or bark chips. One of the more popular mulches is the delightful smelling cocoa mulch which contains a high amount of theobromine, the same chemical as chocolate. Do not use this mulch if you have a dog with access to the garden. While dogs like chocolate almost as much as people do, they can't easily metabolize theobromine. Eating mulch is not good for dogs under any circumstances. It can be fatal to them.

If you are planting bulbs, use a bulb planter – they save time and you find you can easily plant all your bulbs to a uniform depth.

If transplanting seedlings, it's best to do so on a cloudy day or in the late evening. Sun scorch can quickly kill these delicates beings. Remove them from their pot, but keep the original soil around the roots. Dig the transplant hole a bit larger and deeper than the pot was, you need to give the plant plenty of room to stretch and aerate its roots.

Lunar Gardening (When to Sow and Plant)

While many dispute the age-old practice of gardening by the phases of the moon, John Teasdale, director of the US Department of Agriculture's Agricultural Systems Laboratory (Beltsville MD), said, "We know that the moon influences some natural phenomena such as tides…lunar cycles could influence meteorological cycles which in turn could influence crops." And in 1995 Douglas Buhler and his colleague Keith Kohler conducted experiments that showed exposure to light (even moonlight) enhances germination for select species. Kohler said, "Certain species, even though they receive only a flash of light, tend to break dormancy and basically turn on the sequence of germination and establishment." From the National Geographic Website.

Waxing Moon: General Principles

In traditional magic, most things should be sown or planted (and transplanted) during the waxing moon. This is the time of growth. So unless otherwise indicated, sow or plant during the waxing phase of the cycle. Some posit a scientific explanation for this ancient custom: plants are largely composed of water, and the moon exerts her greatest influence on their growth when she is waxing, and her influence is strongest. Some believe it is more likely to rain during the waxing phase of the moon as well. And rain is needed for the seedling to get off to the best start.

This is the time to transplant, and to sow large areas, as well as leafy vegetables and plants noted for their beauty or fragrance. If there is a drought, sow or plant as close to the full moon as possible. **Water** during the waxing moon if possible. This is also the time to graft, and to harvest plants that will be used for their essential oils.

New moon to first quarter: Sow or plant fruits that bear seeds on the outside, such as strawberries.

First quarter to full moon: Sow or plant fruit that bear seeds inside, like peppers and tomatoes. It is also a good time for planting many cane-plants, such as raspberries and blackberries.

Waning Moon: General Principles

This is the time to divide perennials, fertilize with potassium, turn the compost pile, mulch, and weed. Harvest plants destined for long-term storage like apples. This is also the best time to dry herbs.

Full moon to third quarter: Sow or plant vegetables whose roots we eat, such as carrots and potatoes. Trees and some perennials can also be planted at this time.

Third quarter to new moon: Do not sow or plant. Harvest and weed.

I should say, however, that according to one ancient tradition of moon-gardening, trees should be planted during the waning moon, after the last quarter but before the new moon.

Feeding Tips

A well-nurtured plant, like a well-nurtured person, has a much better chance of fighting off disease and insects. And while it's obvious that an undernourished plant lacks the strength to fight off predators, it may come as a surprise to learn that overfeeding can have like results. Most overfed plants have too much foliage for the roots to supply; in consequence, despite its look of blooming health, the plant is weak and a target of opportunity for insect invasion. Using correct amounts of organic fertilizers such as manure, leaf mold and seaweed, will keep your plants sturdy.

Pruning Tips

Pruning is a critical part of plant care. It does more than cut away an objectionable, light-blocking limb. By removing dead, dying, overcrowded, and disfigured branches, it helps focus the plants energies. It improves flowering and fruiting, and also directs the size and shape of the plant. Pruning shears are your friend (and your plant's friend, too!)

Weeding Tips

The best way to control weeds is not to allow them a head start. Use ground covers and thick mulches to choke out undesirable plants, but stay away from pre- or post-emergent chemicals that destroy many garden friends as well as weeds. Keep a careful eye on the garden – when a wayward weeds peeks through your mulch yank it out, and consider mulching some more.

Harvesting Tips

When cutting stems, it is important to always use a sharp knife or secateurs. Simply breaking a stem can be very damaging to the plant. Remember, however, that iron is deadly to all magic and that steel implements should be ritually purified before use.

Many magical gardeners use a special, ritually purified knife for gardening and cutting herbs. The proper implement is usually referred to as a "boline," a sharp, curved blade (traditionally it has a white handle.) Another magical knife is the double bladed, black handled athame (pronounced "ATH-a-may), which is used to cast a magical circle for the plants, but which does not actually touch the plants themselves. When casting a magic planting circle, move the athame in a clockwise (deosil) direction. It is also traditional to be clothed simply, all in white and to be barefoot.

Equally important is the frame of mind of the gardener. If you harbor malice or resentment toward any creature, the purity of the herbs will be injured and their magical properties weakened.

Traditionally, leaves, flowers and berries are picked during the waxing moon, while root crops are gathered during the waning moon. When cutting the top part of the plant, don't take too much, or the plant will not recover. For medicinal or magical purposes leaves should be gathered, as a rule before the flowering period; that is when they contain the greatest amount of active ingredients. They should be young, juicy and spotless. (Spots often signal a viral disease.)

In practical terms it is best to harvest plants in late morning – after the dew dries but before the sun is scorching. However, it is magical tradition to pick plants at night, although you obviously have to be careful when doing this. Make sure you know what you're gathering. When selecting flowers for other purposes, the best time is mid-day, when they are just starting to open. Picking flowers in damp weather is also counterproductive, and the magical properties of herbs are weakened if picked when the dew is on them. Try not to touch the petals when you pick the flowers. Fruits and seeds should be picked when fully ripe, unless counter indicated. In most cases, fallen leaves and seeds are not efficacious in magic; they must be fresh off the plant.

If you must take the entire plant, be sure to replant. In former days, it was common to bring and bury an offering of honey, bread, and wine in the spot from which the sacred herbs were taken, but I don't want you taking wild plants from anywhere unless they are truly over plentiful (like dandelions). If you do harvest something plentiful and wild, you must leave an offering.

Beware of "wild-crafted" plants. This is another name for plant-rustling. Wild plants belong to the earth. Indiscriminate picking of these treasures has led to the decimation and near extinction of many valuable medicinal and charm plants. Please purchase your plants from a reputable organic dealer — or grow your own! I'll show you how. You are justified in collecting rare wildflowers only to save them from land about to be developed — in that case please remove the entire plant and transplant.

Aftercare

Wash all medicinal and magical herbs. You don't need bugs and dirt in your harvest. Use cold water. For most purposes, you'll want to dry your herbs before magical use; so do this during the waning moon. You can use air, oven, microwave, or even a food dehydrator for this purpose. Remember, however, that drying plants decreases some of their most effective properties – both magical and medicinal. For cooking purposes, freezing is better than drying, but for therapeutic and magical purposes, drying is the preferred method. To conserve as much of their power as possible, dry the plants in the shade (if you are air-drying) and try not to disturb them while they are drying. The less you handle them, the better shape they will be in. When air-drying, you can lay them flat on thin sheets of paper towel, or more aesthetically, hang them upside down in a dry, well-ventilated area away from sunlight. You'll know when the plants are sufficiently dry: the stems will break easily. Too much heat during the drying process can destroy the plant's properties. Leaves and delicate plants can't withstand drying temperature above 90°F (32°C); bulbs can tolerate temperature up to about 100°F (38 °C), and tough roots up to about 115°F (45°C). After drying, store the herbs in an airtight jar away from light and oxygen. That's all there is to it, really. Nothing magical about it at all.

Time and Money

One final thing. There is no such thing as a maintenance-free garden. A well-kept garden will always take more time than you think, and will probably cost more than you plan. But it's worth it. Gardening is a spiritually healthful, peaceful exercise, and there are many worse ways to spend your time and money.

Designing the Charmed Garden

Feeling the Magic

All gardens are magic. Anyone who has seen a daffodil push through the snow, crumbled the earth of spring in her fingers, watched a leaf uncurl, or smelled the legendary fragrance of daphne has experienced that magic. But a true magical garden touches something even deeper in us. (While many ancient people built themselves temples in which to perform their rites, the Celts and Aryan people, both of whom were masters of magic, performed their rites in the open air, so as not to be shut away from the great and powerful elements of nature.)

To create a magical garden is to honor not only the blossoms of spring, but also the flowers of our history. To create a magical garden is to explore the odd and mysterious corners of that history, the outposts of our cultural past. And it is to learn the secrets of both the most ordinary and the most exotic of blooms.

There are many kinds of magic. There is the magic of power, the magic of peace, and the magic of beauty. The charmed garden has them all, and calls forth the deepest and sweetest and holiest notes from both the human spirit and the earth that nourishes it.

The garden is a threshold, opening from the world of human beings to the world of nature. It's a fluid boundary, in which wild plants become domestic and old domestic plants escape and go wild. It's the world where magic happens.

Every garden is unique, occupying a particular spot in the universe. The way the sun strikes the plants, the curve of the earth, the qualities of the soil, the play of light and shadow, make your garden a very special place. And when you garden, a living thing enters your care. Not only is every plant a living, perhaps sentient, being with its own particular (and sometimes demanding!) needs, the garden itself slowly develops into an organic whole, not just a collection of disparate plants. That in itself is a kind of magic.

Since the power of the garden intermingles with that of the gardener, I strongly suggest that the magical garden ideally should be one that the participants can walk into, not stand and look at, as in a typical bed or border garden. Bed and border gardens are normally meant to be viewed from the outside. The magical garden is primarily to be entered into and experienced. This is not to say that border and beds cannot contain magical plants. Of course they can. However, I believe such gardens themselves lack the spiritual power of the walk-in, enclosing garden.

From time immemorial, human beings have drawn magic from earth, power from fire, purification from water, and inspiration from the air. One reason that the garden is such a potent instrument of magic is that it presents these elements in harmonious resonance and balance. This is one of the (literally) elemental principles of magic.

Magic is an evocative word. For some, it's a collection of parlor tricks, like pulling a rabbit out of a hat. (For gardeners, it's much harder to make rabbits go away than appear.) But real magic has nothing to do with such degraded versions of "shock and awe." Real magic is a practice that balances precariously between the realm of fantasy and the kingdom of science. It is the stepsister of alchemy, and grandmother of science. Despite the proliferation of technology, we all cling to magic, perhaps without even knowing why. We knock on wood, cross our fingers, and keep a rabbit's foot (rabbits keep showing up both in magic and gardening). We look for four-leaf clovers, and watch out for black cats. Break a mirror and get seven years bad luck. Find a penny and have good luck.

Of course, it's all nonsense, we say in our more "scientific" moods. There is no such thing as good luck – just random happenstance. There's nothing special about moonlight, and love is a neuronal twitch. We all know better. We *know* magic works. We've felt it, seen it, and experienced it. The deeper it enters, the more mysterious it becomes. Where science sees chance magic recognizes intention; where science sees coincidence, magic identifies pattern. Magic yokes the power of nature to the desire of the heart. That's magic, and that's gardening. Magic encompasses the lore of the leaf, the fable of the flower, and the ancient, ancient principles of the **Earth** and **Air**, **Fire** and **Water**. There's magic in them all.

The magical gardener does not reject science, however. She plants with her mind as well as her soul. Magic, science, gardening, they're all after the same thing — transformation. Within many of the simplest plants lie secrets of health, freedom, and beauty.

The wise gardener uses earth magic to heal the body, water magic to purify the heart, fire magic to transform the mind, and air magic to liberate the spirit. All are encoded within every flower, from solid root to evanescent fragrance.

This is *real* flower power! A power rooted in earth, transporting water, displaying color, and giving forth scent. Each individual plant and weed exhibits, in its unique way, the complex inter-relationship of the elements. Put them together in a garden, and the relationship becomes almost unbelievably complex and versatile.

Traditionally both flowers and the gardens in which they grow have been regarded as powerful female symbols. Women find in them a source of their own power, and men are drawn to them as bees to pollen. The rich earth, the seductive blooms and fragrances, breathe the secrets of the feminine power. The connection is so strong and natural that it is silly to pretend otherwise. The concept of paradise as a walled garden, also a famous symbol of woman, only adds to the mystique.

Getting Down to Basics

Size

The wise gardener, the one who loves the earth and sun and moon, knows that before the first seed is planted, before the garden can bloom, even in the imagination, the garden spot must be selected, the soil studied and prepared, the climate and moisture needs taken into consideration.

If you are a beginner, start small and simple. It's easy to get carried away and try to create the best, most magnificent garden ever in your first year of gardening. All too often, however, such over ambitious plans lead to disappointment, overwork, and ultimate (sometimes pricey) failure. If you begin with a small, easy-to-look-after garden, you'll learn so much about your corner of the world that next year you'll be able to add with confidence. Patience is truly your best friend (along with sun and rain). And if you are cramped for space, go multi-level, using a series of raised beds. You'll add vertical interest and increase your space all at once. Herbs often need lots of room to spread out.

Wise gardeners think ahead. Planting is planning! It is the ultimate expression of faith in the future. When you choose your plants, remember that they are living beings. They grow, develop, and change their character as they mature. A hasty, ill-conceived planting will just mean unnecessary digging, replanting, and (horrors!) plant killing later on down the road.

One of the first considerations is space: how much will you allot to your garden? Bigger is not always better. Bigger requires more upkeep, and unless you have a great deal of time, a large garden should be planted with easier-to-care-for plants. (Don't try to include every species known to humankind and the spirit world in your garden. About ten different species should be plenty for a start, even for a fairly large garden.)

One old guideline for garden size is this: the depth of the garden should be twice the height of the tallest plant. This rule is variable, like everything else, although it's common sense that smaller gardens require smaller plants. Be aware that very wide beds are hard to reach into. Some designers, who have a keen eye for practicality, recommend restricting the height of the tallest plants to 4 feet or so. Otherwise, you'll be wading waist high into the midst of the perennial border. But that's part of the fun.

To be sure, the kind of garden you envision will dictate to some degree the spot you choose. For example, my home lies on 5 acres of variable landscape, and I have the luxury of choice. However, many people are less fortunate, and have to take what is offered. This does not have to be a major drawback; there are so many varieties of magical flowers and herbs that you will find many both to your liking and suitable for your garden. In fact, your main dilemma will be which plants *not* to grow.

Purpose

One of the major considerations of designing a magical garden is the overall effect you want to achieve. A magical garden designed to calm and still the spirit will be designed along differing lines from one whose purpose is to tempt, excite, or challenge.

Gardens can, of course, serve more mundane purposes. They can create privacy or invite the neighborhood. They can provide food for the table or curb soil erosion. They can attract butterflies and birds. They can hide an unattractive corner or show off a spectacular view. They can sprout vegetables or provide a quiet retreat. But whatever their purpose, they express the character and spirit of the gardener. (People who hire a landscaper to design their garden may get something very beautiful – but it won't be theirs. Those who plant a garden solely to mask an ugly corner or fill up an unused portion of the yard – or a section where the grass won't grow – are gardening for different purposes than those for whom this book is intended.)

The many purposes gardens serve, however, can be confusing as well as enriching. To make the most of your own magical gardening experience, you'll need to know, as precisely as possible, what you want from your garden. An herbalist has a different purpose than a cook, spell-maker, or aromatherapist, who in turn has a different orientation than someone who uses a garden for spiritual or meditation purposes. Of course a single garden can serve more than one person and more than one purpose, but you, the designer, must have those purposes clearly in mind in order to create that perfect garden. If you have a very large space, one in which the centre garden is not visible all at once, you can include all the effects.

Gardening for different purposes has always been recognized. In the Middle Ages every monastery had its kitchen garden; its medicinal garden, or physic; and its contemplative, or "paradise" garden. The magical garden may combine features of all of them.

Basing Your Design on the Four Elements

One way to plan a garden is by honoring the four elements of the ancients: **Earth**, **Water**, **Air**, and **Fire**. Each has a place in thinking about how to enhance the magical properties of your plants.

Each of the classical elements has its place within each plant. Earth is the root of the flower, Water the stem, Fire the color, and Air the perfume. Each also affects different sense preceptors in its human visitors. Earth is associated with touch, Water with taste and nourishment, Fire with vision and color awareness, and Air with sound and smell. Those skilled in Chinese symbolism can make equal use of the five elements of Taoist philosophy: Water, Wood, Fire, Earth, and Metal. The parallels are obvious, but in the Chinese system, the Metal represents the structural elements human beings add to the natural form of the garden itself.

An ideal garden would contain a perfect balance of **Earth**, **Water**, **Fire**, and **Air** elements, but as a matter of taste, purpose, and practicality, most gardeners will emphasize one or another of the elements. Sometimes, however, something as simple as a statue of a water deity or water animal such as a dolphin, fish, or heron will draw together several important elements.

An **Earth Garden** will emphasize structural features such as trees, and strongly shaped shrubs or vines. It will contain intriguing rocks, paths, and contours. It gives an aura of strength. The magical beings associated with the **Earth** Garden are gnomes and dryads. Its power is greatest in the autumn when many plants fade and the rich brown earth takes possession again of the garden. **Earth** Gardens are most suitable for rites concerning fertility, ancestors, building projects, career, and business. (See the Quick Guide to Magical Uses and Attributes suitable for an **Earth** Garden.)

A **Water Garden** will feature a pond, pool, fountain, waterfall, or stream. (Seashells provide symbolic water, if you are working in a dry area.) In its crystal clarity, water provides an aura of awareness. The magical beings associated with **Water** Gardens are undines. **Water** is an element of winter. In the winter, the deep snows blanket the sleeping garden and the hushed sound of underground springs remind us of the deep water of life in all of us. When the ground is covered with snow, the flowers and their fragrance long gone, water still remains. **Water** Gardens are most suitable for rites involving peace, family, friendship, and contemplation. (See the Quick Guide to Magical Uses and Attributes in the Appendix, suitable for a **Water** Garden.)

A **Fire Garden** emphasizes color by the wise use of tone and shade in bloom and foliage. It imparts an aura of joy. **Fire** Gardens have the most power in the summer, when the garden glows warm with the brilliance of color. (Consider a sundial as well.) The magical beings associated with **Fire** Gardens are salamanders and jinn. A **Fire** Garden is most suitable for rites involving passion, struggle, strength, and rituals involving evil entities. Plants suitable for fire gardens may be so-called "hot" plants by virtue of taste, association with hot places, or stinging powers. (See the Quick Guide to Magical Uses and Attributes for a list of excellent plants for a **Fire** Garden.)

An **Air Garden** features fragrance. This is one of the most difficult kinds of garden to design, as fragrance, which creates a sense of spirituality, is so ephemeral. The magical beings associated with **Air** Gardens are sylphs. The **Air** Garden works its greatest magic in the spring, when the mild breezes carry the garden's fragrance far and wide. You will draw breath about 23,000 times today. It should be a magical experience, not simply a necessity. The **Air** Garden may also profitably include streamers and wind chimes to emphasize their airy quality. **Air** gardens are most suitable to rites involving intellectual or spiritual activity, the arts, and ceremonies involving beneficent entities. (See the Quick Guide to Magical Uses and Attributes for a list of plants suitable for an **Air** Garden.)

In addition to the season when the powers of the earth are at their most beneficent, there is also a season when the elemental powers can become corrupted and dangerous. The fire in the autumn leaves, the raging winds of winter, the floods of spring, and the scorched earth of summer remind us that the powers of nature, while always beautiful almost beyond enduring, function not only to enrich, but to destroy.

Earth Elements

Earth is the foundation of the garden and root of the plant. For human beings, it is associated with touch. In creating your garden, you will need to know what kind of soil you have, how it may be enriched, and what its important properties are. Different plants love different soils, and the wise gardener knows her soil. See "Your Plants and the Four ancient Elements, Soil Quality and Type".

Earth elements of plants include roots and rhizomes. For medical and magical purposes, they are best collected when dormant — in winter or very early spring; that's when they possess the highest level of active ingredients. Although washing roots is a good idea, don't scrub the surface hard for doing so removes some of the most powerful constituents.

Montague Don has said that the garden is a *place*, not a collection of plants. As place, it has an architecture that, while changing through the seasons, maintains a structural integrity that binds together and harmonizes the more ephemeral qualities of the plants themselves. Ignoring the possibilities of architecture means a garden bereft of any winter interest. The magic of the garden should not fade when plants go dormant for the winter.

Location

The first element of place is location. When siting the garden, that is, choosing that particular spot of earth you wish to cultivate, you'll have to take into consideration not only the features of the earth itself, but the purpose of the garden and the overall "feeling" you want from it. A more public garden can be located close to the house, in plain view, with an open inviting path. A more secret garden requires less public access and a fence or wall. The decision is yours – but you must know what you want before you can create it.

Unless your garden is located out of sight and contact with your house, you'll have to take some elements of your house into consideration when designing your garden. A formal style house generally looks best with a formal style garden (and vice versa, of course). A more casual, natural design will support a country style or wildflower garden. And while it is true that plants have powers that go beyond looks, you can't leave appearances altogether out of your considerations. Nature didn't.

Shape and Contours

Earth also determines the shape of the garden itself. Whether you wish to honor the earth by constructing your garden in obedience to its natural contours, or whether you want to assert a more personal influence by changing or overriding the "givens" of your plot of ground, you'll need to understand how shapes create powerful influences on the garden. A formal, rectangular garden presents a different message than a garden with more natural curves and informal shape. And for most charmed gardens, these considerations take precedence over the gardener's desire to impose a particular shape. Magical things happen in unplanned, out-of-way-corners. However, an unplanned, random mass of curves can be confusing rather than focusing. Planning should work with the natural shape and contour of the land; but a garden is, by its nature, a work of design and art.

One favorite way to lay out the curves of an informal garden path is to use a garden hose, which seems to curve itself just about perfectly for human meandering. Another way is what I call the Hansel and Gretel method, which is indeed drawn from that story. Just walk about the your garden or landscape, moving where your eye and heart direct. Drop some lime (it lasts longer than breadcrumbs) as you walk. The resulting trail is the plan for your garden perimeter.

In the ancient Chinese art of feng shui, *Qi*, or natural energy, flows best along natural contours. This ancient art was designed to "bring harmony in the middle"; in other words, to establish the best site for the intermingling of heaven and earth, and for properly balancing yin and yang forces.

Feng-shui practice teaches that straight lines make it easy for evil influences to approach. On a psychological level, you will notice that the strongest focal points occur where visual lines intersect, something to take into account when designing paths. Remember also that the edge of every plant group is a line, whether you intend it so or not.

Those who follow the ancient Chinese art of feng shui believe that a south-facing garden is most auspicious. Careful feng shui gardeners also locate yang energy sources to the front of the garden, and yin energies to the rear. Yang forces include sunny spots and hills; yin forces include shade and water elements.

Paths, of course, are an important and inviting element of any garden large enough to walk in, although many a dedicated gardener has demolished a path in order to plant some particularly desirable shrub for which there is no room elsewhere. (Such gardens have an adventurous character of their own, with the visitor hopping around from one spot to another, trying to find a place to stand.) Most good garden paths curve and lead somewhere, to an important plant, bench, or some other special place. However, if your garden is large and available to children (or dogs), you can bet they will make their own paths. The wise gardener takes these "natural" paths into account.

Paths are best designed so that they form a circle for magical walks and incantations. In general, walking clockwise is done for invocations and walking counterclockwise is used in banishment or exorcising evil spirits. A curving path creates a sense of movement that invites the walker deeper into the garden.

While a brick path positively invites folks to walk upon it, a magical garden does much better with small flat stepping-stones; I like slate for this purpose. Planting delicate mosses or creeping thyme between the stones adds to the effect.

A sloping piece of land may present difficulties in soil erosion or drainage; however, it is always possible to find interesting and magical plants that can cope with it. And if you have heavy soil, a sloping garden may actually improve your drainage! A slope, or sloping places are also inherently interesting and carry more magical potency than most flat places. If the slopes are tricky, you can always add steps. Remember that southeastern and southern slopes get the most sunlight.

Special Shapes

One of the central concerns of the earth-principle is the shape of the garden. Traditional shapes incorporate ancient and powerful motifs that give rhythm, strength, and mystical significance to the space they enclose. Each shape facilitates a different aspect of magic.

The Circle: Unlike a square, triangle, or rectangle, the circle is a natural shape, and manifests itself in objects as diverse as the sun and the daisy. Indeed, many, many flowers bear circular blooms – not triangles or squares. It is symbolically an important shape as well, bringing together opposition and creating healing. This may partly explain why so many plants can be used in apparently contradictory ways, for the circle eventually returns all forces to their starting point. "The eye is the first circle," wrote Ralph Waldo Emerson. "The horizon which it forms is the second…it is the highest emblem in the cipher of the world." The circle is considered a symbol of female and psychic forces in nature. It is the traditional symbol of completion, eternity, and perfection. It is also protective, and magic is most safely performed within its secure psychic boundaries.

A circular garden is an interesting combination of the formal and the informal. Its power partly derives from the fact that it is the shape of the solar and lunar disks. The deity is even sometimes spoken of as a circle whose center is everywhere. The circle is also the emblem of the female, and of the psychic self. It is one of the best places for outdoor magic, especially during the full moon. Its shape is considered protective. Stonehenge, is, of course, circular, as was the legendary Hyperborean Temple of Apollo.

In a large garden design, the circle is best reserved for a particularly sacred place within the total garden. It provides power and focus. An entire large garden of circular design looks distressingly like a crop circle: too overwhelming, strange, and intimidating. The circle works its best magic within a larger design. It is true that some very large formal garden complexes include circular gardens within them. This is the legendary "squaring the circle" and represents the desire to unite the earthly (square) and heavenly (circular) realms. Again, however, this plan is a circle within a larger design; a circular garden out of context is just too strange and imposing. **An oval** has most of the properties as the circle, but is a bit less formal.

The Mandorla: This is an almond shape, and is best used in gardens dedicated to fertility rituals, especially for women.

The Square: The square is a strong shape, emblematic of the four corners of the earth, the solstices and equinoxes, the four seasons, and so on. It is also a powerful symbol of the earth and worldly power. A circle inside a square, however, symbolizes the divine spark within all of us.

An interesting variation on the square is the **diamond-shaped garden**, which is considered to be the sign of the earth before creation. This kind of garden has stronger, more fluid vibrations than the standard square. It is an excellent garden for magic having to do with the family.

The Rectangle: More pleasing visually than the square is the rectangle, and some magical gardeners have obtained remarkable results using the Golden Ratio to design a perfectly proportioned garden. The Golden Ratio is the proportion that results when a line segment is divided so that the smaller is to the larger as the larger is to the whole. In a "golden rectangle" the ratio of the difference of the sides to the smaller equals the ratio of the smaller to the larger. In classical antiquity, this was considered to be uniquely pleasing to the eye, and was called Euclid's Rectangle, considered the most rational, secure, and regular of all forms. Even more intriguingly, it's been discovered than many objects in the natural world, from flowers (roses and sun flowers, for example) to the Milky Way itself make use of the Golden Ratio.

Some people like to place their herbs in a special garden-within-a-garden, choosing one of these special shapes mentioned above. Herbs are a critical part of any magical garden, of course. Most herbs do best on a slight slope facing south or west. Some herbs, such as mints, are highly invasive and may do best in containers or when strictly separated from the rest of the garden.

Triangle: The triangle has a long and powerfully symbolic history in garden design. It is, of course, a strong feminine symbol (the relationship to the so-called "delta of Venus" should be obvious) but it also creates strong lines that can lead to a focal point. To achieve this effect, you don't have to create a perfect equilateral triangle – even a rough or suggested triangular shape has much the same effect. The triangle garden is perfect for magic involving the creative forces.

Pentagram: The pentagram is the uttermost magical shape, and theoretically, a garden in this shape is one of almost unlimited power. Each section can have it own kind of magic, healing, purificatory, protective, and so on. Or you can divide sections into flower colors. Practically speaking, however, a pentagram is hard to design and keep up, unless you have plenty of help. Without proper care, it will be sloppy and difficult to manage. This shape is definitely not for beginners.

Hexagram: If you are ambitious, a hexagram is a lucky shape within a garden. It is composed of overlapping triangles, one of which represents the male and the other the female influence, and also reflects the magic of the sun and moon. As a mandala it is a wonderful meditation aid. A hexagram shape is a perfect way to plant an herb garden.

Crescent: The crescent is not only a pleasing shape in itself, but one that calls forth the strength of the waxing or waning moon. Facing north, a C-shaped garden signifies a waning moon; a backward C represents the waxing moon.

Labyrinth or Maze: While these designs are far too complex and time-consuming for the average gardener, it's important to note that they have great psychological significance. While they became faddish in formal gardens and have been used merely as a pastime to amuse park visitors, their origins reach deep into our cultural psychology. The labyrinth suggests the powerful unconscious, the search for the center, and is a symbol of the intertwining of spiritual and physical realities. Without actually creating a labyrinth, something of its power can be suggested by creating hidden, secret corners that are not apparent as you first enter the garden. Winding paths that first lead away, and then towards the desired object can also achieve some of the same effect.

Specially Shaped, Special Purpose Gardens

The Love Charm Garden

A love charm garden will be based around the shaped of the primordial love charm, a mandorla, oval, or circle. For the more ambitious, you can attempt the Interlocked Heart, here illustrated. Straight lines and sharp angles are best avoided, and the most successful love gardens have an informal, almost casual look. A love garden works best when it includes a prominent water (emotional) element such as a pond, gentle fountain, or birdbath. Statuary is also suitable. Featured plants might include any of the love plants listed in the cross-reference, as well as flowers that have a special meaning for you. Since night and the moon are associated with love, be sure to include some night-blooming fragrant flowers so you can enjoy your garden by moonlight. Lotuses are, I think, essential. (For a list of love plants look in "The Quick Guide to Magical Uses and Attributes under *Love*.)

The Prosperity Garden

Earth features and brilliant colors should predominate in the Prosperity Garden. It is customary to bury several items in the garden representing treasure and valuables. The garden is one in which straight lines and a more formal arrangement of plants can be beneficial; the precise design can be left to your taste. (For a list of love plants look in "The Quick Guide to Magical Uses and Attributes under *Prosperity*.)

The Protection Garden

One interesting shape for the protection garden might be the three-pointed star (a sort of indented triangle), originally from Arabia. Since it is impractical for most people to make the entire garden this shape, you can include a sub-design, even marking it out with pebbles in the middle of the garden.

The three points stand for Underworld, Middle **Earth**, and Otherworld of Bliss, and call upon the powers of each to bless and protect. This is another garden in which strong, powerful colors should predominate. This is indeed a **Fire** Garden. (The flaming cherubs protected the Garden of Eden.) A protection garden should also make good use of sound and wind chimes. For a water element, a waterfall or strong fountain is perfect. For an earth element, select strong vertical lines. A protection garden often benefits from being surrounded by a fence or hedge. (For a list of love plants look in "The Quick Guide to Magical Uses and Attributes under *Protection*.)

The Triple Ring

This is a garden designed for luck. **Air,** the element of transition and change predominates. The interlocking circles symbolize luck (the physical world), meditation (the intellectual world) and divination (the spiritual world). For each ring select plants for their respective powers in this regard. The interlocking areas should ideally contain plants of double or triple benefit. (For a list of love plants look in "The Quick Guide to Magical Uses and Attributes under *Luck, Meditation* and *Divination*.)

The Knot Garden

A knot has powerful significance in magical studies. It is the manifestation of the infinite as it is intertwined with earthly things. It is symbolically related to the maze or labyrinth, but is on a more manageable scale. The knot also traditionally serves as a mandala for meditation. For best visual impact, situate the knot garden in a place where it can viewed from above, as from as upstairs window, so that the pleasing pattern is most evident.

The knot garden was popularized during the Middle Ages (every monastery had one, with an appropriate number of monk-gardeners to care for it) but the symbolism implied by the knot reaches across civilizations. In Buddhism, for example, the knot symbolizes long life uninterrupted by setbacks, so it is a very auspicious symbol. The structural plants for a knot garden should be small-leaved evergreens that form a dense growth.

Box, thyme, hyssop, lavender, and santolina are traditional plants for the knot garden, with box giving the most reliable results. Box comes in several interesting varieties, with different shaded leaves. However, it grows rather slowly, so be patient.

The knot garden traditionally accompanies a more formal house and garden design, but its history and magical qualities are so potent, that, if you are willing to work at the upkeep, a knot garden can be used with into any style of house. There's a problem here, though, at least in my experience. A knot garden of any size is so difficult to maintain that most of the contemplation being done there is likely to be a sullen brooding about how to reshape it. At least, that's been my experience.

Spell Garden

For exceptional control, some people study to design a "spell garden" that conforms to a very specific magical spell. There is no specific required shape for a "spell garden'. This is an individual creation that should reflect the needs and powers of the gardener-practitioner. Some people, especially those aligned with Buddhist or Hindu traditions, create a personalized Yantra, a particular geographical shape that reflects the sphere and powers of the deity invoked. Other people select symbols drawn from alchemy and astrology. The power can be in the shape of the spell garden, or more commonly, in the choice of objects contained in it. Many of these objects should be of personal significance to the gardener. Others can be selected for their magical powers.

Earth Focal Points

While nearly all plants (with the exception of unearthly types like mistletoe) are rooted in earth, for earth notes in garden design, look for woody shrubs, trees, vines, and other strong, powerful plants that serve as anchors and focal points of your garden. Large, interesting rocks also serve this purpose. On principle, I include at least one important rock in every garden. Their rugged durability has always been a sign of divine power and strength, and from time immemorial (consider Stonehenge, and the Pyramids) they have served as emblems of our connection with the divine.

A garden with no focal point is chaotic and distressing to the visitor. And an injudicious arrangement of plants can lead the eye to an unintended (and thus probably wrong) focal point. The best focal points are permanent, or at least durable, like rocks, benches, or trees. A brilliant bunch of daffodils, no matter how powerful and exciting in the spring, turns into a mass of unpleasant foliage in early summer. The same is true, to great or less degree, of most plants.

Look for elements that will command interest and exude power all year round. The good garden is always recognizable as a garden, even in the dead of winter (when some of the strongest magic happens).

All but the smallest gardens have stronger magic when they contain a tree. Trees reach from the earth to the sky, and represent both our aspirations towards heaven and our rooted-ness in the earth. Keep in mind, however, that where trees are concerned, the roots can seriously interfere with perennials. Your job as a gardener is to harmonize the sometimes-competing interests of your plants.

A word about trees, never plant two trees together as a pair. Paired trees never work out well. One is always bigger, better, or weirder than the other. People see them and subconsciously compare them. They make folks feel uneasy. Plant trees in threes or in some other odd number; smaller plants look best in drifts of five to nine. You'll just have to take my word for this, but odd numbers symbolize (unconsciously) spiritual elements; even numbers are worldly. Multiples of three are especially significant; these numbers are sacred to Hecate, the goddess of witches.

A bench for relaxation is essential. For an unusual and magical bench, you can't improve upon a turf seat. Turf seats were a staple of every medieval garden, and there is nothing more magical than a true medieval garden. To make one, build a box (or use a whiskey half-barrel with holes drilled in the bottom for drainage) fill it with potting soil plus a little sand and dolomite chips or shell. When the earth has settled, plant some creeping thyme or another aromatic herb. Sitting frequently on this warm, comfortable bench will release the plant's fragrance.

Earth elements don't have to be permanent. Explore container gardening. The advantages are many; you can change the position and type of plants at will, weeding is easier, and you will have the additional strong decorative elements of elegant or earthy pots.

An accented section of tall plants can also serve as a focal point. Using different aspects of the earth elements gives your garden structure and rhythm, the two alternating aspects of design. It's common in gardening to talk of the foreground, middle ground, and background, with appropriately sized plants (shortest to tallest) for each section. While this is completely appropriate for formal beds and borders, the magical garden, into which one is drawn, can afford to suspend many of these "rules". Looking at the garden from the inside gives an entirely different effect from "outside" viewing. When people will be viewing a group of plants from all sides, it often makes sense to put the tallest plants in the middle, preferably a single large plant or a group arranged in a circle, rather than a ridge-like affair in the middle. Angelica and lovage are tall herbs that serve this purpose well.

Drifts of flowers, a focal tree, statuary, an arbor, a bench, an alter shrine, or a gazebo, carefully arranged, supplies a pleasing asymmetrical balance to the garden. You don't have to put a bench at each end, for instance, unless you want a very formal effect. You can achieve a much more dynamic balance by putting, for example, a shrub of the same visual weight as the bench on the opposite side. This is one case where separate but equal really makes sense.

I like the idea of using pillars in gardens. They have ancient and complex meanings – from simple phallic symbols to magical and occult meaning. In alchemy, three pillars stand for wisdom, strength, and beauty. In Masonic symbolism, a black pillar represents the god of darkness while a white one symbolizes the god of light. In any case, they make an excellent accent and powerful focal point in any magical garden. What's more they are easy to find; you can buy them (in varying heights) at a local home improvement or garden store.

Many gardeners like to enclose their "special" gardens with a fence; this serves not only as an important earth accent, but also to remind all who enter that the garden is a special place, and of supreme value in itself. Fences also possess the undeniable advantage of keeping out charming but predatory guests like rabbit and deer.

To make a narrow border look wider, point up the differences between the short plants in front and the taller plants in back, by selecting plants with more noticeable differences in height.

By the same token, rounded shapes are generally more pleasing in the smaller garden than vertical ones. And don't forget — trees grow so plan for the future. You'll need to take into account the tree's mature height, width, growth rate, and amount of shade it casts. If the tree doesn't have enough space or light, it will grow scraggly and over-tall in a desperate attempt to reach the light. However, even a crowded garden can usually accommodate a few charming vines, which with their supporting arbor, also add vertical interest.

Sometimes it's hard to figure out exactly how much space to allow a plant. Each plant has a unique architectural quality that structures and adds a degree of permanence to its beauty. Each plant is different, of course, but there is a general rule of thumb. A rounded or vase-shaped plant requires the same ground space as its height. A mounded plant requires 1.5 times as much, whilst a prostrate or creeping plant needs, on average, 4 times its height. However, a narrow, columnar plant needs a ground space only one-third its height. Don't worry if your garden has some bare spots. That's not necessarily a bad thing. In garden design, as in art, empty space has a power of its own, and makes its own magic. And of course, if you have a spectacular view, you don't want to plant anything that will interfere with its own powerful magic. If you do need "filler", unobtrusive, cool-colored plants are usually the best choice.

Texture

Since **Earth** elements heavily affect the sense of weight and touch, you will need to consider not merely obvious things like size and color but subtle qualities like texture, a "feeling" word that refers to the character of the plant's foliage, its form, and its "visual weight." Combining and complementing textures is a more subtle and exacting art than doing the same with color, but the results are longer lasting, and, in a way, more satisfying. Delicately textured plants are fine for small gardens, especially when you want them to look more spacious. Coarse textured plants like rhododendrons serve to make a big area more intimate. Coarse textured plants include peonies, comfrey, foxglove, and iris. Fine textured plants include thyme, carnation, and many types of marigold. Medium textured plants include the pot marigold and verbena.

Huge rhododendrons in a small garden, however, create a too-bold, almost claustrophobic effect. Of course, that may be what you want. Combining different textured plants, such as feathery and bold, usually produces a pleasing effect. Very fine textured plants, planted en masse, tend to create a solid, mat-like effect. In general, large leaves equal coarse texture; small leaves equal fine texture. Variegated leaves tend to give a bolder, coarser texture to the plant. Delicately textured plants include shade-loving ferns, astilbes, columbines, sweet cicely, and bleeding heart. For the sun, try fernleaf peonies, feverfew, achilleas, artemisias, mountain mints, tansy, dog fennel, and asparagus fern (not a fern).

Water Elements

The Significance of Water

Water has a powerful practical and symbolic significance that reflects its critical role in all life. It falls from sky, bubbles up from the earth, and gives life to every being. It symbolizes life, purity and cleansing. Nearly every garden visitor is drawn first to its pond, fountain, or spring. The Garden of Eden was blessed by four rivers, and nearly every medieval monastic garden featured a *fons vitae*, or fountain of life, in the middle of the garden. In fact, some of the early walled church gardens were actually called paridaezae, or Paradise gardens, a deliberate attempt to recreate either the Garden of Eden or the gardens of the Song of Solomon.

Plan your garden so that plants by the pool will be blooming during the hottest part of the summer, when people are most drawn to water.

In addition to its symbolic and psychological value, a pond or water feature has a practical application in the garden. It not only provides a cooling element, but also by humidifying the air near it, can actually create a moister microclimate in that corner of the garden.

Other practical water considerations include availability (natural or irrigation), depth of the water table and drainage. An amazing amount of the available drinking water in both the US and UK is used for landscaping; by carefully grouping plants with similar water needs you can cut down on what you use by about half. It's worth it.

In design terms, water refers to any water elements you may include, such as ponds or streams. I cannot imagine any garden without at least one water element. Even a birdbath offers a moment of reflection. As Emerson wrote in his journal about water: "It is no matter what objects are near it – a gray rock, a little grass, a crab-tree, or alder-bush, a stake – they instantly become beautiful by being reflected. It is rhyme to the eye…and suggests the deeper rhyme or translation of every natural object into its spiritual sphere." One of the most lovely of water elements is a free-form rock pool. Such a pool has the mystical aura of the Celtic sacred well. If possible, situate the pool or pond is such a way that it is not visible at once. This helps create a mystery. Even the dew that glorifies a morning garden represents spiritual illumination from heaven.

Still water adds an element of calmness, running water supplies drama and excitement. If you are fortunate enough to have a suitably sized pond or stream in your garden, a bridge over it should be included in the design. A bridge is not only practical and charming (in more ways than one), but it is also symbolic as a division between the secular and sacred world. In fact, the Latin word for priest *pontifex* literally means "bridge-builder." **Water** of any size may attract frogs, who are lunar animals and sacred to Hecate and Venus. (Lunar magic performed in the presence of frogs increases its potency.)

A garden statue of the Egyptian goddess Isis is one way to show how you honor this important element. Isis, the great mother and creator, has long been considered a guardian of water sources. Of course, you may choose a deity of your own spiritual tradition instead.

Although water lilies and lotuses are dramatic water flowers, the wise gardener does not forget to adorn at least one edge of the pond with bog plants, most of which have striking foliage. (You do need at least 6 inches of mud for them to "set" right, however, so be forewarned.) You can make your own mud by placing the liner of your artificial pond under the level of the surrounding soil, so the pond water seeps out.

I am a firm believer in goldfish, which are inexpensive and charming. A fishless pond provides a perfect environment for mosquitoes and other horrible beings. In addition, goldfish supply color, interest, and great good luck. They enliven even the shadiest corner of your garden with a splash of color. If your pond is 18 inches or deeper, your goldfish can over-winter with ease. And if you need a metaphysical reason to cultivate goldfish, you will be interested to know that they symbolize the unconscious, as they dwell in the depths of the water.

Foliage

Within the plant itself, the foliage and stems represent the element of water. Walt Whitman said that every leaf was a miracle. How right he was. Good foliage adds a serene, deep beauty to every garden — and remember good foliage is by no means always green. In fact it's surprising how many different shades of foliage there are! Several varieties of iris and sedum come to mind. For additional sparkle, try plants with variegated foliage.

Many amateur gardeners overlook the critical importance of foliage, although the recent popularity of hostas shows that it is at last getting some recognition. Recall that the foliage lasts a lot longer than the bloom; a week of pretty flowers may not compensate for months of drab or ugly foliage.

Good foliage (and evergreens) also serve as a wonderful background for both seasonal flowers and the brilliant leaves of autumn.

However, the real trouble comes not from the plants that people buy for their foliage, but from the undeserved popularity of many showy flowers that lack attractive foliage. (Too often, even the flowers are short lived.) This is all avoidable. The wise gardener keeps her garden in balanced harmony by carefully selecting plants with handsome foliage as well as those with attractive flowers. To do otherwise is to end up with a straggly, unpleasant garden of baneful influence.

Of course, one can endure unremarkable foliage in plants with long-lasting blooms or powerful magic, but one should never have to settle for anything positively ugly or grotesque. In the case of a treasured or powerful plant with unfortunate foliage, your recourse it to camouflage the poor foliage by carefully placing the plant among better leaved specimens. Then everyone is happy.

Not only should the gardener choose plants with good foliage, but she should also take care to protect that foliage from the blights of slugs, bugs, and disease. Caring only for flowers is shortsighted and self-defeating. Plants need foliage to survive.

Fire Elements

Fire refers to both flower color and sunlight in the garden. It is the most obvious kind of magic.

COLOR

Fire is the most transformative of all the elements, and in the garden too, color (which symbolizes fire) transforms the dark winter garden into a blaze of light and glory.

Color touches the emotions as well as the eyes. To change the emotional tenor of the garden, you can simply change the color, something easier to do than changing the texture or design. The blending of colors can calm, tease, or excite, and reward the eyes in many ways.

Color is true magic, for it adheres to the principle that things are not what they seem. A red rose is called red because it absorbs all colors except red. Red is the one color that it reflects. Biochemical compounds in the plant cause this phenomenon. Chlorophyll and chloroplastids produce green, carotene and xanthophylls produce yellow and orange, while anthocyanins produce red, blue, purple and violet.

In general, color is defined in terms of three characteristics: *hue,* or the actual pure color (white, yellow, red, or whatever); *tone,* a *value* (how much light the color reflects or its brightness); and *saturation* (the purity of the color). A *tint* is what happens when white is mixed into the color, while a *shade* is the color mixed with black.

Colors are often divided into warm and cool. Warm colors are the yellows and reds, while the blues and violets are cool, or at least cooler. Warm colors do tend to give the psychological impression of warmth and closeness. Most are assertive and seem as if they are marching towards you. They also attract more attention, and have more "visual weight." In fact, a small brilliant flower is often more noticeable than a larger pale one Cool colors have the opposite effect, encouraging the visitor to enter the mystery, and many magical gardens use a more muted color scheme. Lots of hot colors "advance" on the viewer and make the garden seem smaller; dim, cool colors draw the eye away and make the garden seem larger.

Hot colors can always be "cooled" by an admixture of white; this is what turns them into pastels, soft, pale, "chalky" colors. Pastel flowers are probably the most versatile of all, and draw the eye and feet of the visitor into their part of the garden, not by shouting, but by softly whispering. Darker natural shades are obtained by the adding of black to the "palette." Only nature can do this, of course. Even the most magical gardener can't very well tiptoe through the tulips swabbing down garish flowers with black paint. Although I have been tempted.

Color Symbolism

Color symbolism runs very deep in the human psyche. As the palette of flower colors is almost infinite, and dozens of species can be found for any one color, lists of specific flowers are only given for those colors that are somewhat more unusual.

Red is the longest wavelength of the visible colors. Like white, it is ambiguous in nature. It is a "hot" color and is associated with material and physical forces, especially in magic. It represents power, energy, and robust health. Lots of red produces strong emotional stimuli in the viewer. Of course, there are many shades of red, including scarlet, crimson, vermilion, and claret, but all are identifiably red.

In alchemical lore, red stands for the primal substance sulfur. For the ancient Maya, red represented east, the place of sunrise. Gardeners who choose a Mayan influence might group a drift of red flowers on the east side of the garden. In the Brazilian spiritist traditions, red signifies the direction north and the element **Earth**. In Chinese gardens, on the other hand, red represents the south. (The ancient Egyptians disliked and feared red; they tried to avoid it as much as possible. They associated it with the evil god Seth and the vile serpent Apophis. A garden with strong Egyptian magical accents should use red sparingly if at all.) The ancient Babylonians associated red with the planet Mars (which is indeed the red planet).

In China, however, red is a sacred color, the color of life. It was the emblem of the Zhou dynasty (1050-256 BCE) and is also the color of the People's Republic of China.

In Christianity, red and green are Christmas colors, of course, but red alone is linked with both the blood of martyrs and with hell. The Beast in the biblical book of Revelation is described as "scarlet." On the other hand, red in the church calendar represents the passion of Christ and the fire of Pentecost.

In western popular culture, red stands for love and passion, and a garden with many red notes suggests a strong, passionate nature. (Annuals tend to produce the hottest, most vivid reds. It's important for them to attract attention in a hurry.) The darkness and purity of the red used in the garden makes a difference in the color effects. Lighter, clearer, purer shades denote affection. As the color deepens, desire and passion are suggested. Very dark, muddy reds can present an aura of anger. Interestingly, red is not visible to bees at all. It looks black to them. In general, red looks best against a rich green background.

For Renaissance thinkers, red stood for the metal iron and the planet Mars, both rather unsettling influences. Of course it also represents blood in both the positive and negative senses. For the Celts, a red flower represented the Goddess in her mother form.

Orange, another "hot" color, stands for ambition, personal glory, strength, and striving. (The name of the color comes from the name of the fruit, not vice versa.) It is a combination of red and yellow. Some people have an instinctive dislike for this brash color, and it should be used sparingly in a spiritual garden for that reason and because of its traditional worldly associations, although some

people consider it healing. Orange is also difficult to harmonize with other colors; it overpowers them with its brashness. Aesthetically, orange gives its happiest effects when paired with more restrained colors, and combining it with blue and green pulls all three colors together in a harmonious whole. The ancient Babylonians associated orange with the planet Jupiter.

Pink is a mixture of white and red. Different shades and amounts of red produce different tones of pink. Pink is soothing in small doses and a garden with occasional areas of pink is calming and, in fact necessary. A garden with no pink at all can be strident. For some, pink represents honor and friendship.

However, an entirely pink garden can be cloying, and may even arouse aggressive instincts. A garden with many pink notes suggests romantic love and affection. Warm pinks harmonize well with other warm colors; paler pinks do well with cooler colors. Pink is very passive color in that it has little power to influence or modify the colors that border it. However, pink itself can be greatly influenced by the surrounding palette. White and silver make pink look darker, green makes it look redder, and gray makes it brighter. Pink and yellow do not go well together, as rule. If you must combine the two, try using very pale yellows.

As pink heats up, it becomes *magenta*, a color disliked by many people. The great gardener Gertrude Jekyll described it as malignant, for reasons impossible to know. (She didn't care for purple either.)

Yellow, also a "hot" color is associated with the intellect, esteem, and majesty. In the medieval church, yellow (golden) flowers represented revealed truth. In China it suggests progress and fame, and traditionally, it is the color of divination and clairvoyance. It has the opposite physiological effect from blue, its complement. In Mayan-influenced gardens, yellow stands for the south. In Chinese gardens, yellow stands for the center, while in the Brazilian spiritist tradition, yellow signifies the west and the element water. For Renaissance thinkers, yellow represented gold and the sun itself. Many yellow notes in the garden suggest strong mental activity. For the ancient Babylonians, yellow represented the sun, a very natural association. A garden with lots of yellow looks cheerful even on cloudy days.

However, too much yellow in a garden has rather sinister connotations, especially in the summer. Spring yellows are beautiful against the tender green of new foliage, but in summer yellow looks better mixed with other colors (except pink). One great thing about yellow is that since you can find yellow plants blooming from mid-winter (witch-hazel) through the fall, you can always count on a splash of it in your garden.

Blue, a decidedly "cool" color has similar connotations to violet, in both western and Indian lore. (The Indian god Krishna is described as blue.) On most surveys, people report that blue is their favorite color. Interestingly, blue is the rarest color among flowers, and for that reason, is exceptionally prized. (There's a million dollar reward for the first true blue tulip. There's no true-blue rose either.) In color therapy, blue is one of the most beneficial of all colors, helping to lower blood pressure and relax breathing.

In many traditions blue, especially dark blue, stands for truth and good health. Lighter blue suggests psychic awareness, intuition, and tranquility. A lot of blue in a garden produces emotional moderation, the ability to master one's drives. In a similar vein, blue also tends to make one reflective, so it's a good choice for a meditation garden, especially for a Buddhist garden, since it promotes detachment. A garden with many blue notes suggests healing and peace. Too much blue in a garden, however, can bring on sadness or even make one feel uncomfortable. Since blue is so rare, however, there's little chance your garden will have too much of it.

In the Brazilian spiritist tradition, blue signifies the east and is associated with the element air. In Chinese gardens, blue also stands for the east, and a garden based on Chinese magic might include a drift of blue in the east. In Chinese thought, however, blue flowers are considered inauspicious. (It is even unlucky to wear blue flowers in the hair.) So it is probably best to avoid them in a Chinese-inspired garden. For Renaissance thinkers, it stands for the metal tin and the planet Jupiter. The ancient Babylonians, however, considered blue to be the color representative of Mercury.

In western symbology, blue represents faithfulness and devotion, as in "true blue." In Christian thought blue symbolized immortality, faith, and heaven, and both Jesus and Mary are frequently shown in blue. Since blue represents water, blue flowers are also an excellent choice for a water garden. Blue flowers include cultivars of anemones, bachelor's button, cranesbills, hyacinth, iris, forget-me-not, phlox, primrose, veronica, periwinkle, and pansy.

Violet, which has the shortest wavelength, is a mixture of blue and red. It symbolizes spirituality and enlightenment — the opposite of the materialistic striving represented by orange. It is considered a "cool" color, and is sometimes linked to the idea of sacrifice. In the Christian liturgical calendar, it represents repentance, and was used during Lent and Advent. Violet or purple flowers can include cultivars of anemone, crocus, daphne, cranesbill, hyacinth, iris, phlox, primrose, lilac, tulip, valerian, violet and pansy, and wisteria.

Purple, in its purest, brightest aspect, is the color of transmutation. It perfectly combines red and blue. It also represents power. But it's a tricky color, shading away to mauve on one hand and blue or violet on the other. A purple (containing more red than violet) signifies the east in the Celtic tradition, in Renaissance thought, purple stands for the planet Venus and the metal mercury. It is also the traditional royal color, and magically very powerful. It is often used for ceremonial magic. In China, purple symbolized not only the emperor, but also heaven itself. Related to purple is *lavender*, a color that traditionally symbolizes spiritual development and divination.

Symbolically, light, pure shades of red/violet suggest friendship, but as the color becomes muddier, greed is suggested. Purple symbolically represents the deeper mysteries. Famously purple plants include iris, lavender, cultivars of clematis, and the buddleia.

Brown is not brown, not really. Thinking of brown, one gets a mental image of a monochromatic, dull mouse-like color. But the brown of the earth is a rich and imposing tapestry of bronze and copper, cinnamon and nutmeg, coffee and chocolate. Brown is hazelnut and chestnut. It is burnished gold. It symbolizes the whole fruitful earth, and while not common in flowers, it is, of course, the main color of twigs and stems, as well as of the earth itself. It is therefore a foundation color of garden design. It has a warm and comforting influence, and is associated with strong animal magic. It is the color of endurance.

White, which reflects all colors, is associated with divinity itself. Maybe too divine for some, there's a lot of folklore that says bringing white flowers indoors or to sick people will result in a death. In alchemy, white stands for the primal substance mercury. In Maya symbology, white signifies north; gardeners wishing to create Maya magic may want to emphasize white on the north side of the garden. However, in the Brazilian spiritist tradition, white signifies south and is associated with the element fire.

White also signifies south in the Celtic tradition. In Chinese-influenced gardens, white stands for the west and the season of autumn. For Renaissance thinkers, white represented silver and the moon. The ancient Babylonians also linked white and the moon. In western thought, white traditionally represents innocence, blessings, and joy, and in church symbolism white flowers represent the resurrection of Christ and were used in the sacraments. White represents purity in both pagan and Christian traditions. White flowers also represent the Virgin aspect of the Goddess.

As a design element, white can bring an illuminating note to a shady garden. However, this is just a note – and a note doesn't make a song. A patch of white flowers in a dark corner serves to make the *surrounding* area even darker – and if you're like most magical gardeners, that is just the effect you want. And nothing is more wonderful than a white or moon garden for a magical aura. Choose plants with large white blooms. Yucca is one traditional choice, along with white lilies and daisies. And make sure there is sufficient green for the white plants to appear in their purest elegance. Remember, however, that like every other color, white is a matter of degrees. Some flowers we call white are really cream or biscuit, or palest yellow, and whites look their brightest and purest against a green backdrop.

Gray is a wonderful harmonizer of other colors. It is also a symbol of serenity. Many gray-foliaged plants are native to the Mediterranean, and so do well in a dry climate. A gray-green shade stands for the west in the Celtic tradition. Plants with gray foliage enrich a white or moonlight garden. Such plants include dusty miller, lamb's ears, lavender, buddleia, and artemisia. Plants with gray foliage may also harbor fairies.

Green is of course *the* color associated with nature and fertility. "A green thought in a green shade" (Andrew Marvell, The Garden) is the very essence of the garden itself. It is associated with natural, calm vigor. At the same time it suggests renewal and rebirth.

Green is the stem and leaf color for most plants, and so it's the dominating note of any garden, especially in the winter when the green stands alone clothing the hollies and yew. In the garden, green is a neutral color. In alchemical lore, green is a powerful solvent. For Renaissance thinkers, green stood for the metal copper and the planet Saturn. For the ancient Babylonians, green represented the planet

Venus. In much of the ancient pagan world, green represented wisdom. In Christian symbolism, green stands for immortality, a victory of spring over winter's death. It was also used to represent the trinity. For everyone, it seems, it represents freedom and beauty.

In garden design, however, it is well to remember that green comes in various shades, from pale yellowish-green to deep, dark green. A garden with many green notes suggests serenity, prosperity, and comfort. In addition, most flowers look their best against an evergreen background. While green is understandably a rare color for flowers, some do indeed bear green blooms, including some cultivars of zinnia, hellebore, and clematis.

Black is almost unknown in the world of flowers. It is the dark place, the color that absorbs all others, the mystery of mysteries. In Mayan symbology, it represents the west, the dark place where the sun goes down. While it's not possible to plant black flowers, Maya-conscious gardeners may use the west for a shady corner by planting a tree there. In Chinese and Celtic gardens, black stands for the north. In the magical tradition, black is used in exorcisms and in the breaking of hexes. The ancient Babylonians associated black with the planet Saturn.

Color Schemes

Conventional garden design involves the use of one or more color schemes. For example, a mono-chromatic color scheme uses one predominant color, such as white or blue throughout the garden, while a dichromatic one is based on two colors. (You can also choose one dominant color for spring and another for summer.) For a subtle effect, use colors near each other on the "color wheel", like blue and violet; for a more dramatic effect use colors further apart. But be careful. Used over large areas, opposing primary colors like red and blue can clash.

If there is flower whose form and habit you like, but which comes in a loud, unpleasing color, look around. Most such plants have a paler or white variety you can substitute.

Some sources advise those not sure about how colors go together to buy a small sample of flowers and arrange them in a vase. This is a dodgy technique, in my opinion. What may look interesting and arresting in a vase may be shocking when spread over a large area. And a subtle vase flower arrangement may be deadly dull in a large garden. The best way is to visit other gardens in your area, either those of your friends or large public gardens. (It does little good to travel to a climate zone outside your own for this purpose. In fact, soil conditions can vary widely even within a small area.) Note what looks good to your eye, and don't be afraid to imitate effects that appeal to you. As you grow more confident in your own magic, you will find it easy to be more creative.

If you like a bold effect, but are completely unsure about what complementary colors "go together," you can't go wrong with blue and yellow. These are the warm and cool colors of the sky and sun, and traditionally represent joyfulness. Every shade of blue looks good with every shade of yellow, so have confidence. If you wish to add a third color, use white sparingly. (Those are the clouds.) Pink, blue and white also make a pleasing threesome. One simple rule is: the brighter the color: the less of it you need to achieve an effect.

If you find you've made a ghastly mistake by introducing too much contrast into your garden, don't rip out everything by the roots. Try planting some silver or gray foliage plants to harmonize softer colors, and some deep green foliage plants to harmonize more brilliant hues and tone down the rest of the garden. White flowers can also help.

If you choose to be stylishly conservative in your garden design, and want to stick with one basic color (with, of course, various shadings to avoid monotony), it's easier on the eye and better preserves garden rhythm to arrange the changing shades gradually, not in discrete clumps of flowers at opposites ends of the saturation scale.

In this, as in all things magical, consult your own taste. Some people like harmony, some like contrast. Sometimes you can have the best of both worlds. If you want to develop a more harmonious effect, yet have a variety of colors, you can consider growing several colors of one type of flower, or at least use flowers of similar shape. Or, if you like varieties of a single shade, choose different species of that color. That way, you get some interesting variety in form while retaining a harmony of color.

Sunlight and Shade

Fire also refers to the amount of light and shade in the garden. How the sun travels across the sky is not something even the greatest wizard can alter – although even the humblest among us can plant a tree or construct a barrier to create shade. If your garden is too small for a tree, use vines to create the important vertical element essential for any garden. It's also important to consider not simply how long, but when the sun shines into your garden. Afternoon sun is generally much more intense (and hot) than morning sun.

Remember also that the angle of the sun varies from season to season. If you have the luxury of time, the best thing to do is to let the prospective garden lie fallow for a year, and record the passage of light and shade as the year goes by.

If possible, all observations and record keeping should be done before the planting, but if this is not possible, just do the best you can. Stand in the center of your site, or proposed site, and face south. Learn where on the horizon the sun rises and sets in summer. Where is the sun at midday in the summer? What might block it? The farther north you are the more difference there will be between summer and winter sun positions. Don't be afraid to get some help in learning the path of the sun. Try to determine how much direct sunlight your garden will get during the growing season.

It is easy to confuse direct sun with general brightness, but don't do it. When a leaf is in direct sun, it will cast a shadow. In general full sun means more than 6 hours of direct sunlight a day.

It's important also to realize that summertime, with its intense light, is also the season of the deepest shade, since the shading plants are in their glory. Although most plants thrive in full sun, there are enough exceptions to make shade-gardening an enjoyable and truly magical experience.

Choose plants whose habits allow them to thrive in the area you plant them. Plants with large leaves usually need more shade (and moisture). It is a charming fact of nature that most shade-loving plants have shallow root systems that enable them to flourish beneath a tree, while sun-loving plants usually have deeper roots, allowing them to suck up all available water in the soil. In generally the soil beneath trees is quite dry.

If you have too much shade, you can sometimes ameliorate the situation by careful pruning of overhanging trees. However, don't despair, some of the most magical of all gardens are the outwardly subdued, but inwardly dynamic, shade gardens. Of course, it's always possible to cut a tree down, but unless it is diseased, I wouldn't do it. You can inherit a very heavy load of karma by sawing them down. Trees are powerful magic, living air conditioners, and anchoring points. Work around them. Harming the environment is not a way to create good magic.

Many people like a ground cover in parts of their garden, especially under trees. Ground cover is attractive, especially in a magical garden. However, it's only fair to warn you that some common ground covers can be quite invasive, quickly spreading to parts of the garden where it is distinctly not wanted. In general, a combination of sandy soil, lots of rain, and plenty of warm sunshine make it more likely that your ground cover may become invasive. Some kinds of ground cover, like periwinkle and oregano, will allow plants to grow through them. Others like ivies are much less forgiving, although some exceptionally tough plants might be able to sneak through.

If your over-shady garden is caused by immoveable buildings and trees too sacred to cut, you have an easy solution: Pots! You can put the desired plants in containers and rotate them into a sunny position every week or two. You can choose pots with special designs or personal meanings that increase their magic, and enjoy sun-loving flowers all season.

Shade tolerant magical plants include astilbe, forget-me-not, monkshood, columbines, foxglove, sweet woodruff, daylilies, cranesbills, periwinkle, and violets.

Air Elements

Climate and Weather

In a metaphysical sense, air represents spirituality. In horticultural terms, it refers to weather and climate.

If your garden is in a low pocket, it may be an entire zone colder than the surrounding areas. And within your garden, there may be warmer microclimates. In my own garden, I have a white wall that protects the plants in its purview from northwest winds. The hot, sunny area it protects will grow plants I can't grow 3 feet away.

In one sense, of course, you are stuck with your climate — unless you are willing to move! And all of us must ultimately bow to the exigencies of day length, average temperatures, and, first and last, frost. Nowhere, however, is a little practical magic more useful than in manipulating the streaming elements of air. But before rushing into attempting to control the winds — learn to live with them. Bountiful nature has supplied us with a rich array of plants for every climate. From rough and tumble daffodils to exotic tropical plants, your corner of the world is well supplied with native plants. The wisest of gardeners trusts nature, and works with her to establish a garden that changes with the seasons, rather than one that attempts to conquer them.

To this end seek out what riches each season brings to your region. Think beyond blooms to roots, shapes, and berries. Thus, when winter wind rips the color and fabric from your plants, the true beauty of their "bones" remains. The true glory of the air garden is the way it honors the seasons.

But you can still cheat a little. By taking careful heed of he way the wind blows, and the microclimate created by a wall or hedge; you can coax into bloom that special magical plant everyone said was impossible to grow in your area.

Gardeners in areas with long-blooming seasons (and lazy or busy gardeners) often do best growing flowering shrubs rather than flowers; such shrubs give a high return for relatively little labor. If you have to tend a garden for nine months or so – easy care is a definite consideration!

Sound and Scent

In design, air provides the sound (along with water) and fragrance. It may seem odd to think of a garden's sounds, but the rustling wind, the chimes, or the sound of water offer a special quality to every garden. Even, perhaps especially, the tiniest garden should offer the gentle refreshing sound of a fountain. And the bamboo, they say, laughs in the wind. Birdsong and bee-hum adds a living note that is absolutely essential to the magical garden. A garden that does not draw bees and birds is a dead garden. No garden should be without yet another sound, that of your own voice, your songs, chants, whispered secrets. Everyone by now knows that talking to plants makes them grow — and it will  make you grow too. As the biblical book of Job states, "Speak to the earth, and it shall teach thee" (12:8). As you enter into this rich relationship, you will find yourself growing ever more sensitive, intuitive, and magical.

The rich perfumes or delicate scents of your garden are sensuous and inviting. This most subtle of sensations releases the most subtle magic within each of us. The most fragrant flowers include hyacinth, lilac, lily-of-the-valley, many roses (English and some hybrid teas), lavender, dianthus, and peonies.

Different Types of Gardens

There are myriad ways to order a charmed garden. You can follow the seasons, or organize by color, fragrance, texture, or shape. You can use your knowledge of plant history, culture, signatures, or powers, or follow your intuition. The choice is yours.

To plan the garden, you can draw a "bird's eye" view or a ground level view. Some people even take a photograph of the present site and draw the future plants on it to imagine how they would look. This sort of thing works very well for the professional designer, but I have never had any luck with doing any of these things. Somehow the "bird's eye" view never transforms itself into what I really want. I use my imagination, and instinct, and simply try to get the feel of the place. Of course I have made plenty of mistakes, but they are hard to avoid in any case. By the way, never forget that even you are not allowed to set foot on your neighbor's property – there's nothing stopping you from making use of his "view" if it's a pretty one. Your vision doesn't stop at the border of your garden.

This section of the book is not meant to be a step-by-step guide to how you should plan your garden. As I mentioned earlier, your garden is a unique spot in the universe, and you are a unique person. You know your own earth and your own spirit. I will, however, provide ideas to stimulate your creative instincts.

The Path of the Sun: The Seasonal Garden

One of the most time-honored and rewarding ways of designing a garden is to base it around the seasons. Nothing in a garden stays the same from moment to moment, and planting a garden in accordance with the seasons is a wonderful way to pay homage to the irrevocable passage of time. The thrill of spring surrenders inevitably to the richness of summer, the glory of fall, and the somber strength of winter. To each season belongs its own beauty.

Little is more satisfying than observing the passage of snowdrops, crocus, daffodils, and tulips, peonies, roses, asters, chrysanthemums, on to the rich harvest of brilliant fall and winter berries. (In gardening, we refer to this process rather majestically as "order of bloom.") This is such a natural way of thinking about a garden that it only remains to decide what plants suit both the season and your own magic.

While we tend to associate gardening only with flowers, a year-round approach reminds us that bark, foliage, fruit, and berries add not just color, but structure to the garden. The noble beauty of the winter garden also provides one of the best places to exhibit your garden's statuary and garden art!

Speciality Gardens

The Bee and Butterfly Garden

While you certainly don't need a garden that is swarming with bees, especially if anyone in the family is allergic to them, adding a few plants specifically designed to attract them is good sense and powerful magic. Bees play a critical role in the pollination of many plants, especially fruiting varieties; they also have strong magical significance.

Bees have long been the symbol of hard work, purity, and diligence, as well as of royalty. Napoleon Bonaparte, who was not of royal blood, chose bees for his new coat of arms. The Pharaohs of ancient Lower Egypt were considered to belong to the tribe of bees. Bees also are reputed to lead men to their proper brides, an interesting piece of folklore that pops up in both Chinese and European stories. In Christian iconography, they represent the spirit and the resurrection. (St. Bernard of Clairvaux thought they symbolized the Holy Spirit.) Bees are ambiguous, however. While associated with honey, sweetness, and flowers, their stings remind us that nature always guards her treasures. Interestingly, the honeybee is not native to either North America or Britain, yet it plays a greater role in pollination than any other insect in our gardens. Other beneficial insects include wasps, hornets (really!), hoverflies and ladybugs. In fact, some species of ladybugs feed only upon aphids.

As for butterflies, they are the immemorial symbols of the soul, and the Greeks used the same word, *psyche*, for both. Still, one needs to be practical. Get a copy of the *Field Guide to Butterflies*, published by the National Audubon Society.

Although most butterflies are elegant, spiritual, and graceful visitors to the garden, they weren't *always* butterflies. Caterpillars, no matter how charming, often devour the leaves of your most important plants. You can and should have both butterflies and flowers, but you will need to find out which caterpillars eat which leaves, and plant accordingly. Sometimes you'll have to make a choice; other times you will find that caterpillars of desirable butterfly species may nibble at, but not decimate, your garden. For example, the larvae of desirable monarch and fritillary butterflies enjoy the common milkweed (*Asclepias syriaca*). Dill (*Anethum graveolens*) is also a favorite of monarch.

Traditionally, butterflies are symbols of transformation, for obvious reasons. In this connection, too, they are associated with the soul. The Greek word for butterfly *psyche* makes a great deal more sense than "butterfly." Butterflies have nothing to do with butter. In Japan, a butterfly represents a young woman; a pair of butterflies suggests marital happiness. Much the same was true in China, except that the butterfly represented a young man in love. In Aztec Mexico the butterfly was the emblem of the god of vegetation; thus it is the perfect accompaniment to any garden! One who creates a butterfly garden is creating magical opportunities for the transformation of the soul.

The Wildlife Garden

The best magical gardens are welcoming to wildlife. But before you begin, you'll need to decide which animals will – or won't – be invited. Some of the most beautiful and interesting creatures like deer and raccoon can devastate a garden, while some of the most terrifying, like spiders and snakes can be beneficial; not only that, but many of these frightening creatures have profound magical value. The snake, for example, is a representative of secret wisdom, and, indeed, of immortality. Some underground creatures like earthworms and ants help aerate your soil. Others, such as certain beetle larvae, gobble plant roots. But not all larvae, not even all beetle larvae, are so destructive. Some help recycle deadwood back into a usable form and some ground beetles hunt slugs, snails, and caterpillars.

But I think the most important inhabitant of the magical garden must be the toad. Not only are toads a catalyst for magic, and but they also perform helpful work in the garden, gobbling up cutworms, slugs, snail, and other dastardly pests. Unfortunately, they eat the beneficial earthworm as well, but I suppose you can't have everything. Although certain old texts made reference to the killing of toads for various magical potions, this is unnecessary, dangerous, and wrong. Toads work their best magic while living peacefully near you in your garden. The witches of old apparently made charming costumes for their toads of red or green velvet and bells, but this is not necessary. Toads are more magical in their natural warty outfits.

Frogs can be harder to come by, since they are very particular about water cleanliness and extremely sensitive to even low levels of pollution. Sometimes you can attract a bullfrog or green frog, but they often stay only for a while before migrating elsewhere. This is their nature. Frogs are sacred to Hecate and Venus.

When you decide what your levels of interest and tolerance are, you can plan a garden designed to attract the species you like. To do this, you'll have to create a habitat niche suitable for the species of interest. A habitat niche includes proper shelter from predators and wind, a water source, the right kind of food, and perhaps a nesting area. A welcoming and well-designed wildlife garden contains secluded areas where shyer visitors can relax until they discover you mean them no harm; a careful planning of shrubs and paths can lead them directly to your viewing window. Even if you live in a dry area, having a fountain or pool in your garden is sure to be a main event as far as wildlife is concerned! Keep feeders and birdbaths full, and sooner or later, your guests will arrive.

The Sun Garden

Many are the principles by which to design a sun garden. A sun garden helps the magic practitioner find power and strength. On the simplest level, a sun garden is simply any garden planted in a sunny spot. Another way to create sun magic is to plant yellow and orange flowers, which psychologically suggest the sun to the eye. Indeed, many yellow and orange flowers do indeed prefer a fully sunny area. There is a more subtle way, however; that is to plant the so-called herbs of the sun. Anciently, plants were characterized by their affiliation to various celestial bodies and the magical powers associated with them. Some plants (and this is a mere sampling) magically associated with the sun include almond, angelica, ash, bay laurel, chamomile, dittany, eyebright, grapes, ivy, juniper, mistletoe, oak, peony, potentilla, rosemary, scarlet pimpernel, St. John's wort, strawberry, sunflower, thyme, viper's bugloss, and walnut. (For more Sun plants see the Quick Guide in the Appendix.)

Always make sure what you plant is suited to your area. If the plants come in a choice of colors, yellow and orange have stronger sun powers than white or blue/violet.

The Moon Garden

The night is the kingdom of the moon. It is both a time and place. Here lies the deepest magic, and only the night garden can evoke its full mystery. As the moon is considered a feminine symbol, the most powerful moon gardens are best for feminine magic. On a more prosaic level, the moon garden is considered the very best for relaxing and unwinding. The traditional color for the moon garden is white.

In the night garden, fragrance makes up for lost color. Some plants release their sweetest scents with the moonlight, and all plants take on an added majesty. (Many night blooming plants release their fragrance at night to draw the moths that pollinate them.) Some of these plants include honeysuckle, gardenia, stock, nicotiana, tuberose, and the evening primrose. Other excellent plants for the moon garden are betony, rosemary, thyme, and mugwort. Many night-bloomers are of a solid, pale color, to make them easier to see.

As the sun sets and the moon rises, the night garden begins to glow. Perhaps the best bloomer of all is the tobacco plant (*Nicotiana sylvestris*).

If you have the funds, you can add dramatic lighting to the night garden; many easy-to-install kits are available. This increases the practical use of your magical garden, enabling you to hold special ceremonies even when the moon is new or obscured by clouds. Certain kinds of lights also cast dramatic, mysterious shadows, adding to the overall aura. If you shun modern embellishment, torches are available that accomplish much the same thing.

Choose white or cream flowers to catch the moonlight, and be sure to include night bloomers. The evening primrose (*Oenothera*) is a particular favorite of mine. It has sweet-smelling white flowers. In the ancient magical tradition these are some plants associated with the moon: cabbage, lettuce, lily, loosestrife, moonwort, poppy, privet, pumpkin, water lily, willow, and wintergreen. (For more moon plants see the Quick Guide in the Appendix.)

Again, plant only things that are suitable for your area. If cultivars come in different colors, the white variety has the greatest magical power.

Other Planetary Gardens

You may wish to design a garden (or part of a garden) to honor other planetary forces. Many plants have associations with more than one planet or with Sun and Moon. (For plants associated with more than one planet, look under the planets' name in the Quick Guide to Magical Uses and Attributes in the Appendix.)

A garden devoted to Mercury strengthens the intellect and communication skills. Mercurial plants often have delicate and divided leaves. They include acacia, anise, azalea, basil, bittersweet, bryony, caraway, carrot, celery, chicory, coltsfoot, foxglove, dill, fennel, fenugreek, flax, ferns, garlic, honeysuckle, horehound, lavender, lily-of-the-valley, mandrake, myrtle, oat, oregano, parsley, parsnip, santolina, southernwood, trefoil, valerian, and wormwood.

A Venus garden will enhance your powers of love and spirituality. Venus-governed plants include alder, artichoke, birch, blackberry, bramble, cherry, chickpea, coltsfoot, columbine, cowslip, daffodil, daisy, figwort, foxglove, goldenrod, hollyhock, ivy, linden, mint, mugwort, orchid, peach, pear, pennyroyal, plantain, plum, raspberry, rose, sorrel, strawberry, tansy, violet, and wormwood.

A Mars garden promotes energy and courage. Plants of Mars include all-heal, anemone, basil, box, bryony, catnip, chives, dead nettle, garlic, gentian, hawthorn, honeysuckle, hops, leek, lettuce, lupine, oak, onions, pine, tarragon, and woodruff.

A Jupiter garden brings prosperity. These lucky plants include agrimony, apple, apricot, asparagus, basil, blueberry, borage, carnation, centaury, chervil, coltsfoot, comfrey, dandelion, fennel, fir, flax, ginseng, horse chestnut, houseleek, maple, meadowsweet, mullein, myrrh, potentilla, raspberry, sorrel, sycamore, tansy, and tomato.

A Saturn garden is one devoted to the deepest inner mysteries. Many plants governed by Saturn are toxic; others live in the deep woods. Plants under the influence of Saturn include amaranth, barley, beech, belladonna, blackthorn, centaury, cypress, elm, foxglove, fenugreek, hawthorn, holly, iris, monkshood, mullein, periwinkle, pine, quince, Solomon's seal, water hemlock, willow, wintergreen, and yew.

The Fragrance Garden

Air governs the fragrance garden, but of course the plants themselves produce the fragrance. While most plants have a distinctive scent, it is their subtle and complex combinations that produce the magic that is the fragrance garden. Only experimentation will show you the way to maintain that special magic through the seasons, but certain plants have an important place in any such endeavor: these include daphne, honeysuckle, hyacinth, jasmine, lavender, narcissus, pine, rose, viburnum, and various herbs…. many silver-leaved plants (several species of artemisia and yarrow, for instance) have fragrant foliage, so don't despair of scent when the blooms have faded.

In general flowers with a single row of petals are sweeter scented than the double form, unless the double form occurs naturally. Single-petalled flowers that have been hybridized into a double form often lack the intense fragrance of the simpler variety. (Apparently, in nature many plants have to choose between looking snappy and smelling sweet. There's only so much energy available.)

The Fairy Garden

Fairies are said to represent the supernormal powers of the human soul. If you want to draw fairies, the following plants are reportedly very attractive to them. However, fairies are not always the sweet benevolent things they are sometimes made out to be. They can be not merely mischievous, but downright dangerous, and are famous for making off with human children. Several species bite. However, if you are determined to have them, plant some of the following (with the possible exception of foxglove; which is questionable see Foxglove in Encyclopedia of Magical Plants): alder, apple, ash, aspen, betony, blackthorn, borage, bramble, broom, carnation, chamomile, clover, daisy, elder, foxglove, hawthorn, holly, hollyhock, hyssop, juniper, lavender, lemon balm, lilac, linden, lobelia, maidenhair fern, oak, pansies, pine, primula, rose, rosemary, St. John's wort, silver birch, sunflower, sweet pea, thyme, vervain, violet, yarrow, or zinnia.

Do not include peonies or dill in a fairy garden. Fairies can't stand either one of them, and will not enter a garden that contains them no matter what else you have. Most fairies don't like mistletoe, either.

The Zen Garden

A world apart is the Zen garden. Instead of fertile earth, there is sterile sand. Instead of birdsong and bee-hum, there is silence. Nothing grows, nothing lives, and nothing dies. Instead of plants, there are rocks. Instead of welcoming paths, there are formal, carefully raked lines of sand that forbid walking. The Zen garden is a garden of the mind. It doesn't invite the senses; it stills them. And yet.... once over the culture shock of experiencing a garden without (or almost without) plants, one comes face to face and heart to heart with the deep mystery of self and un-self-ness. Truly, as poet Marianne Moore wrote, "The mind is an enchanting thing." The Zen garden's pure, solemn strength, its intense emptiness, draws forth the spirit. Spend an hour in a Zen garden, and you'll emerge strangely calm, oddly refreshed, and weirdly poised.

To design a Zen garden of your own, you must first properly immerse yourself in Zen meditation techniques, which to some extent parallels incantatory and spell-making traditions of western magic. Only after you have obtained the proper state of mind should you even begin to study Zen gardening design. It is an art of its own, for the mastery of which you will need to consult another book.

Beyond the Garden (The Meadow Garden)

One of the most delightful of recent gardening trends is the concept of creating a "meadow", or meadow garden instead of the classical garden. I use the word "creating" advisedly. Simply neglecting your garden will not automatically produce a fragrant, beautiful, and spiritually potent place; instead a tick-ridden, burr-studded wasteland will result, making enemies of your neighbors. A meadow garden is not for the lazy, but for the environmentally committed who are willing to work with (and put up with) nature.

Over most of America and Europe, meadows are not natural phenomena. They are clearings (often made by humans) that are constantly threatened by encroaching forest. The exception is the vast prairie lands of the American Midwest, so gardeners living there may have the best luck with a magical meadow garden. If you decide to go the meadow garden route, you'll have the best luck choosing native plants or at least ones that grown wild in your area. (Many "wild" flowers are actually escaped and naturalized imports). Check with a local plant society to find out if it is a good idea to plant an "exotic" plant in your area; in some places they become pests.

Of course you don't want to include anything that might become a nuisance, such as (in my area) honeysuckle and multiflora rose. Some of the best magical plants for most areas include asters, foxglove, and yarrow. Use just a few well-chosen plants, and look for species that don't need staking or other excessive care (including watering and regular division). Plants that form thick mats will be less likely to allow in weeds.

You'll probably have the best luck if you kill off the existing vegetation, but try not to shake up the soil too much; that only encourages latent or dormant weeds. You can smother the area with a heavy mulch and wait a year, or you can just burn it off (get the permits first) or kill it off with a non-persistent weed-killer. See, already it's turning into a project – and all you thought you had to do was gaily toss a packet of wildflower seeds in to the grass.

If you are lucky enough to have wooded area on your property, many lovely and magical plants prefer the shade, and you can judiciously add the ones you like or need. All woods are full of powerful magic – and those lucky enough to share their lives with a forest truly lead a charmed life. The sacred grove is an ancient magical tradition of both the Greeks to the Druids.

Dedicating and Consecrating the Garden

Every enchanted garden requires a dedicatory ceremony. Some people prefer to celebrate the ceremony before the first spade of dirt is turned; others wait until the garden is planted. There are no rules. Nor are there any rules about having the ceremony by yourself or with friends, by the light of moon, dawn, or midday. The only sensible requirement is the honoring of the Fours: The Four Directions, the Four Seasons, and the Four Elements. These are space, time, and substance – and of these our cosmos is made.

This is what I do: I dedicate the garden at the full moon closest to the time of planting my first plants of the year. I bow to each of the Four Directions, holding in my hand a symbol of each season: a bud for spring, a flower for summer, a brilliantly colored leaf for fall, and a root for winter, collected in a small bag. I pass the bag through the air, pass it through a candle flame, dip it in water, and bury it in the earth, thus honoring each of the elements. As you do this murmur the holy name of Airmid, the Celtic goddess of herb-lore. She will bless your efforts.

Encyclopedia of Magical Plants

Introduction

Obviously, this listing cannot include all plants, not even all magical plants. Many common garden flowers have been omitted simply because there is no magical tradition associated with them. In other cases, I have included herbs of comparatively minor magic, but for which I have a special fondness. I have also included several plants that are by no means garden flowers – such as dandelions and thistles. While many of these plants are rightly considered weeds, they do have some interesting properties and can be gathered safely from the wild. In addition, I have included several species of trees, many of which can be planted on your property outside the garden proper.

Most, although certainly not all, of the magical plants listed here are of European origin. This is because Europe was the birthplace of the western magical tradition, which is the focus of this book. In addition, Europe and the Americas share many of the same types of climate. Thus only a few tropical or subtropical plants are included. As time goes by, we will see Native American plants develop a rich magical tradition of their own. Indeed, we have already seen some of this occur and Native American plants seem to have absorbed some of the magical traditions of related, similarly named, or closely resembling, European plants.

Because my specialty is classical European witchcraft I have omitted many Native American magical plants. The Native American people have used native plants for their healing properties for millennia. Native Americans have a rich spiritual tradition, the magical underpinnings of which are just beginning to be studied. For the same reason – and because of the particular kind of magic associated with it – I have omitted many plants used in the New Orleans Hoodoo tradition. (Hoodoo, while a very exciting magical practice, has little of the transcendent/immanent visionary quality of the classical European tradition, which is central to this book.)

Some of the plants mentioned here are not commonly grown, either because of special climatic requirements or because they are difficult and need special care (sandalwood, for example). I am listing them anyway, both for their inherent interest, and because commercial preparations of many of them are available for herbal magic. Using herbs in this way is not the same as growing them yourself and having the joy and special magic that only a garden brings, but practical constraints make the home growing of some plants impossible. It is frequently possible, however, to replace exotic or rare plants with more common ones, but sometimes no adequate substitute is readily available.

Do not even attempt to use all the plants listed. Ten carefully chosen species will be sufficient for all but the most advanced spell-casters and magicians. Learn as much as you can about the growing habit, history, and powers of each plant before proceeding to the next. Let your visionary eye guide you.

Medicine, Magic, and Spirit

While most plants in this encyclopedia have documented medical uses, they can also be dangerous if mishandled. Only a trained medical herbalist (which I am not) should prescribe herbal remedies; this should be done in concert with your regular medical practitioner. This book focuses on the spiritual and magical, rather than the medicinal powers of herbs. Although we may describe a plant by its size, habit, color, and fragrance, these things do not encompass its meaning and import. The power of the plant breaks forth from its physical being; its true root is not in the soil, but in the spirit.

It is in this, I find the most important function of the plant. While not every plant in and of itself has spiritual meaning, many do. And placing the different plants in the right order and in the right garden design creates a powerful and unique spiritual whole. The powers of plants are synergistic; they work together to create a potent atmosphere of great spiritual strength.

The magical power of the plant can be tapped only by one versed in its secrets. This usually requires study, practice, and ideally an apprenticeship. Secrets are not easily yielded, and the magical practitioner must know that magical plants are tools that can be utilized only by one skilled in their ways and the ways of the ancient craft. This book is a guide only — a showing forth of what can be achieved by the diligent and creative practitioner.

What I write here is what I have confirmed from my own experience or from that of people (ancient and contemporary) whom I trust (especially in the case of plants with which I am not well acquainted or in the case of plants whose magical powers are anciently and universally acknowledged.)

But use your own judgment. This book is not a Bible; it's a guide. Don't strain your eyes with reading it. Stain your hands with the soil of the earth. If the earth and its products do not confirm my words, trust the earth and your own wise spirit. Be true to your experience, and the magic will never fail you. I promise.

Planetary Associations and Spiritual Affinities

Unfortunately for the beginning student, many modern books on magic simply echo each other on the planetary and spiritual associates of herbs. Herb X, for example, is an herb of "Venus," referring to the planet, not the deity. And why? Largely because Nicholas Culpeper, an interesting and entertaining herbalist of the seventeenth century, declared it to be so. Since Culpeper was unaware of the existence of the outer planters (Uranus, Neptune, Pluto, etc) they are not included in his classification, and are usually omitted from most contemporary classifications as well, even though we know these planets exist. A few people have made desultory attempts to include the outer planets, but are usually driven to assigning to them rare, tropical, or New World plants unknown to poor Culpeper. This does no one any good. Culpeper was an amazing herbalist of his day, a charming writer with a keen eye and captivating style. But, like everyone else, he was a creature of his time. While I don't believe that a particular planet "rules" a plant in having an effect on its growth, much magical tradition asserts a spiritual connection in magical rites between certain herbs and certain celestial objects. Therefore I have included instances where I believe it empowers the magical rite if it is performed when a certain planet is actually visible in the sky. Those who do find planetary associations usable in horticulture will find them listed in the Quick Guide to Magical Uses and Attributes in the Appendix.

This book is written partly from my own experience, and partly from years of study in the history of magic. But I do know this. I know every herb has a *principal spirit,* a secret affinity, a special excellence, derived not from some distant planet, but from our own earth. This power is listed in bold next to the plant's scientific name. Sometimes that bit of magic is unique to the herb; in other cases other herbs may share the power, but it is particularly strong in the one I indicate. That spirit is the focus of magical power. Sometimes the spirits seems replicated in several different plants. This makes sense, since many of them come from diverse parts of the world, and everyone – no matter where they may live, needs the same magical help. It only becomes a bit confusing in the contemporary world where we have access to plants from every continent and every climate. However, this confusion covers a great blessing – we have an abundance of magical tradition with which to work!

Key

The plants in this encyclopedia are listed alphabetically, for the most part by common name. Each entry includes a common name, the scientific name, and a master-property, or attribute of that herb. There are, for example, hundreds and hundreds of herbs that offer protection. I have chosen just one, Angelica as an example. For other, perhaps better choices for you, see the Quick Guide to Magical Uses and Attributes in the Appendix. Experiment.

Each entry is divided into two sections: Horticulture, which is concerned with cultivation, and Magic, which is concerned with the magical heritage of each herb. Neither section is etched in stone or written in blood. The most sensible use you can make of this encyclopedia is to adapt it to your own needs and desires.

The Horticulture section contains a brief **Description** of the plant including height. In many cases, I have to be extremely general, as there exist several species of the plant, all of which are used for magic. In a few cases, I have found it desirable to separate out certain species and given them their own entry.

Then follows **Name Lore**, in which I give a little history or some interesting facts about the derivation of the common or scientific name. **Other Names** lists alternate cognomens of the herb in question. **Similar and Related Species** lists other plants in the same genus or by the same name, which may be confused with (or used instead) of the herb listed. **Colors** refer to the colors of the flowers, resin, bark, leaves, or whatever seems appropriate. You can use this guide to help you color your garden or to use color symbolism for various magical works. **Fragrance** describes (as best I can) the smell of the plant – sometimes of the flowers, sometimes of the foliage, and sometimes of the resin. Fragrance is extremely subjective and what is more, the smell of incense made from the plant often smells nothing whatever like the fresh plant. Peppermint is a perfect example. Nice when fresh, rather nasty when burned, at least in my opinion. Again, experiment. **Bloom Time** refers to when the flowers (if any) bloom. This is extremely variable depending upon your climate zone. Some plants, especially tropical ones, seem to bloom whenever they feel like it. **Origin** refers to the plant's original home. (Sometimes we just don't know.) **Habitat** refers to the sorts of places the plant is found in the wild. Some long-domesticated plants don't seem to have any wild relatives, however. In most cases, it is better to garden than gather. Exceptions may be made in cases of truly noxious or ubiquitous plants like dandelions. **Earth, Water, Fire,** and **Air** refer to the herb's growth requirements. **Earth** usually refers to soil quality, **Water** to moisture needs, **Fire** to sunlight requirements, and **Air** to proper climate zones. (See Climate Zones [**Air** Element] page 12.) Every one of these can be managed to some extent by good gardening.

Tips and Warnings is a transitional section that includes special gardening advice, historical lore, and warnings (horticultural and magical) about the plant under discussion. Some of the plants are toxic in one way or another. If you don't know compost from mulch, a hoe from a spade, or elder from alder, consult an encyclopedia of gardening for complete information about cultivation.

The second section is **Magic**. Since many different traditions may converge upon one herb (Celtic and Pagan lore often cover the same plant) you may find many different, even opposing attributes ascribed to an herb. Don't let this worry you. Use the information as guidelines, and do what makes sense to you. Let your own intuition guide you. In several cases I have included some suggestions about appropriate rites, invocations, colors, and so on. This is not meant to be inclusive or definitive in any way. If you have no god to invoke, don't invoke one. If you can't stand orange, either don't wear it, or select a different plant for your rite. Magic is freedom.

Acacia *(Acacia senegal and others)* This is the herb of **Victory over Death**.

Horticulture

Description: Small, spiny, gum-yielding, fast-growing tree with alternate bipinnate leaves, ball-shaped flowers in loose clusters, and fruit in pods. Some varieties evergreen. Height 20 feet. *Name Lore:* The King James Bible calls the acacia, rather unprepossessingly, the "shittim tree." *Other Names:* Egyptian thorn, cape gum, hachah, gum arabic, wattle. *Similar and Related Species:* Over 1000 species. Acacia can be grown in the milder parts of Britain, especially in sheltered spots. One acacia, the *A. longifolia*, or Sydney golden wattle, is commonly grown in the United States, especially in California. It has the same magical properties as the classic *A. Senegal*, but is evergreen and showier. A sub-variety, the *A. longifolia floribunda* is similar but with bluish leaves. *Colors:* Foliage gray; bark gray; blooms yellow. Other varieties have yellow-brown, white, or pink blossoms. *Fragrance:* Some cinnamon scented; others grassy or bittersweet. *Bloom Time*: Flowers late winter or early spring; gum is collected from December — June. *Origin:* Tropical Africa and Australia.

Habitat: Hot sandy places. **Earth** (soil type): Sandy, slightly acid, well-drained. **Water** (moisture needs): Low. **Fire** (sun/shade requirements): Full sun. **Air** (climate): Enjoys a very warm, dry climate. *A. Senegal* cannot handle temperatures below 60°F (17°C), although the *A. longifolia* grows as far north as US Climate Zone 8; one variety, the straggly evergreen *A. farnesia*, actually makes it up to Zone 7.

Tips and Warnings: Acacia should be planted on Sunday. It is an excellent plant for the **Air** Garden. Good garden varieties of acacia include *A. baileyana*, *A. dealbata*, and *A. melanoxylon* if you have the climate for them. Some jurisdictions have statutory restrictions on the cultivation of wattles.

Magic: The acacia is perhaps most familiar to Europeans and Americans as an unearthly TV image – a lonely thorn tree baking on the Serengeti or Australian Outback. Its welcoming branches are the only shade for miles, and it thrives in inhospitable deserts that would kill any other tree. The acacia is so dedicated to the sun that it dies without its blazing warmth. As the sun is life itself, the acacia is holy to resurrection deities like Osiris, solar gods such as Ra, warrior goddesses like Astarte, and those who haunt lonely places like Diana. The acacia is our assurance of the power of life over the most difficult of situations, even over death itself. In Hermetic doctrine, it symbolized the Testament of Hiram, the murdered Masonic Master Builder, whose teaching was: One must know how to die in order to live again in eternity. Today in Freemasonry, death notices still bear the image of this immemorial tree, and acacia branches are placed in the grave. Modern practitioners of our ancient Craft traditionally keep implements of magic in a box of acacia wood, to symbolize a movement that has been persecuted, "put down," and exterminated a thousand times, but which blooms again like this fierce desert tree. The Ark of the Covenant was likewise kept in a box of durable acacia wood. Acacia herb products are traditionally used during Lughnasa (the Celtic harvest festival); acacia can also be used to seal pacts. Acacia (combined with sandalwood) can be used in a scented oil to aid meditation, bring harmony, provide protection, and develop psychic powers. *Acacia may be used as incense or amulet. Invoke the name of Astarte, Diana, Osiris, or Ra. Clothe yourself in orange.*

Adder's Tongue (*Erythronium americanum*) This is the herb of all **Serpent Deities.**

Horticulture

Description: Perennial growing from a bulb. Nodding flowers at first funnel shaped, then with reflexed petals, and large, lanceolate, mottled leaves. Fruit an oblong capsule. Height 4–10 inches. *Name Lore:* The name "trout lily" refers to the spotted brown of the leaves, resembling the mottling of trout. *Other Names:* Dog-toothed violet, yellow-fawn-lily, trout lily, yellow snowdrop, serpent's tongue, adder's mouth. *Similar and Related Species:* There is a white trout lily, whose leaves are seldom mottled. *Colors:* Flowers bright yellow, or creamy with yellow inside. Leaves shiny green but mottled with brown. *Fragrance:* Faint tulipy smell. *Bloom Time*: February–May. *Origin:* Eastern United States.

Habitat: Rich open woods and meadows. **Earth** (soil type): Deep, moist, loamy, and slightly acid. **Water** (moisture needs): Needs to be kept moist. **Fire** (sun/shade requirements): Part shade to full shade. **Air** (climate): US Climate Zones 3–9.

Tips and Warnings: Although a wild flower, adder's tongue can be grown easily in the garden. Plant 4 inches deep in the autumn. You may collect the leaves any time (the foliage dies back in summer but reappears in spring), but the roots are best gathered in the fall. Leave the flowers alone. Be patient with adder's tongue, it takes four to seven years to mature. Do not harvest wild adder's tongue; it is a precious resource. (Besides, you might get bitten.) Incidentally, the whole plant is edible.

Magic: Like the snake, this secretive plant has a mysterious, hidden beauty that suddenly illuminates the spring. While traditionally supposed to protect against snakebite, adder's tongue actually honors the serpent. Adder's tongue is frequently used in magical healing rituals, for the skin-shedding serpent is a potent emblem of the renewable resources of the body. Just as the snake casts off its old skin, the body heals itself. Unfortunately, the power of this homegrown American herb is largely overlooked by those irretrievably wedded to the European witchcraft tradition. While occasionally mentioned as a healing herb, its true qualities are magical not medical. Use the leaves or roots in workings concerned with a sudden decision or life change. Wear boldly patterned clothing and an opal for rites. It can also be used in chthonic initiations. Adder's tongue partakes of the energies of sun and moon, making it an extremely powerful herb. Folklore says said that if you throw adder's tongue into your neighbors' yard during the waning moon, they will stop talking about you. *Rites involving adder's tongue are efficacious in the spring or in summer during the sign of Cancer.*

Agrimony *(Agrimonia eupatoria)* This is an herb of the **Unconscious.**

Horticulture

Description: Perennial with an erect, mostly unbranched, somewhat hairy stem, long, divided leaves, and small, five-petalled, star-shaped flowers on spikes. Fruit is burr-like. Height 3-5 feet. *Name Lore*: The species name eupatoria is in honor of Mithradates Eupator, King of Pontus, who is credited with many herbal remedies. *Other Names:* Sticklewort, cocklebur, church steeples, garclive, philanthropos. *Colors:* Flowers yellow. *Fragrance:* Grassy, lemony, or apricot-like, slightly bitter, but mild, dry, and pleasant. *Bloom Time*: June-September, with the seeds ripening soon after. *Origin:* Europe, now worldwide.

Habitat: Clearings, field margins, damp thickets, hedgerows, roadsides. **Earth** (soil type): Ordinary moist garden soil, preferably slightly alkaline. **Water** (moisture needs) Moderate. **Fire** (sun/shade requirements): Light shade. **Air** (climate) US Climate Zones 2–9.

Tips and Warnings: Harvest at midsummer, before the burrs start to develop.

Magic: Although agrimony has no known narcotic properties, persistent traditions credit it with being able to lock a person into a deep, sound sleep simply by being placed beneath a pillow. The sleeper cannot awaken until the agrimony is removed. In a medieval English manuscript are written these words:

> *If it be leyd under mann's heed,*
> *He shal sleepyn as he were deed;*
> *He shal never drede ne wakyn*
> *Till fro under his heed it be takyn.*

It is obvious from these lines that agrimony has strong connections with our deepest psyches. And although the traditional use of the herb suggests that the "victim" is being put temporarily out of commission, while the perpetrator goes about his or her mission, there is a deeper message – that we may be always in some way asleep, unconscious. It's no accident that the herb carries a subsidiary meaning of secrets kept, for the Unconscious is where all deepest secrets lie. The other use of the herb is equally instructive: it is used for counter-magic, to detect witches, evil spirits, and goblins. Goblins and their kin are more likely to be found in the Unconscious than anywhere else. While the herb is beneath the pillow, it seeks out these destructive psychic goblins and lays them to rest – for good. *Agrimony can be used in a bath, wash, or oil. Those born under the sign of Cancer are most likely to succeed with agrimony.*

Alder *(Alnus* species) This is the herb of **Unity**.

Horticulture

Description: Deciduous shrub or tree with rounded, inverted, serrated, heart-shaped leaves that are very sticky in spring. Tiny flowers (catkins and cones) appear before the leaves. The alder is the only broadleaf tree to bear cones. Alders can live for 150 years. Height 50-70 feet. *Alnus glutinosa* is the black alder, a conical tree with deep green leaves and yellow catkins *A. uncana* is the grey alder. (It has gray, pointed leaves.) *A. cordata*, the Italian alder, has glossy heart-shaped leaves. *Name Lore:* The word alder comes from the Old English *Ealdor*, meaning chief. *Colors:* Bark brown to blackish; buds purple; flowers yellow or white. *Fragrance:* Subtle or scentless. *Bloom Time*: March-April, with the seeds ripening in September. *Origin:* Native to Europe, Britain, Asia, and North Africa. Brought to America in colonial times.

Habitat: Wet open woods, by streams and rivers. **Earth** (soil type): Deep, moist – will not tolerate alkaline soils. **Water** (moisture needs): High. **Fire** (sun/shade requirements): Full sun. **Air** (climate): US Climate Zone 2-8, *A. glutinosa* grows throughout Britain. Prefers cool climate.

Tips and Warnings: Gather bark and fruits before the first frost. The roots enrich the soil by fixing nitrogen. The alder is suitable for an **Air**, **Fire**, or **Water** Garden. Once established, the alder is not easily uprooted. The alder is an excellent tree to have among grasses, as its roots don't hurt grass, and actually help feed it. It is thus an excellent tree for a damp pasture where livestock are kept. Careful pruning will keep the alder bushy and handsome.

Magic. The alder may not look like much, but it is a tree of wonder. It not only enriches the soil whereon it grows, but also cleans and purifies any water it is near; fish find safe haven near its roots. The alder has connections with Io, who became a cow. (It's one of these long, apparently pointless stories, which serve to point out, however, some interesting connections.) To this day, the alder is considered a good plant for damp cow pastures, for reasons already mentioned.

In ancient magical tradition, the alder was considered a tree of fire, yet it has strong affinities with weather magic and the air. (An alder whistle can conjure up the North Wind). Thus the delicate alder unites all four traditional cosmic elements. At the same time, the alder is friendly to human beings, yielding several beautiful dyes: brown from the twigs, red from the bark, green from flowers, the last of which is favored by fairies for their own clothes. It is also said to protect one from drowning. The alder imparts strength, not the rigid strength of the oak (which is so often destroyed by a lightning blast), but a giving, helping, nurturing strength, the kind that can survive any storm.

This gentle plant is even planted on graves as a protection measure, and at one time alders were used to measure people for the coffin. But because of this sad task, in parts of Ireland it was dangerous to touch an alder unless one was a priest. Another reason why the alder became "untouchable" is that the cut tree turns red, giving a rather alarming bloodlike appearance. I can assure you, however, that it is perfectly safe. No tree is more forgiving. The red serves to remind us, however, that we are indeed all linked, and that we should not cut down any tree without a very good reason. Most famously, the alder is connected with the great hero Bran the Blessed, for whom it was the totem tree. While Bran didn't win every battle, he was never completely defeated, showing us again the balance in the nature of things characteristic of the alder. *No special preparations are usually necessary for alder rites; a bit of the tree, honored and invoked, is sufficient. Rites performed with alder are most efficacious when performed in the autumn, in January, or from March 1–April 15. The best day is Saturday.*

Alfalfa *(Medicago sativa)* This is the herb of **Plenty.**

Horticulture

Description: Herbaceous perennial with pinnately trifoliate leaves and oblong clover-like flowers. Attains a height of two feet, but its roots can reach 30 feet! Alfalfa is the world's most valuable forage crop. **Name Lore:** *Alfalfa* means "best forage" in Arabic. **Other Names:** Lucerne, buffalo herb, purple medic, Chilean clover, Buffalo grass. **Colors:** Flower colors can range from yellow to violet-blue. **Fragrance:** Fresh, hay-like. **Bloom Time**: June–August. **Origin:** Asia Minor, now cultivated all over the world.

Habitat: Edges of fields. **Earth** (soil type): Well-drained – pH 6.5–7.5. **Water** (moisture needs): Drought resistant because of its deep roots. **Fire** (sun/shade requirements): Full sun. **Air** (climate): Variable – very dependent on other conditions.

Tips and Warnings: Although we think of alfalfa in the waving-fields-of-amber-grain mode, you don't need a farm; you can grow just a bit (even in a pot) for nutritional or magical use. It's easy. Harvest when the moon is full.

Magic: Simply placing a jar of alfalfa in the cupboard is said to keep poverty and hunger away. You can also burn it and scatter it around the property for the same purpose. However, the herb is best seen as a symbolic representation of the plenty of the earth. It is extremely unlucky to perform a magical rite for our own advantage unless we at the same time make an effort to help those less fortunate. *Keep alfalfa as a reminder of the wealth that lies everywhere around us – and also of those who are hungry and thirsty while we eat and drink.*

Allspice *(Pimenta officinalis)* This is the herb of **Vitality.**

Horticulture

Description: Fruit of the tropical evergreen pimento tree. Tree much branched, with dense foliage and opposite, oval, leathery leaves and small four-petalled flowers borne on racemose cymes; berries globular. Height 40 feet **Name Lore:** Allspice was so named because the flavor of the dried berry resembles a combination of cloves, cinnamon, and nutmeg. **Other Names:** Jamaica pepper, pimento, new spice, clove pepper. **Similar and Related Species:** Sometimes confused with "Carolina Allspice" which, however, is in a different genus. **Colors:** Flowers white to greenish-white; berries reddish brown (when dry). **Fragrance:** Berries highly aromatic. **Bloom Time**: Late spring and early summer. **Origin:** West Indies and tropical Central America.

Habitat: Wet limestone forests. **Earth** (soil type): Tolerant. **Water** (moisture needs): Drought tolerant. **Fire** (sun/shade requirements): Full sun. **Air** (climate): Tropical. Can handle wind.

Tips and Warnings: Unless you live in the tropics, you probably can't grow allspice. In Hawaii, as an alien introduction, it is becoming a threat to the environment. Trees do not produce berries until they are about eight years old and don't mature until they are about fifteen. Allspice can irritate the skin of some people.

Magic: You can't be somber about this energizing, cheerful herb with its flavorful berries (Jamaican are the best). *Anoint yourself every day with an extract of its oil, and you'll find yourself brimming with health and energy. You can also burn allspice as an incense. Use it whenever you need extra energy or determination to complete a task. Allspice may be used as an amulet.*

Almond *(Prunus dulcis)* This is the herb of **Duality**.

Horticulture

Description: Deciduous shrub or small tree with thorny branches, lanceolate, finely serrated leaves, and large flowers growing in pairs. It is closely related to the peach. Height 10–20 feet. *Name Lore:* Interestingly, the Hebrew word for almond also means diligence. *Other Names:* Greek nuts, shakad, Jordan almond. *Similar and related species:* There is also a bitter almond that produces a slightly toxic oil. Sweet almonds are used for eating, and bitter almonds for their essential oils used in the cosmetic and liqueur industry. *Colors:* Bark reddish; flowers white, rose, or pink; fruit light green. *Fragrance:* Rich, fruity, sweet. *Bloom Time*: March-April. It is among the earliest trees to blossom in Israel. *Origin:* Middle East; Mediterranean countries. Now cultivated over much of the world where it is sufficiently warm and dry.

Habitat **Earth** (soil type): Deep, well drained, loamy with pH 6-7. **Water** (moisture needs): Drought tolerant. **Fire** (sun/shade requirements): Full sun. **Air** (climate): Require hot dry summers and mild winters, although almonds can take cold winters better than wet summers.

Tips and Warnings: All else being equal, plant almond to the east in the garden. Bitter almonds contain cyanogenic glycosides in seeds, bark and leaves, which, if eaten in large quantities, cause convulsions and death. Fifty to seventy bitter almonds cause death in adults, seven to ten in children. Three can cause severe poisoning.

Magic: As an herb that is both sweet and bitter, the almond alerts us to the puzzling ambivalence of life itself. Its traditional associations of sexual love *and* virginity reflect our own confusion about the duality. The Talmud probably came the closest in understanding the complex nature of this herb, when it suggested that the sweetness and the bitterness of the almond reflect the joy and suffering of the children of Israel. Indeed, the shape of the almond tree was taken as model for the menorah, and almond oil was used for ceremonial occasions. (Pliny suggested that eating five almonds before drinking would prevent drunkenness. This remedy, of course, is useless for people who drink in order to get drunk.) *Use almond as anointing oil or incense in your rites when you are faced with ambivalence or conflicting feelings — love and anger, pride and fear. The almond understands. Almond may be used as an amulet. When working magic with almond, select a time when Jupiter is visible; it strengthens the magic. Leos have particular luck with almonds. Invoke the name of Hermes, Attis, Mercury, or Thoth.*

Aloe *(Aloe barbadensis, A. vera)* This is the herb of **Healing**.

Horticulture

Description: Tender evergreen perennial, with narrow, fleshy, spiky leaves and tubular flowers. When broken the leaves exude a sticky sap. There are over 325 species, ranging from very small to large. Leaves usually 1–2 feet. Other Names: Agave (especially in symbology), bitter aloes, cape aloes, Barbados aloe, Aloe vera, Curacao Aloe.

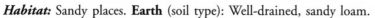

Name lore: The word *aloe* is said to mean "bitter and shiny," which certainly describes the plant. (Sometimes you hear the word *aloes* rather than *aloe. Aloes* is the dried juice of the plant.) *Similar and related species:* The aloe proper should not be confused with the New World aloe, or agave *(Agave Americana)*. Other true aloe plants include *A. latifolia, A. perryi, A. saponaria,* and *A. tenuior*. **Colors:** Flower yellow to purplish. Leaves gray/blue/green. *Fragrance:* Semi-sweet, a little strange. *Bloom Time:* The aloe flowers only once. *Origin:* East and south Africa, islands in the southern Mediterranean, East Indies.

Habitat: Sandy places. **Earth** (soil type): Well-drained, sandy loam. **Water** (moisture needs): Low to moderate. **Fire** (sun/shade requirements): Sunny, but can tolerate some shade. **Air** (climate): This plant needs winter protection.

Tips and Warnings: For best results, plant on Thursday. The plant enjoys crowded conditions. To harvest aloe for its healing gel, split the largest outer leaves and scrape out the gel.

Magic: No plant works its medicinal magic so obviously and quickly as the soothing aloe. Under the gentle influence of the moon and associated with the merciful Virgin Mary, aloe has long been known for its protecting qualities. In fact, it is apparent that some hoped the aloe's rejuvenating qualities would last beyond the grave; one variety of aloe *(A. succotrina)* was used in Egypt for embalming, and the Gospel of John mentioned aloe being used to embalm the body of Jesus. Aloe is even said to relieve loneliness. However, the aloe has a dark side: it has been traditionally used in the initiation ceremonies of werewolves. The aloe teaches us another virtue: patience. Although the plant is long lived, it blooms only once. The same can be said of many of us! *For best magical effect, perfumes incorporating aloe should be worn on Tuesday. Aloe may be used as an ointment or amulet. Rites using aloe are most effective when performed when the moon is as close to full as possible. Invoke Mars during rites with aloe.*

Amaranth *(Amaranthus* species) This is the herb of **Paradise**.

Horticulture

Description: Most are annual herbs with upright habit and alternate, oblong-lanceolate pointed leaves and clustered flowers. About 400 species. Height 3–4 feet. *Name Lore: Amaranth* means, "never fading flower" in Greek. The correct spelling is amarant, not amaranth, but the latter has embedded itself in usage, and may not now be disturbed. *Other Names:* Pigweed, velvet flower, love-lies-bleeding *(A. caudatus)*, Joseph's coat *(A. tricolor)*, lady bleeding, lovely bleeding, pilewort, spleen amaranth, prince's feather. *Similar and Related Species:* Numerous species, some grown for gardening, some for seed, some for magic. *Colors:* Leaves reddish green with a purplish spot; flowers red. *Fragrance:* Flowers scentless, but the seed head has a woodsy or corn like smell. *Bloom Time*: August–frost. *Origin:* Warm places in several parts of the globe, including South America, India, and Greece, depending on species.

Habitat: Open areas. **Earth** (soil type): Average garden soil. Tolerates poor soil, but bad drainage causes rot. **Water** (moisture needs): Tolerates drought. **Fire** (sun/shade requirements): Full sun for best color. **Air** (climate): Tolerates heat. Frost tender.

Tips and Warnings: Plant in warm soil after all danger of frost has passed. This plant is extremely visually stimulating, so plant with this in mind.

Magic: Paradise is the abode of the deathless, and the amaranth is its flower. As John Milton wrote in *Paradise Lost:*

> *Immortal amarant, a flower which once*
> *In paradise, fast by the tree of life,*
> *Began to bloom; but soon for man's offence*
> *To heaven removed, where first it grew, there grows,*
> *And flowers aloft, shading the fount of life…*

Its long-lasting flowers are typically fashioned into a wreath that imparts to its wearer the ability to perform rites of spirit-conjury or invisibility. (The amaranth is the smallest of grains, symbolic of invisibility). So sacred was it to the Aztecs and Incas they considered Amaranth a god. *For practitioners in the neo-pagan traditions, it is proper to call upon Artemis during these rites; scatter the flowers upon the grave of the deceased. Amaranth may also be used during death rites, to help the decedent's invisible sprit find its way into Paradise.*

Here is an old ritual to protect you from being killed by a bullet, using amaranth. Pull up a whole amaranth (including roots) on a Friday during the full moon. Leave an offering for the plant you took, and then fold the entire plant in a piece of white cloth. Wear this against your chest – you'll be bullet proof. I haven't actually tested the efficacy of this myself, and suggest you don't either. *Amaranth may be used as an amulet.*

Anemone (*Anamone patens* and **Windflower** (*Pulsatilla vulgaris*) This is the plant of **Forsakenness.**

Horticulture

Description: These two genera are frequently confused and at one time they were included in the same genus (*Anemone*). Both are members of the buttercup family and they have identical magical properties. The main difference in them lies in the shape of their flowers: *Anemone* has an open to shallowly cup-shaped flowers with prominent stamens and *Pulsatilla* has cup-shaped or bell-shaped flowers. There are about 120 species of *Anemone* and about 30 of *Pulsatilla*. Anemones include small spring-flowering species like the wood anemony (*A. nemorosa*), with its palmate leaves, creeping rhizome, and white to pinkish star-like flowers;

the tuberous Mediterranean species, like the Grecian windflower (*A. blanda*) and the florist's anemone (*A. coronaria*), with its brightly colored, showier blooms, and the tall, handsome Japanese anemones (*A. hupensis* and its hybrids), which are so valuable in the border in late summer and early fall. Pulsatillas include, among others, the pasque flower (*P. vulgaris*), which has ferny foliage and silky, hairy, bell-shaped flowers, usually blue to purple but, in some cultivars, red-purple or white. The Eastern pasque flower (*P. patens*) has hairy, palmate mid-green leaves and cup-shaped blue to violet flowers. *Name Lore:* The word *anemone* is Greek for "wind." The reason for the name is uncertain. One suggestion is that these flowers prefer windy places, although this is not proven. The old herbalist Nicholas Culpeper wrote, "The flowers never open but when the wind bloweth." Then, perhaps thinking better of the statement, he hedges it. "Pliny is my author; if it be not so, blame him." But there's another possible derivation for the word, from Naaman, another name for Adonis. The name pasque flower comes from paschal, meaning "relating to Passover or to Easter." *Colors:* variable according to species. *Bloom Time*: Variable. *Origin:* Europe, North America, and Asia.

Habitat: Variable. **Earth** (soil type): Rich, well drained, with plenty of organic matter. **Water** (moisture needs): Moderate. **Fire** (sun/shade requirements): Partial shade to full sun. **Air** (climate): US climate zones 5–9.

Tips and Warnings: Culpeper writes, "They are sown mainly in the gardens of the curious," which I find charming, if not completely clear. If the prevailing wind is from the south, says an old legend, the blooms will come out double. Whether or not this is true, it is true that the anemone is not a particularly hardy plant, and clumps of them tend to gradually diminish over the years. They need replenishing. Planting spring-blooming anemones, such as the Grecian windflower (*Anemone blanda*) beneath flowering dogwood creates a lovely picture.

Magic: Both Anemone and pasque flower claim to have sprung from the blood of Adonis, or alternately from the tears of Aphrodite when he was killed. A competing theory states that the goddess Flora turned the nymph Anemone into a windflower because she attracted the attentions of Zephyr, Flora's husband. In either case, these are the flowers to be used ritually in times of abandonment or loss. Their loveliness reminds us that even sorrow gives birth to beauty. *Use only perfect blooms for these rites. Invoke the names of Aphrodite and Adonis.*

Angelica   (*Angelica archangelica*) This is the herb of **General Protection.**

Horticulture

Description: Hardy perennial or biennial resembling celery or parsnip with a round, grooved, hollow stem branched near the top. Height up to 6 feet. *Other Names:* Garden angelica, masterwort, choraka (Ayurvedic), archangel, dong quai, Chinese angelica for *Angelica sinensis*; the Chinese call it the "empress of herbs." *Similar and Related Species:* A. atropurpurea; A. sinenis. There is also a wild angelica, *A. sylvestris*. *Colors:* White or greenish-white flowers; seedpods yellow-green; stem tinged with blue or purple. *Fragrance:* Light, honeylike. *Bloom Time*: June–August. Traditionally, it is said to bloom on the Feast of the Apparition of St. Michael, May 8. (This is different from his regular Feast Day, September 29, which is called Michaelmas and is the bloom time of the Michaelmas daisy.) *Origin:* A. archangelica is widely distributed throughout Europe, especially in the colder regions.

A. atropurpurea is native to North America. *A. sinensis* is native to China.

Habitat: Damp meadows, marshy areas, streambanks, or coastal regions. **Earth** (soil type): Deep, moist, well drained, and fertile. **Water** (moisture needs): High. **Fire** (sun/shade requirements): Partial or light shade preferred. **Air** (climate): US Climate Zones 6-8.

Tips and Warnings: Easy-to-grow angelica is most suited to the informal garden. If sowing from seeds, sow in late fall or early spring when soil is still cool. Don't cover the seeds. This tall, dramatic herb can be used as a focal point or background plant, or simply grown against a fence. Angelica resents transplanting. The leaves, which can be harvested all summer, can be added to soups and stews. Various parts of this flower have been used to flavor candy, pork, baked goods, gin, jam, vinegar, Benedictine, Absinthe, and Chartreuse. The essential oil, derived from the root, can be added to baths or lotions. And as an extra benefit, the foliage is striking in floral arrangements. For superior magical effectiveness, angelica should be planted on Sunday, and if possible to the east in the garden. There is a definite toxicity risk associated with the powerful *A. sinensis*. Unless you are working with a trained herbalist, I would stick with *A. archangelica*. People with diabetes should not use angelica internally. The flavor is somewhat like licorice at first, then tart or bitter. When handled, it can make the skin photosensitive.

Magic: Many herbs, of course, have protective properties, but angelica may be the most powerful of all. In the Middle Ages, angelica was an essential component of every monastery garden. (At one time it was known as the Root of the Holy Ghost and has been anciently associated with the great warrior Archangel Michael). Angelica is truly the master-herb of protection; it is effective against evil spirits, disease, evil beasts, enchantments, witchcraft, sorcery, plague, mad-dog bites, and lustful thoughts. In fact, it fights off negative energy of every sort. The leaves can be scattered around a room, or the root can be worn around the neck. It can also be used in a purifying bath. According to Culpeper, "It resists poison, by defending and comforting the heart, blood, and spirits." He believed the garden-variety angelica was more effective than the wild kind.

In addition, this multi-faceted plant can be used in rites of consecration, divination, prosperity, purification, and knowledge, hex-breaking, facilitating contact with the Otherworld, and changing bad luck to good. Many practitioners include it as a decoration at Imbolc (February) and for burning and decorating at Beltaine (May). Angelica may be used as an amulet or incense. *Leos have very good luck with angelica. Clothe yourself in white and invoke the name of Venus.*

Anise *(Pimpinella anisum)* This is the herb of **Handfasting** (Weddings).

Horticulture

Description: Annual with a weakly erect, branched stem, delicate, feathery leaves, and small flowers. Height 18-24 inches. *Other Names:* Aniseseed, anneys, Florence fennel, finocchio. *Similar and Related Species:* Star anise (*Illicum* species) is a different plant altogether, but shares the same magical properties. *Colors:* Flowers white. *Fragrance:* All parts of the plant are fragrant, – bittersweet, licorice-like, or nutty. *Bloom Time*: July–August. *Origin:* Mediterranean and Asia Minor.

Habitat: Open places. **Earth** (soil type): Light, dry; pH about 6. Enjoys poor soil. **Water** (moisture needs): Low–moderate. **Fire** (sun/shade requirements): Full sun. **Air** (climate): US Climate Zone 4-9

Tips and Warnings: Easy to grow, but you'll need four frost-free months from seed. Grow closely together (in clumps) so the plants can support each other. Plant it close to coriander; the two get along well together. The seed is a baking spice and can also be used to flavor soup. The fruit is used to flavor liqueurs and in candy and perfume. It is also a breath-freshener. Medieval people used anise to bait mousetraps. Luckily, anise helps clear your conscience if you have killed something. Because of its sweetness, anise was once frequently added to other medicines. Rather oddly, anise is poisonous to pigeons; so don't invite any to your wedding.

Magic: From ancient Roman times onward, anise has been an important ingredient in wedding cakes. Before the wedding, both the bride and groom bathe in anise water. Even after the wedding, place some anise seed in your wallet as a love charm. Such use not only enhances the joy of the wedding, but you will be able to benefit from other famous uses of the anise as an herb of purification, prosperity, happiness, and consecration.

Later, put a sprig of anise over the bed (or the seeds in the pillow) to ensure a refreshing, nightmare-free sleep with prophetic dreams. Scatter anise leaves around the bedroom to keep it free of evil spirits, especially those that destroy your sense of well being, equilibrium, and self-esteem. The leaves also attract the help of good spirits and protect against the evil eye. *Anise may be used as an amulet, incense, or potion. Scorpios are most successful making magic with anise.*

Apple *(Malus sylvestris* and others) This is the herb of **Desire**.

Horticulture

Description: Broadleaf fruit tree with heart-shaped leaves, and single or double blossoms, depending on the variety. As apple trees age, their bark becomes gnarly, and the trees lean at delightfully crazy angles. Some varieties hold their fruit throughout the winter. Over 2000 species worldwide, including the magically powerful crab apple. Height 30–40 feet. *Name Lore:* In China, apples are never given to invalids, as the word for apple, *ping*, closely resembles that for illness, *bing*. *Other Names:* Silver branch, silver bough (from Irish legend), tree of love, and fruit of the gods. *Similar and Related Species:* A true crab apple has small (1–2 inch) fruit (pomes), with a deep depression at each end, that hang in clusters on long stalks. If other characteristics prevail, you have some variety of regular apple, perhaps gone wild. *Colors:* Fruit green, yellow, red, russet. Leaves usually green and semi-glossy but some forms have bronze or reddish purple summer foliage.

Fragrance: Sweet, similar to honeysuckle but not so strong. *Bloom Time*: May. *Origin:* Europe and Asia.

Habitat: Moist soils in the openings of forests. **Earth** (soil type): Deep. **Water** (moisture needs): Moderate. **Fire** (sun/shade requirements): Full sun. **Air** (climate): US Climate zones 4-8.

Tips and Warnings: Plant during the third or fourth quarter of the moon. Apples were an important feature in every medieval orchard. If you want your apple tree to bear fruit for many years, ask a woman who has borne many children to eat the first fruit. (A good year for apples is also supposed to be a good year for twins.) Apple seeds do contain cyanide, and if you gobble up a cupful of them, you'd get pretty sick. But people seldom eat cupfuls of apple seeds.

Magic: Apples are potent for all love spells, and it is wise to share an apple with the one you love. Likewise, a gift of apple blossoms or apples is an offer of love. Apple blossoms were once traditional wedding flowers.

Apples have long been associated with beauty and erotic passion, possibly because of their resemblance to breasts. The apple core cut in half is also thought to resemble the vulva. (In ancient Greece, the newlyweds divided and ate an apple before entering the marriage chamber.) The fruit's spherical quality suggests totality, but its historical associations are with desire and indulgence. The earth-goddess Gaea gave Hera an apple to symbolize fertility when she became engaged to Zeus. Adding apple blossoms to love spells increases their power; the blossoms may be burned as incense for love, and apple wood makes an excellent magic wand for use in love enchantments. And to call someone, the "apple of one's eye" means they are the source of all love and desire. But the desire symbolized by the apple goes well beyond love enchantments. While the Bible does not specify the apple as the fruit of the Tree of Knowledge of Good and Evil, it is customary to consider it so, as it symbolizes all desire, even though apple trees don't grow in Iraq, where the Garden of Eden supposedly was. (Apples were also the featured tree in the Garden of Hesperides, the Greek Paradise.) As the forbidden, yet all-desirable fruit, there exists a plethora of fairy tales in which poisoned apples are offered to fair maidens by evil old crones – who, of course, are connected with Samhain (Halloween). It is said that burying apples beneath the ground at Samhain provides food for the dead. Pretty soon we are dunking for apples. One thing is sure: rubbing an apple before eating it banishes the evil spirits.

The Druids also considered the apple tree sacred and of all trees it is the one most likely to bear mistletoe. From that tradition we know that cutting down an apple tree brings ill fortune. And if any unicorns still remain, they may be found browsing beneath an apple tree. (Others can be found in ash wood.) Apple trees are attractive to fairies as well.

But apples have their dark side. In Greek myth, a quarrel over a golden apple started the Trojan War. (Eris, a rather contentious goddess, tossed out a golden apple to Paris, and told him to give it to the most beautiful. Paris decided that Aphrodite was the winner and as a result won the beautiful Helen as a wife.) And Nemesis, the goddess of divine vengeance, carries an apple bough as present to heroes.

European myth watches apples trees carefully as well. Apple trees that bloom in the autumn are said to presage death. In fact, if a single apple remains on the tree after harvest and does not fall to ground till spring, it is a death omen for those living on the property. A similar legend says that leaving an apple on the tree will call up spirits and ensure success. On the other hand, leaving an apple on the tree (for the Old Apple Man) is supposed to insure good harvests. This is a conundrum. In Norse myth, the goddess Iduna guarded the apples of immortality. There is a strong connection between desire and immortality, and for good reason; immortality is the most desired of all gifts, even over love, as least for most of us. In seasonal celebrations, apples are used at wassailing on the Winter Solstice and on Twelfth Night. They are also a traditional decoration at Yule. *Apple may be used as an amulet.*

Invoke the name of Aphrodite, Apollo, Athena, Diana, Hera, or Olwen. Librans and Leos have especially good luck with apple. Wear mouse-colored clothing. Friday is the most auspicious day.

Arbor Vitae *(Thuja* species) This is the herb of **Cleansing** (See also Cedar).

Horticulture

Description: Slow-growing evergreen with small, flat, and scale-like needles. Arbor vitae can grow into a medium-sized tree (Height 40 feet), although most horticultural forms are smaller. *Name Lore: Thuja* comes from a Greek word meaning "sacrifice." *Other Names:* Also called the tree of life; American arbor vitae; northern white cedar; eastern arbor vitae; white, swamp, or yellow cedar. *Colors:* Needles green or yellow-green; cones brown. *Fragrance:* Spicy, most noticeable on warm days. The western red cedar is said to smell like pear. *Bloom Time*: Mid spring (reddish male and yellowish brown female flowers). *Origin:* Cool, northern areas of the eastern United States. Introduced into Europe.

Habitat: Sunny, open places. **Earth** (soil type): Neutral to alkaline. Most are very tolerant, but prefer deep, loamy soil. **Water** (moisture needs): Variable. **Fire** (sun/shade requirements): Best in full sun, but will tolerate light shade. **Air** (climate): Does best in cool climate, and many new cultivars are resistant to snow and ice damage. US Climate Zones 4–8.

Tips and Warnings: Most cultivars, especially the common *T. occidentalis*, do best where summers are humid.

Magic: See Cedar. Arbor vitae and cedar have identical magical properties.

Artemisia

Over 400 species; for more specific information see Mugwort, Southernwood, and Wormwood, each listed as separate entries. Tarragon and dusty miller are also artemisia species. Most kinds of artemisia thrive in US climate zones 4–8 in average to poor, well-drained soil. Horticulturally, they are generally prized for their foliage. Magically, they have many uses. All these plants are sacred to Artemis, or Diana, and so are especially important in all witchcraft. Some varieties are very attractive to butterflies.

Asafedita *(Ferule fetida*; also spelled asafeotida) This is the herb of **Exorcism.**

Horticulture

Description: Coarse umbelliferous plant with cabbage-like flowerheads, a large fleshy root covered with bristly fibers, numerous stem leaves, and oval fruit. This herb is a kind of giant fennel. Height 6–10 feet. *Other Names:* Devil's incense, devil's dung, ferula, narthex, hing. *Colors:* Flowers greenish-yellow. *Fragrance:* The gum or sap is strong and rank, rather like rotten meat. *Bloom Time*: The juice (oleoresin) is collected in June from the roots. *Origin:* Central Asia, Afghanistan, and Iran.

Habitat: High plains and moist wooded areas. **Earth** (soil type): Regular garden soil. **Water** (moisture needs): Moderate. **Fire** (sun/shade requirements): Sun or shade. **Air** (climate): US Climate Zones 6–10. Temperate regions, will tolerate some heat.

Tips and Warnings: The great majority of asafetida is collected wild or even poached, although there is some commercial production. This is probably not something you can manage in a home garden, but its traditional importance as *the* herb of exorcism makes it impossible to exclude.

Magic: While many herbs can be successfully used for exorcism, the really rank odor of this plant makes it the herb of choice if you are really serious about getting rid of malign spirits. The stuff smells so bad that even the demons can't take it. (In a way, asafetida breaks the rule about bad smells drawing demons and good, pleasant smells chasing them away. Asafetida gets rid of everything.) Interestingly enough, it's eaten raw by people in Afghanistan, and is in fact quite a popular dish with vegetarians worldwide. When cooked it loses most of its nasty odor, and is said to be a delightful accompaniment to roasted mutton.

Believe it or not, asafetida is used as a flavoring in Worcestershire sauce. Asafetida is also used in related magical workings such as purification, counter-magic, consecration, death rites, and protection, despite (or because of) its odor. A lot of people can't handle it, because of the smell, preferring to go to more pleasant herbs. But magic is not for cowards. If you can't take the smell, you may have to put up with the demons. Some texts suggest adding garlic for extra effect. Believe me, with asafetida you don't need any extra effect. The big drawback is that once you use it, it destroys the magical properties of everything in the area, and it all has to be re-consecrated. Such is the nature of this incredible herb. It should be mentioned that in ancient Siberia, asafetida was one substance used in the initiation ceremonies of werewolves. Like other canines, werewolves are not put off by bad smells. Worn in a bag around the neck, it is rumored to prevent colds. (It's better to have a cold. Only demon banishment is important enough to use the stuff.) Asafetida may be used as incense or an amulet. *Rites with asafetida are most effective when Saturn is visible. Geminis are most successful in handling this difficult herb. Clothe yourself in white.*

Ash *(Fraxinus* species) This is *the Axis Mundi*, the World Tree.

Horticulture

Description: Large, straight, deciduous fast-growing broadleaf tree with smooth bark, compound tooth-edged leaves, and small flowers. The flowers have no petals or sepals, only stamens. The gray bark is smooth when young, but develops ridges and cracks as the trees ages. Height 140 feet. *Other Names:* Nion, common ash, weeping ash. *Similar and Related Species:* The American mountain ash, *Sorbus americana* and the closely related European mountain ash, *Sorbus aucuparia,* are not true ash trees. But they have magic of their own. (See Rowan.) In Norse myth the first man was made from ash (and woman from alder). *Colors:* Bark grayish-green. Flowers reddish-brown; leaves light green at first, darkening over the season, turning yellow or purple in autumn. *Fragrance:* Subtle.
Bloom Time: April–May. The flowers appear before the leaves. The leaves are some of the last to appear (along with those of the oak). *Origin:* Britain. Grows throughout Europe and the United States.

Habitat: Mountains and slopes, forests. **Earth** (soil type): Limey, deep, well drained. Dislikes dry or rocky soil. **Water** (moisture needs): High. **Fire** (sun/shade requirements): Full sun. **Air** (climate): US Climate Zones 3–9. It can handle strong winds, being one of the least "breakable" of trees.

Tips and Warnings: Most species are too large for a garden. In addition, it's a greedy tree that robs the soil of many nutrients. Planting too near a building can undermine its foundations. The best use for ash is as a landscape plant; it makes a very handsome specimen indeed. If you must cut down an ash, you have to beg its pardon first. One good thing about ash wood is that is does not require much aging, it can even be burned green.

Magic: From time immemorial, ash has been recognized as the original World Tree, Yggdrasil, the Axis Mundi, which connected the underworld, middle earth, and heaven. From this tree the god Odin created the first human being, and from it he later hung himself as a sacrifice in order to receive ultimate wisdom. The magical powers of the ash are legion: it is renowned as a tree of protection, psychic healing, divination, wisdom, knowledge, hex breaking, and counter-magic. Magic wands made from ash wood are especially powerful for healing and prosperity spells. The Druids carved images from its roots to use in their rites. To invoke the powers of the elements, cast ash leaves in the four directions. Because the ash is such an incredibly powerful tree, I would not use it for merely personal requests. The magic of ash should be reserved for great events and crises affecting numerous people. Remember this is a *World-Tree*, even if it grows in your back yard. Use it with prudence.

Magical rites with ash are most efficacious if performed in the summer. Ash leaves or wood may also be burned in rites at Beltaine. The ash makes a superior Yule log, bringing summer light (and prosperity) into the darkness of winter. The ash is frequently used as a Maypole, replacing the original birch for this purpose. *Invoke Gwydion, Poseidon, Mars, Neptune, Uranus, Thor, or Woden. The most auspicious day is February 18. Sagittarians are best at dealing with ash. Wednesday is the most auspicious day. Ash can be used as an amulet.*

Asphodel *(Asphodelus* species) This is the herb of the **Underworld**.

Horticulture

Description: Perennial with showy flowers and long, leathery, narrow leaves. Height 3 feet. (Actually many people are rather surprised to learn that the asphodel is a real plant, as it has been so often mentioned in myth.) *Name Lore:* The name is derived from a Greek word meaning "scepter." *Other Names:* Royal staff, branched asphodel, king's spear. *Colors:* Flowers white or pale yellow, usually with a dark red stripe. Dark green leaves. *Fragrance:* Heavy. *Bloom Time*: May and June. *Origin:* Mediterranean, southern Europe, and South Africa.

Habitat: Usually grown in gardens nowadays. **Earth** (soil type): Sandy humous, well-drained soil. **Water** (moisture needs): Moderate. **Fire** (sun/shade requirements): Full sun. **Air** (climate): US Climate Zones 5–10.

Tips and Warnings: This powerful and lovely plant deserves to be more widely grown.

Magic: According to Greek mythology, the asphodel brings the spirits of the dead, their only happiness. "And rest at last where souls unbodied dwell, /In ever-flowing meads of Asphodel." (The Odyssey of Homer. Book xxiv. L. 19.) Supposedly they ate it, and indeed the root is edible. In modern enchantments, the blossoms of the asphodel are used in death rites, as is its more commonly grown cousin, the lily. Leos have the best luck with asphodels.

Aster *(Aster novae-angliae, A. novi-blgii)* This is the herb of **Mabon.**

Horticulture

Description: Perennial with hairy stems, and clasping lanceolate leaves. Over 600 species, with the *Aster novae-angliae,* New England aster, and *A. novi-belgii,* Michaelmas daisy, the parents of most of the commercial garden types. Height 3-4 feet. *Name Lore: Aster* is the Latin word for "star," and refers, of course, to its star-like shape. *Other Names:* Eye of Christ, starwort, Michaelmas daisy (mostly in England), Christmas daisy. *Colors:* White, blue, pink, pale blue lavender, purple, violet. Leaves light green. *Bloom Time*: August–October. A few cultivars bloom earlier. *Fragrance:* Pungent. *Origin:* North America and Europe. The two species were hybridized. There is also a Chinese aster, which is grown as an annual.

Habitat: Stream banks and roadsides. **Earth** (soil type): Variable. Most like average, moist, well-drained soil. **Water** (moisture needs): Moderate. **Fire** (sun/shade requirements): Most like full sun; some can handle shady places. **Air** (climate): US Climate Zones 4–9 for most varieties.

Tips and Warnings: Asters need to be divided every couple of years. You can do this in the spring, when the shoots first appear. Pinching back encourages blooming. Cut off the flowers when they have finished blooming. Asters attract butterflies and birds; toads seem to like them as well. In the garden, the cultivation of asters symbolizes the gardener's knowledge of the darker side.

Magic: In mythology, Asteria ("Starry") was pursued by Zeus, and to escape him, leaped into the sea. However, Asteria is an important figure in the history of magic. She was the mother of Hecate, the goddess of witches. The aster is Hecate's flower, and thus has exceptional symbolic significance for Wiccans who serve this goddess. Although she has a rather bad reputation, Hecate has not always been associated with evil. In her earliest historical appearance (in Hesiod) she is benign, but always mysterious, enigmatic, and powerful. Her darker self emerged only during the fifth century B.C. *Rites with asters are usually performed in honor of Hecate, and within a pentagram. You may also invoke the name of Venus. The most propitious time is Mabon, the sabbat of the Autumn Equinox. Burning asters is also said to keep away evil spirits and snakes; aster is said to make a superior love potion, as well.*

Bachelor's Buttons *(Centaurea cyanus)* This is the Herb of **Release from a Painful Past.**

Horticulture

Description: Hardy annual herb with a wiry, erect stem, lance-shaped leaves, and fluffy round solitary flowers. Some varieties have coarse foliage. Height 12-30 inches. *Name Lore:* The scientific name *Centaurea* is derived from the tale that the plant healed a wound in the foot (or hoof, as it were) of Chiron, one of the centaurs. The name "bachelor's button" is given to a surprising variety of flowers, including Kerria. The name "cornflower" is given because it grows in wheat fields along with wheat. (In Britain wheat crops are called "corn."). *Other Names:* Cornflower, bluebottle, hurtsickle, or devil's flower. *Similar and Related Species:* The centaury is another flower of this genus, also with magical properties, although it looks quite different. *Colors:* Most have blue flowers, but some varieties have yellow or violet flowers; leaves grayish. *Fragrance:* Blooms have a delicate floral scent. *Bloom Time*:

May–August, depending on the cultivar. *Origin:* Mediterranean, now found all over Europe.

Habitat: Meadows and open woods. **Earth** (soil type): Average, well drained soil. **Water** (moisture needs): Low. Tolerates drought. **Fire** (sun/shade requirements): Full sun but can tolerate some shade. **Air** (climate): US zones 3–8 for many varieties; some can handle more heat or cold.

Tips and Warnings: This plant draws bees to the garden. Frequent deadheading keeps the flowers blooming. Medieval monks used the petals to make blue ink.

Magic: Bachelor's Button is traditionally used to help overcome the memory of past oppressions and pain. It can be used to combat all harmful magic. As a plant of general magical power, it can be used to energize all magical spells. It encourages the development of psychic abilities. *Used at Beltaine. Invoke Flora or Chiron.*

Bamboo *(Phyllostachys* and *Bambusa* species) This is the herb of **Flexibility.**

Horticulture

Description: Over 1200 species. Woody, shrubby grass, most with hollow stems. *Colors:* Various. One species, the *Phyllostachys nigra,* or black bamboo, has white, waxy flowers and stems that are at first olive green, then turn black. *Fragrance:* Sweet, grassy. *Bloom Time*: The bamboo flowers very rarely. *Origin:* China.

Habitat: Mostly tropical areas. **Earth** (soil type): Average garden soil. **Water** (moisture needs): Moderate. **Fire** (sun/shade requirements): Full sun to partial shade. **Air** (climate): US Climate zones 4–9.

Tips and Warnings: They say when the wind blows; the bamboo laughs so this plant may be added (with care) as a sound element in the charmed garden. The leaves rustle with the slightest breeze, and it is essential to any garden with an oriental theme.

Despite the modesty associated with this plant, most cultivars are extremely aggressive, and as they are not native to either the US or the UK they should be planted only with extreme care. Choose only varieties specifically developed for gardening use, those with a less invasive habit. Many varieties of bamboo can be grown in pots and placed safely within the garden that way. For the most magical effect, plant bamboo on Thursday. The roots are edible when young.

Magic: In China, the true home of bamboo, its "hollow-heartedness" denotes the gentle modesty of the plant, its ability to sway gracefully in the wind, rather than be broken by it. Guan-yin, the Bodhisattva of mercy in Chinese lore, often holds a bamboo branch as a symbol of her modest nature. But there's more to bamboo than this. Look carefully at the joints of the bamboo; each represents a step towards higher spiritual knowledge! The flexibility of the plant applies not only to its ability to withstand crises, but also to meet the challenges life brings us every day. Because it is supple, it represents youth, because it is gaunt, it represents age, and because it is evergreen, it represents eternity – the complete circle. "Two live as one/One live as two/Two live as three/Under the bam/Under the boo/Under the bamboo tree." Faithfulness, good luck and fertility are added to its attributes, and Chinese wizards of old used bamboo wands to call up spirits. On the other hand, fireworks made with bamboo were used to ward off demons. Rites involving bamboo are most effective if performed the third day of the third lunar month, the fifth day of the fifth month, the seventh day of the seventh month, and the ninth day of the ninth month. Otherwise select an auspicious day in winter.

The ancient Taoists texts tell of a powerful rite using bamboo. The ancient wizards used a nine-segment bamboo, each segment named after a constellation. To perform the rite, go to a clean and quiet place and face south. Slightly bend the first segment of bamboo to the left and to the right. Then open four holes below the first segment and insert the secret names of the Four Sacred Mountains, and open one hole in the center at the top of the bamboo to insert the secret name of the Sacred Mountain of the Center. Place a sacred scripture (I suggest something from the Tao Te Ching) in the middle part and seal the opening with wax. It is said one can summon spirits and destroy hells, if you follow the rules, with magical staffs made in this way. Point to heaven with the staff and the heavenly spirits will pay homage; point to earth with the staff and the earth spirits will welcome you. Point to the northeast with the staff and the bodies of all the ghosts will be controlled. Magically, the wand changes at the moment the hells are destroyed into a pillar in the form of the dragon's head (yang aspect) and the tiger's tail (yin aspect). The dragon is brilliant and holds a splendid streamer in its mouth. Numinous winds and auspicious clouds coil around the dragon, shining limitlessly. If you are a Buddhist you may also invoke the name of Guan-yin.

Basil (*Ocimum basilicum*) This is the herb of **Reconciliation**.

Horticulture

Description: Fast-growing annual herb with a square, branched stem and beautiful habit, with over 150 varieties. Height 1–2 feet. ***Name Lore:*** The name "basilisk," a terrifying mythical monster whose glance was fatal, is said to derive from basil. There is a complicated connection between basil and basilisks (transmogrified into today's salamander), and some say that basil bred basilisks. ***Other Names:*** American dittany, alabahaca, devil plant, herb of kings, St. Joseph's wort, sweet basil, herb of kings, witches' herb, tulsi. ***Colors:*** Blooms pale yellow, white, or red. Leaves often reddish. ***Fragrance:*** Green, herby, heady, pungent, sweetly spicy, especially after it rains. All parts of the plant are aromatic. The so-called holy basil, *O. sanctum,* is very fragrant; pious Hindus used to plant it about their temples and later cut the stem base into rosaries. ***Bloom Time***: August. ***Origin:*** India and Mediterranean, now grown worldwide.

Habitat: Open places. **Earth** (soil type): Rich, well drained, moist, composted earth. **Water** (moisture needs): Moderate. **Fire** (sun/shade requirements): Full sun. **Air** (climate): US Climate Zones 4–10. Tolerates heat; frost tender.

Tips and Warnings: For the most efficacious magic, basil should be planted on Tuesday or Sunday. It should be planted near tomatoes, onion, chives, garlic, or oregano but kept away from other herbs. Harvest frequently, but autumn basil is best for magic. Oddly, the Romans thought that basil would grow only if it were roundly abused and snubbed. Fresh basil is of course used with tomato paste for sauces and can be used to flavor soup. The longer you cook it, the stronger the taste. It is also said to discourage flies. Some say that basil has the power to raise scorpions in the brain. Others claim contrarily that basil protects against scorpion stings.

Magic: This good-natured, peaceful herb brings harmony, especially between quarreling lovers. In fact, it's an all-around love and fertility herb. In the old days, a woman would place basil outside her window or wear a sprig of it when she is ready for her lover. Spanish prostitutes used to wear basil as an aphrodisiac to attract customers, but that is perhaps a different thing, although basil does bring money as well as love. Sprinkling powdered basil over the heart will ensure fidelity.

But basil has other virtues as well. Carrying it protects one in a crowd, brings wealth and success, and supplies courage in times of spiritual danger. Basil blesses and brings luck and joy to a home, especially a new one. To this end, it is sometimes placed in a bowl as potpourri. As incense, basil restores a sense of equilibrium; the very scent of it brings happiness, restoring health to head and heart. The same basil that we grow alongside our tomatoes may be a new component in grocery bags because of its ability to slow the growth of certain bacteria, including *E. coli* and listeria!

In India, basil is a sacred funeral herb helping to direct the deceased into the next life. It is associated with Vishnu and his avatar Krishna. In the Orthodox Church, basil is used as an altar plant during Easter. (Constantine's mother said she found one growing in the place where the cross once stood.) Basil can be used as an amulet and in consecration rites. *Rites involving basil are most effective when performed on Tuesday, best of all when Mars is visible. (Why this charming and friendly herb should get so much power from Mars is a mystery to me.) Invoke the name of Vishnu. Basil is burned at Imbolc. Scorpios have a particular affinity to basil.*

Bay Laurel *(Laurus nobilis)* This is the herb of **Oracle**.

Horticulture

Description: Tender perennial with leathery leaves and inconspicuous flowers. Height 60 feet in the wild, but can easily be trimmed to a more convenient height (even into a pot) ***Name Lore:*** The term "poet laureate" comes from the name of this plant. ***Other Names:*** Sweet bay, bay, bay tree, Grecian laurel, Indian bay, or true laurel. ***Similar and Related Species:*** There is also the so-called California laurel *(Umbellularia californica)* of the same family (Laurel) but a different genus. There is also the West Indian bay *(Pimenta racemosa)* and the bayberry *(Myrica cerifera)*. These trees are quite different. ***Colors:*** Flowers yellowish or whitish. ***Fragrance:*** Leaves fragrant and herby, most noticeably on warm days, or when broken. (The leaves of the California laurel are very strong smelling and not always pleasantly so.) The wood of the bay laurel is aromatic; it is said that King David had his room paneled with it. ***Bloom Time***: April–May. ***Origin:*** Mediterranean region.

Habitat: Damp, partially shady sites. **Earth** (soil type): Well-drained, rich in organic matters; pH 6.2. **Water** (moisture needs): Moderate. **Fire** (sun/shade requirements): Full sun to partial shade. **Air** (climate): US Climate Zones 7–10. Can be kept in large pots in colder areas. Needs protection from wind and cold.

Tips and Warnings. Bay laurel should be planted on Sunday. Prefers humid conditions. If a bay laurel in the garden suddenly withers, it is considered a bad sign. According to famous magical herbalist Scott Cunningham, bay laurel should be planted to the south. In colonial America, farmers placed bay leaves in strategic locations to ward off caterpillars.

Magic: The bay laurel is one of the most ancient, glorious, and powerful of all magical herbs. The Oracular Priestess of Delphi chewed and perhaps burned laurel in her visionary trances. In her trance, the Priestess was able to receive and impart the special wisdom of Apollo, who held the trees sacred and whose sacred groves were surrounded with them. (The nymph Daphne, of whom he was enamored, was changed into a laurel tree.) Some of the old divinatory power is left to the laurel, even today. It aids memory, the development of psychic powers, and empowers wish-magic. The leaves placed under a pillow bring prophetic dreams. The smoke can also be inhaled to bring on prophetic dreams. Keeping a bay leaf between your lips will cause you to prophesy. The prophetic powers have descended through folklore into love queries. If you etch your lover's name with a pin onto a bay leaf, and pin it under your nightclothes, when morning comes, a brown bay leaf means your lover is true. If it remains green, however, beware! Your lover is false. A similar rite will tell if your lover will marry you: etch your lover's initials on a bay leaf and place it in your left shoe. Wear the shoe all day, and check the leaf the next morning. If the initials have grown darker, your marriage is assured. If they have grown fainter, the wedding will not take place. But this is a degraded use of this great and ancient herb.

Because of its exalted status in Greek society, laurel came after a while to symbolize victory, honor, and success. From time immemorial laurel has crowned victors of athletic and military events. Symbolically, the laurel garland represents glory, honor, greatness, artistic achievement, victory, success, wealth, wisdom, and perseverance.

Laurel leaves also wash away guilt; Apollo and Orestes both made use of this property of the plant after they shed blood unlawfully. For this reason, the laurel remains a magical herb of justice and is used in exorcisms. Magically, bay laurel is a strengthening herb used to grant wishes, and to protect against witches, demons, Satan, lightning, and death, by simply being hung on the door. Bring a few leaves in the house (or just scatter them around) to ward off illness and dispel hexes, especially family curses (the old House of Atreus problem). Since bay laurel is difficult to grow in most places, you can use the store-bought leaves, although they don't work as well. Old-time midwives touched an infant's feet with it to protect the child from lameness. Roman legend tells us that putting a bay leaf behind your ear will prevent you from getting drunk at parties. although since getting drunk is the point of many parties, this seems a fruitless endeavor. Laurel can be burned at Yule/Winter Solstice and Imbolc. *Rites performed with bay laurel are most efficacious on Sunday, especially during the new moon. Bay laurel makes a good potion or an amulet. The name of Apollo, Pan, Ceres, or Adonis should be invoked for utmost efficacy.*

Beech (*Fagus sylvatica*) This is the tree of **Ancient Knowledge.**

Horticulture

Description: Deciduous, long-lived, shallow-rooted broadleaf tree with smooth bark, pointy-oval leaves, and luxuriant foliage. Beeches can live for 300 years. Height up to 140 feet. *Name Lore:* The old Anglo-Saxon word for beech was *boc.* This becomes book, and solidifies the reputation of this tree as a tree of knowledge. The scientific name comes from *Fagus* a Celtic god of beech trees. *Other Names:* Bog, boke, faggio, fagos, the "mother of the woods." Sometimes, it is also known as the "queen" of the woods to contrast with the "kingly" oak. *Similar and related species:* The so-called copper beech is a popular European park plant and is featured in a Sherlock Holmes story, "The Copper Beeches." *Colors:* Bark silvery gray, twigs purplish and tassels red and pink. The wood is yellow-pinkish. In fall, leaves turn orange, yellow, and russet. Copper beeches have purple foliage. *Fragrance:* Woody, masculine. **Bloom Time**: Late April–early May. Fruit ripens in September. ***Origin:*** Europe. Introduced into America during colonial times.

Habitat: Woods. **Earth** (soil type): Moist, well drained. Some types like a slightly acid soil; others prefer one, which is chalkier. Beech improves soil for other trees. **Water** (moisture needs): Moderate. **Fire** (sun/shade requirements): Sunny to shade. **Air** (climate): US Climate Zones 3–9.

Tips and Warnings: There are garden-size cultivars considerably smaller than the wild variety. Some kinds of beeches can be formed into hedges. Beech leaves make excellent mulch. Beech is a slow grower.

Magic: "They will not hush, the leaves a-flutter round me, the beech leaves old." (William Butler Yeats "The Madness of King Goll".) It is very helpful to the practitioner of magic to meditate within a beech grove, which will lead to personal growth and development. *Beech wood makes a good amulet. Perform rites using beech when Saturn is visible. Invoke Bacchus.*

Belladonna *(Atropa belladonna)* This is the herb of Silence.

Horticulture

Description: Perennial herb with branching stems, fleshy white root, and bell-shaped flowers. Height 2–6 feet. ***Name Lore:*** *Belladonna* means "beautiful woman" in Italian and supposedly comes from the old habit of women using belladonna drops to enlarge their pupils and making themselves more attractive. It gave them glaucoma, too. The scientific name reminds us uncomfortably of *Atropos*, the eldest of the Three Fates, and the one who cut the thread of life. **Other Names:** Deadly nightshade, death's herb, great morel, devil's berry, naughty men's cherries, woody nightshade, dwale. *Colors:* Stems are purplish; flowers brown or purplish; cherry-sized fruit black and shiny. *Fragrance:* When crushed, belladonna gives off a strong odor. ***Bloom Time***: May–August. *Origin:* Europe, Asia, and eastern North America.

Habitat: Hedges, woods, thickets, abandoned fields, waste places. **Earth** (soil type): chalky, limey, well drained. **Water** (moisture needs): Moderate. **Fire** (sun/shade requirements): Prefers part shade. Too much sun stunts it. **Air** (climate): US Climate Zones 4-8.

Tips and Warnings: For best results, plant on Sunday. It has most magical effect if planted to the south. Harvest at dawn. This plant contains several potent alkaloids, including atropine. It is deadly poison, causing damage to the central nervous system. Two or three berries can kill a small child, and children are attracted to its beauty. Even rubbing it on the body, as in the famous "flying ointments," can produce delirium. Because of its danger, it should be avoided except in extreme cases, and even then used only by knowledgeable practitioners.

Magic: Belladonna is so deadly that it is said that during the witch-hunts, fellow practitioners of the Craft would attempt to give some to the condemned witch on the way to the stake, in the hopes of easing the passage to the Otherworld. Placing nightshade anywhere on the body banishes the memory of old lovers and dispels evil of all kinds. Belladonna has traditionally been used as an ingredient of the "flying ointment" made by witches, especially on May Eve (Walpurgisnacht), when whole covens reportedly took off, at least in spirit. This is the original astral projection. Legend says that this plant belongs to the devil, except on the witches' Sabbath, when it is sacred to Hecate. On the other hand, belladonna guards against evil spirits, and is hung over the beds of the sleeping household. Farmers also used it to protect their livestock. Today it can be used in love magic, but it should be guarded carefully like the poison it is. Belladonna was formerly used as a drug, but should not be so used now. *If you dare use it, invoke the name of Bellona, Circe, and Hecate. Librans are really the only ones who have the balance to deal with this very dangerous herb.*

Benzoin *(Styrax benzoin; also Lindera)* This is the herb of **Purification.**

Horticulture

Description: Fast-growing deciduous tropical tree with pointy-oval leaves and bell-shaped flowers. The aromatic resin comes from the bark. Height 60 feet. *Other Names:* Benjamin, friar's balsam, spice bush, Sumatra gum, snowbells, storax. *Similar and Related Species:* The *S. benzoin* and the true storax, *S. officinalis,* are closely related. *Colors:* Flowers white; leaves pale green above and cream below. *Fragrance:* Sweet, balsamic, flowery. *Bloom Time*: Spring. *Origin:* Southeast Asia

Habitat: Tropical rainforests. **Earth** (soil type): Moist, well drained. **Water** (moisture needs): High. **Fire** (sun/shade requirements): Sun to partial shade. **Air** (climate): Tropical.

Tips and Warnings: The resin can only be extracted from older plants. Benzoin is nearly always purchased commercially.

Magic: Benzoin is a visionary herb (technically, of course, a balsamic resin) that establishes peace of mind and harmony. Its purpose is primarily to banish evil sprits and perform weather magic, but it is also a mood enhancer and promotes generosity. It is a good herb to burn while reading Tarot. Benzoin is used as incense, usually during exorcisms, Imbolc (Candlemas), and Mabon (Fall Equinox). *Rites using bezoin are most effective when performed at Beltaine or as close to the full moon as possible. Open all windows during rites concerned with benzoin. Capricorns have a particular affinity for this herb. Clothe yourself in white or blue.*

Bergamot *(Monarda species)* This is the herb of **Material Success.**

Horticulture

Description: Perennial upright plant with tubular flowers popping from the terminal head. It has paired, opposite leaves and square stems. It is member of the mint family. Despite one colloquial name, bee balm it is not pollinated by bees. Height 3 feet. *Other Names:* Bee balm, Oswego tea, Indian plume, fragrant balm, monarda, mountain balm, mountain mint. *Similar and related species:* *Melissa* or lemon balm is also sometimes called "balm," just to confuse things more. *Colors:* Red flowers, reddish brown bracts. *Fragrance:* The leaves are richly fragrant. *Bloom Time*: June-August. *Origin:* North America.

Habitat: Rich woods, moist meadows, streambanks. **Earth** (soil type): Adaptable to most soils; prefers rich, moist, slightly acid. **Water** (moisture needs): Moderate–high. Does not like dry conditions. **Fire** (sun/shade requirements): Prefers full sun. **Air** (climate): US Climate Zones 3–9.

Tips and Warnings: This mint is most suitable to informal gardens. Needs plenty of room. Bergamot is attractive to hummingbirds and some butterflies. The hummingbird moth seems especially fond of it. It will spread rapidly in fertile soil.

Magic: Bergamot, when worn on the palm of each hand attracts both love and material objects, but especially the latter. It is said that carrying a few leaves of bergamot in the wallet – or rubbing money with it before you spend it will insure its return. It brings money, justice, compassion, protection, and success. Like many New World plants, bergamot hasn't had a lot of time to develop an extensive magical tradition. *Clothe yourself in orange or pink.*

Betony *(Stachy officinalis)* This is the herb of **Home Protection.**

Horticulture

Description: Perennial small herb with erect, square stem and spiked flowers. This plant is grown for its hairy foliage, which resembles that of a woolly lamb's ear. *Other Names:* Lamb's ears, wood betony, bishopwort, lousewort, wood betony, hedge nettle, purple betony. *Colors:* Foliage silver gray; flowers reddish-purple. *Fragrance:* Leaves tart and spicy, especially when dry. *Bloom Time*: June–September. *Origin:* Europe and Siberia.

Habitat: Open woods, meadows, and hedges. **Earth** (soil type): Well-drained, average soil. Tolerates poor soil. **Water** (moisture needs): Moderate; tolerates drought. **Fire** (sun/shade requirements): Full sun, part shade, or shade. **Air** (climate): US Climate Zones 4-9.

Tips and Warnings: Betony was an important feature in every medieval herb garden. Its silver foliage creates a beautiful softening effect in the garden. Plant in the west for the best magical effects. It also makes an excellent ground cover, and is a fine choice in a moon garden. Supposedly betony loses all its powers if it is touched with iron.

Magic: Betony has such powerful magic that merely planting the herb in the garden protects the entire house and its residents from witchcraft, evil spirits, despair, nightmares, and ghosts. It has even stronger powers if burned at Midsummer. One old saying is "Sell your coat and buy betony." Betony also protects against drunkenness, draws the fairy folk, attracts men, and promotes psychic awareness. Bits of betony in a cachet are said to be a sure man-attractant. Stuffing a pillow with betony (or at least putting some under the pillow) is said to prevent nightmares. Sprinkling some around the doorway dispels despair. Betony also cures "elf sickness." Some old sources say that if two snakes are put into a ring of betony, they will fight to the death. Considered magically powerful against evil spirits. *Capricorns are most successful with this herb. Clothe yourself in brown.*

Birch *(Betula* species) This is the herb of the **Feminine Spirit.**

Horticulture

Description: Deciduous, straight, smooth-barked broadleaf with slender branches, and inconspicuous flowers. The bark of the birch proper, of course, is papery and peels easily. Flowers are small and inconspicuous. Leaves of most species are pointed, small, spade shaped, with double-toothed edges. They are shallow rooted and rather short-lived. Height 30–50 feet. **Name Lore:** The word "birch" probably derives from the Anglo-Saxon *beorc,* meaning white and shining. **Other Names:** Lady of the Woods. **Similar and Related Species:** The common names of birches are particularly exasperating. For instance, *B. alleghaniensis* is commonly known as the yellow birch. However, it is sometimes called the gray birch or silver birch. (There are other silver birches too, *B. pendula* or *B. alba.*) *B. lenta* is usually known as the sweet birch, but it is also called the black birch or the cherry birch. *B. nigra,* is often called the river birch, but can also be known as the red birch or the black birch, while the *B. occidentalis* is *also* sometimes called the red birch or the black birch. I could also talk about the white birch, the European white birch, the paper birch, and the wire birch. Don't lose heart; I won't. All have the same magical powers. **Colors:** Flowers are greenish. Bark may be white, gray, or almost green, depending on the species. New leaves delicate green, turning rich yellow in the fall. While usually white, some species have gray, black, or orange-brown bark. Inner bark is often russet. **Fragrance:** The twigs and leaves of some species are spicily fragrant. The resinous sap has a characteristic fragrance. **Bloom Time**: Early spring. **Origin:** Northern hemisphere.

Habitat: Edge of wood, woods. **Earth** (soil type): Light, loamy, moist. Dislikes alkaline soil. **Water** (moisture needs): High to moderate. **Fire** (sun/shade requirements): Full sun in the north, partial shade in the south. **Air** (climate): US Climate Zones 2–9.

Tips and Warnings: Plant in early spring, but do not plant close to borders or fences. Many fungi (important for magical use but not considered in this book) may be found beneath birch trees. Most deer don't care for the taste of birch and leave it alone. One story says that you can never take the bark from a birch unless Thor has kissed it. Thor kisses trees by striking them with lightning.

Magic: This birch is considered the "wife," of the oak, or masculine spirit. It is an herb of fertility, creativity, grace and protection, all under the aegis of the Great Mother. Hanging birch in the home protects one from infertility, lightning, and the evil eye, especially when red ribbons are tied to it. It was also held to have powers over evil spirits, the evil eye, witchcraft, and all other negative influences. It is especially protective of children and animals. If you don't want elves to ride your horses, tie red and white rags to a birch strand. And believe me, you don't want elves riding your horses. They ride them to death and knot up their manes. (If there's one thing worse than a dead horse, it's a dead horse with a knotted up mane.) Using birch bark to write magical formulas will render them more efficacious as long you are careful to select only as much bark as will not harm the tree. Birch twigs also make a wonderful witch's broom for cleansing and purifying a sacred area. Birch wood wands are especially efficacious for rites of purification, fertility, and blessings. Birch also provides protection against witches. Wreaths made of birch are a traditional lover's present. Birches made the original Maypoles, and wearing a sprig of birch on Beltaine will assure a young woman of finding a perfect suitor. In a few cases, evil spirits inhabit birch trees; they have the power to make people crazy– also (perhaps) a singularly feminine ability. *Birch wood makes an excellent amulet. Invoke the name of any suitable goddess, especially Cybele, or the name of Thor. Rites involving birch are most effective on January 20, May Day, Whitsuntide, and when performed on Friday or Sunday, during daylight hours. Sagittarians work best with this herb.*

Bittersweet (*Celastrus scandens*) This is the herb of **Expulsion.**

Horticulture

Description: Woody, twining, rambling vine with glossy leaves. Height 15–20 feet. ***Other Names:*** American bittersweet. ***Colors:*** Flowers greenish to yellow; fruit orange/red. ***Fragrance:*** Subtle. ***Bloom Time***: Blossoms in spring, berries in fall and winter. ***Origin:*** Eastern and central United States.

Habitat: Woodland areas, thickets, rocky slopes, bluffs. **Earth** (soil type): Poor to average soils. **Water** (moisture needs): Moderate. **Fire** (sun/shade requirements): Full sun. **Air** (climate): US Climate Zones 3-8.

Tips and Warnings: Please plant only the American bittersweet (*C. scandens*), not its invasive Asian counterpart (*C. orbiculatus*), which has already escaped and is naturalized in some places. Bittersweet should be planted on Sunday. Do not collect from the wild, as the wild species are already seriously depleted. Bittersweet comes in male and female versions, and generally a male is needed to pollinate the female, which has the showy berries. Unfortunately many nurseries don't distinguish between the two. Be sure to inquire. Bittersweet attracts wildlife.

Magic: Bittersweet is used to rid people and pets of witchcraft and sudden ailments. Rites are generally performed by scattering the berries, but if you put bittersweet under your pillow, all memories of an unhappy love affair will fade away. It is said that sprinkling bittersweet in your neighbor's yard will make them move away. (Of course, the new neighbors might be worse.)

Blackberry (*Rubus villosus, R. fructicosus*) This is the herb of **Lughnasa.**

Horticulture

Description: Slender, deciduous thorny, creeping vine or shrub with five-petalled flowers. They use hooks to latch onto their supports. Noted for its seedy, sweet berries. Many species. Height 4–7 feet. ***Other Names:*** Bramble, brameberry, bly, bramble-kite, brambleberry, brummel, bumble-kite, common blackberry, European blackberry, scaldhead, ***Colors:*** Flowers white; fruit black. ***Fragrance:*** Subtle. ***Bloom Time***: Blossoms May; fruit ripens in late July. ***Origin:*** Widespread over the world.

Habitat: Wood, hedges, scrub. **Earth** (soil type): Average to rich. **Water** (moisture needs): Moderate. **Fire** (sun/shade requirements): Full sun. **Air** (climate) US Climate Zones 5–9.

Tips and Warnings: Plant during the second quarter of the waxing moon. Blackberries attract wildlife. Blackberries are ready to eat when they lose some of their glossiness and are a bit soft, pulling off the vine easily. Blackberry pies are traditional at Lughnasa.

Magic: Brighid the ancient Celtic goddess of fire, the seasons, and metalworkers held blackberry sacred. Blackberry is also one of the many herbs with magical healing powers, and is famous for promoting wealth. However, its most unusual power is that of protecting folk against the power of evil runes. There is an ancient spell (immortalized in Michael Drayton's *Nimphidia*) using blackberries to make someone well. A sick person must crawl backwards and forwards (oriented from west to east), three times under the natural arch made by a blackberry rooted at both ends and the patient will be made well. I would have more faith in this cure if it weren't for the fact that very sick people (or anyone else, for that matter, are not usually capable of crawling around under blackberry bushes). But blackberries do make nice arches, even when they aren't rooted at both ends. And here is a traditional chant to soothe burns. Dip nine blackberry leaves in spring water and laying on the burn gently, while saying three times to each leaf: "Three ladies came from the east/ One with fire and two with frost/Out with fire, in with frost." In Brittany, the blackberry is said to belong to the fairies. No one else can touch it. Blackberry wreaths about a grave will keep the ghost from rising.

The blackberry carries an obvious symbolism as well, which is nevertheless important to repeat. Only by braving the thorny canes (and blackberry thorns are worse than almost anything imaginable) can one hope to achieve the sweetness of the berry. Use blackberry whenever you face a difficult challenge that yet brings sweet rewards.

The blackberry does have its detractors, of course. One legend claims that the devil stumbled into a blackberry plant and forever put his curse upon it. An English story adds that picking the fruit after October 11 (the date the devil cursed it, and also the date of Michaelmas in the Old Calendar) will bring bad luck. Since blackberries ripen almost precisely on August 1 (Lughnasa), at least at my house, any berries in October would be shriveled, rotten, or long since eaten by the birds. So it is an empty curse. Blackberry makes an excellent amulet for those brave enough to wear it. *Rites involving blackberry should be performed invoking the name of Brighid and in her honor. Lughnasa is the most auspicious day.*

Black Hellebore *(Helleborus niger)* This is the herb of **Frenzy**.
See also *Hellebore* and *Lenten Rose*.

Horticulture

Description: Perennial evergreen herb with palm-like leathery leaves. *Other Names:* Christmas rose, true hellebore. *Name Lore:* Black hellebore because of the blackness of the root. Christmas rose because it blooms in mid-winter. *Similar and related species:* Lentern rose *(H. orientalis),* green hellebore (*H. viridis*). White hellebore, or false helleborine (*Veratrum album* and its variants), is really a member of the lily family, but is also poisonous. *Colors:* Flowers white or pinkish. *Fragrance:* Subtle. ***Bloom Time***: Late fall, winter, or early spring, depending on climate. *Origin:* Southern and Central Europe.

Habitat: Woods, rocky slopes. **Earth** (soil type): Limey, humous, rich. **Water** (moisture needs): Moderate. **Fire** (sun/shade requirements): Partial shade to full sun. **Air** (climate): US Climate Zones 5–8. This plant needs to be protected from wind.

Tips and Warnings: It is considered bad luck if picked; the only safe way is to face east and curse while you're doing so. This empowers the plant. It resents division, and does best in a sheltered spot if winters are cold. All parts of the plant are extremely poisonous.

Magic: Ancient sorcerers used black hellebore to whip up their followers into madness. Hellebore conferred invisibility if the magic-worker walked upon the powdered plant or if she tossed it into the air with suitable accompanying spells. If the plant was dried and burned, it would banish ghosts and possessed creatures. It was also used for astral projections. (It is sometimes unclear from old texts as to which variety of hellebore was efficacious for magical purposes.) Despite the fact that this plant is quite poisonous, it was been used for centuries to cure everything from worms to madness.

Blackthorn (*Prunus spinosa*) This is the herb of **Darkness**.

Horticulture

Description: Deciduous, many branched, crooked, spiny shrub with extremely long, sharp thorns and star-shaped flowers that bloom before the foliage appears. *Other Names:* Sloe (the name of the fruit). *Colors:* Bark brownish black; flowers pure, dazzling white; fruits bluish-purplish-black; leaves dark green, but turning yellow in autumn. *Fragrance:* Musky and powerful. The scent has been described as "erotic." *Bloom Time*: March–May (flowers), September (sloes). *Origin:* Europe.

Habitat: Hedges, wood margins, thickets. It is sometimes found with hawthorn. **Earth** (soil type): Poor, stony. **Water** (moisture needs): Low. **Fire** (sun/shade requirements): Sunny. **Air** (climate): US Climate Zones 5–8.

Tips and Warnings. The fresh fruits can be eaten. And the sloes are used to flavor sloe gin.

Magic: Traditionally, this plant is the sister of the hawthorn; they were twined together in Mayday celebrations. Crowns of blackthorn were also worn during the New Year festivities, and were then burned and scattered on the fields as a fertilizer. In Ireland blackthorns were used to make the traditional shillelaghs as well as the magicians' "blasting stick." However, in general, the blackthorn has a sinister reputation. It has even more vicious thorns than the blackberry, without the latter's sweet reward. Supposedly the devil used blackthorn prickles to mark the bodies of witches. Blackthorn is unlucky to bring into the house, although fairies are quite attracted to it. It is suggested that the thorns that grew up around the castle of Sleeping Beauty were blackthorn, although no one can be certain. By carving a candle roughly into the shape of a person and piercing it strategically with three thorns from the blackthorn, you will cast a hex back to the person who made it. Chant the appropriate formula, of course. Most magic rites with blackthorn involve fate, or other powers outside the practitioner's ordinary sphere of influence. *These rites are most efficacious at Beltaine, Imbolc (February 1), Samhain (October 31), or in the winter. The rite should be performed at night. Wear bright colors.*

Bladderwrack

(Fucus vesiculosus): This is a seaweed, common off the coast of Scotland and other places, used in weather control, summoning sea spirits, and to forestall accidents at sea. Obviously this is something that is not possible to grow in a garden.

Blessed Thistle (*Carduus benedictus,* also *Cnicus benedictus* and *Carbenia benedicta*) This is the herb of the **Mother Goddess.**

Horticulture

Description: Annual hairy, spiny herb with a branched, spreading stem. Flowers solitary and terminal. Height 2 feet. *Other Names:* St. Benedict thistle, Our Lady's thistle, bitter thistle, spotted thistle, cursed thistle, blessed cardus, spotted cardus, and holy thistle. *Colors:* Flowers yellow. *Fragrance:* Subtle. *Bloom Time*: May–July. *Origin:* Mediterranean and nearby parts of Asia.

Habitat: Roadsides, moist areas, wastelands. **Earth** (soil type): Tolerant. **Water** (moisture needs): Moderate. **Fire** (sun/shade requirements): Prefers full sun. **Air** (climate): US Climate Zones 4-7.

Tips and Warnings: As Shakespeare wrote in *Much Ado About Nothing,* "Get you some of this distilled Carduus Benedictus and lay it to your heart: it is the only thing for a qualm ... plain holy thistle."

Magic: The blessed thistle is associated with all tender aspects of the Mother Goddess, and of all-powerful protective magic associated with her. It is also an herb of consecration, love, and counter-magic especially when the practitioner is the victim of anger or envy. When carried, it brings joy, strength, and safety, and has traditional use in magic wands; it is an energizer. It also keeps thieves away. *Rites involving blessed thistle are particularly effective at Yule. Invoke Pan, or St. Benedict, if you are a Christian. Arians work best with this herb.*

Bo Tree

See Ficus. The Bo Tree was a particular tree under which the Buddha sat to achieve Enlightenment. The word Bo means "Enlightenment tree."

Borage (*Borago officinalis)* This is the herb of **Courage.**

Horticulture

Description: Fast-growing annual hairy herb, with star-shaped flowers and rough leaves that form a basal rosette. Height 18–24 inches. *Other Names:* Bee bread, starflower. *Colors:* Flowers bright blue or purple and pink, with black anthers. *Fragrance:* Light, cucumber-like. *Bloom Time*: June–September. *Origin:* Mediterranean area, naturalized all over the region (Crusaders carried it around).

Habitat: Where escaped, can be found in waste places. **Earth** (soil type): Rich, well-drained, sandy. Needs lots of room. **Water** (moisture needs): Needs to be well watered. **Fire** (sun/shade requirements): Sun or part sun. **Air** (climate): US Climate Zones 5–9.

Tips and Warnings: Borage should be planted on Thursday. It is a very good herb to plant near strawberries, as it seems to help them. Borage draws bees. In former times, borage was made into a refreshing drink. Borage flowers may be candied, and turned into jellies and jams. It was also used to flavor claret. The young leaves, whose flavor resembles cucumber, can be added to salads and soups

Magic: Roman soldiers used to drink a wine made from borage before going off to battle. The Greeks said that steeping borage in wine induced forgetfulness. It has the power to impart joy and goodwill. Borage tea may aid psychic powers, and carrying a few leaves is said to be protective. Use in a bath or as incense for rites invoking courage during a difficult situation. *Leos have a particular affinity to this herb. Clothe yourself in red or purple.*

Box *(Buxus* species) This is the herb of **Eternity.**

Horticulture

Description: Broadleaf evergreen shrub or small tree, dense branching habit, with small flowers and glossy leaves. Height up to 20 feet. *Colors:* Flowers whitish-green; leaves dark green or blue. *Name Lore:* Its wood is indeed famous for making boxes (it doesn't warp), and that's where our word "box" comes from. *Fragrance:* Love it or hate it, box has an unforgettable smell, which some liken to cat pee, but which Oliver Wendell Holmes called the "flavor of eternity." This gives one pause to think what eternity might be like. *Bloom Time*: March–May. *Origin:* Central and Western Europe.

Habitat: Woody areas. **Earth** (soil type): Lime, deep, moist well-drained. **Water** (moisture needs): Moderate. Will not tolerate drought. **Fire** (sun/shade requirements): Sun to part shade. **Air** (climate): Many varieties of box are hardy in US Climate Zones 5–10. Protect from drying winds.

Tips and Warnings: Easy to grow, but the plant grows very slowly. Box shears easily to any desired form, but needs to be mulched heavily. Dangerous if taken internally. All parts of the plant are poisonous, most especially the leaves and seeds.

Magic: This evergreen was planted along the edges of ancient cemeteries (as was cypress and yew). In ancient times it was frequently used to make wooden statues of the deities, especially Apollo, and in more modern times is the wood of the master hammer in Freemasonry. It was once used to cure malaria. The green leathery leaves symbolize immortality. In Europe, box greens were traditionally placed in churches to replace Christmas holly until Easter. "Down with rosemary and bays,/Down with mistletoe./Instead of holly, now upraise/The green Box for show." (Robert Herrick, "Stoicism"). *In rites involving boxwood, invoke the gods of the Underworld and Cybele, the mother goddess.*

Bracken Fern *(Pteridium aquilinum)* This is the herb of **Invisibility**.

Horticulture

Description: Large, coarse, perennial, deciduous fern growing from a rhizome. The leathery blades of the frond divide into pinnae, each further divided into pinnules. Often forms large colonies. Height up to10 feet. *Name Lore:* The scientific name *aquilinum* means "eagle," while the *Pteridium* simply means "fern." *Bracken* is an Old English word for all ferns, but is particularly applied to this one. *Other Names:* Female fern, brake fern, fiddlehead fern, eagle fern, pasture brake, hog brake. *Similar and Related Species:* See male fern, maidenhair fern. *Colors:* Dark green. *Fragrance:* Ferny. *Bloom Time*: Ferns have no flowers, of course. Spores produced August through September. *Origin:* Global, except for deserts (either tropic or arctic).

Habitat: Woods. **Earth** (soil type): Moist, woodsy, acid, humous. However, it succeeds on soil too dry for other ferns. **Water** (moisture needs): Prefers to be well watered. **Fire** (sun/shade requirements: Sun or shade. **Air** (climate): Most are hardy to US Climate Zone 8.

Tips and Warnings: For most magical results, plant on Thursdays. For strongest magic, gather on Midsummer's Eve. Ferns provide an excellent, textured foliage plant to serve as backdrop or contrast in most gardens. Bracken fern aids soil fertility by bringing large amounts of phosphate, nitrogen, and potassium into circulation. Most mammals can't stand the stuff, so it's pretty safe from grazers. Ferns were used as rent-currency in the Middle Ages, also as thatching and kindling. Supposedly ferns can cause vitamin-B deficiencies if eaten in large amounts. Few people eat large amounts of ferns, although fiddleheads are considered tasty. (It's an acquired taste.) For herbivores, the plant is more dangerous. It can cause poisoning that affects the bone marrow of both cattle and sheep, causing anemia and hemorrhaging, blindness and tumors of the jaws, rumen, intestine, and liver.

Magic. "We have the receipt of fern-seed, we walk invisible…" Shakespeare, *Henry IV.* It may also be used in rites of love, protection, counter-magic, prosperity, and vision. Ferns are associated with invisibility; to accomplish this one is supposed to gather fern seeds. This is trickier than it sounds, since ferns have no seeds. (One assumes the early writers meant spores, rather than seeds.) Ferns may help find hidden treasure; this is easier to do if you are invisible and no one notices you are looking. Once invisible, you can also enter the fairy realm (generally a bad idea). Keeping a fern amulet will protect your privacy.

But ferns have additional benefits. They are supposed to bring immortality and are often used to banish evil spirits. When burned outside, they bring rain. When placed beneath a pillow, bracken fern will bring not just garden-variety prophetic dreams, but a solution to your problems. The spores will help you improve your finances. *Bracken fern is useful in all exorcisms, protection, and female fertility rites, and makes a good amulet. Fern is frequently used as decoration at Samhain. Taurians have the best luck with it.*

Bramble
See Blackberry.

Broom (*Cytisus scoparius*) This is the herb of **Wind and Storm.**

Horticulture

Description: Deciduous, free-flowering erect shrub with long, tangled branches and oblong black fruit pods. ***Other Names:*** Link, genista, asphaltus, banal, Scotch broom, broom tops, Irish broom. ***Colors:*** Flowers yellow or pink; fruits black. ***Fragrance:*** Some varieties (*C. x praecox*) are unpleasantly (musty) scented. Others are bittersweet. ***Bloom Time***: Long-flowering; May–July. ***Origin:*** Europe.

Habitat: Sunny hillsides, open woods. **Earth** (soil type): Dry and sloping; prefers acid soils. **Water** (moisture needs): Low. **Fire** (sun/shade requirements): Sunny. **Air** (climate): US Climate Zones 4–8.

Tips and Warnings: All else being equal, plant broom to the east in the garden. The flowering broom tips should be gathered before midsummer. It was once believed to increase the potency of beer. Broom is an excellent plant for a **Fire** or **Air** Garden. All parts of this plant are poisonous.

Magic: In general, it is considered unlucky, although some wedding traditions include broom. Broom does protect against sorcery, but when brought into a home, especially in May (a very dangerous month in general) it brings bad fortune. (There is a rival tradition that claims broom is protective when hung indoors, but that's definitely a minority opinion. Use something else.) Throwing broom into the air will raise the wind; burying it will calm the winds. Some Christians considered broom cursed. (It's a long story to do with the crackling of broom seeds threatening to betray Mary and Joseph on their flight into Egypt.) Broom is one of the few yellow flowers that the Welsh and Manx Fairies can tolerate. Other varieties of fairies detest it. *Broom is used in weather rituals, weddings, and exorcisms, and is frequently used as a decoration during Samhain. Rites using broom are most efficacious when performed outdoors.*

Bryony *(Bryonia alba; B. dioica)* This herb is **Protection Against Lightning.**

Horticulture

Description: Fast-growing perennial climber with a thick root, and angular, prickly, branching stems. **Other Names:** Wild bryony, bryony, lack-berried bryony, tetterberry, wild hops, English mandrake, wild vine, wood vine, ladies' seal, white bryony. **Related Plants:** White bryony is *B. alba*. Red bryony is *B. dioica*. **Colors:** Flowers yellow-white with green veins. *B. alba* produces black berries; *B. dioica* produces red. **Fragrance:** Berries have a distinctly unpleasant odor. **Bloom Time**: May. **Origin:** Eastern and southeastern Europe but naturalized in other places.

Habitat: Waste areas. **Earth** (soil type): Tolerant. **Water** (moisture needs): Moderate. **Fire** (sun/shade requirements): Sunny. **Air** (climate) US Climate Zones 6–9.

Tips and Warnings: Both species of bryony are extremely poisonous; the sap causes itching, and a dozen berries can kill a child.

Magic: Augustus Caesar wore a wreath of bryony to protect himself from lightning, and sure enough, he was never struck. However, because of its root's resemblance to that of the magically dangerous mandrake, the plant is sometimes considered bad luck. On the other hand, bryony can be used in place of mandrake most of the time, when that herb is needed. Hence the name English Mandrake. True mandrake is hard to come by and very tricky to work with. *In using bryony for magical rites, invoke the name of Dionysus. Gemini have an affinity to bryony.*

Buckeye *(Aesculus species)* Buckeye is the herb of **Gamblers.**

Horticulture

Description: Deciduous tree or bush with a rounded habit. Several species range from 20 to 90 feet in height. **Name Lore:** The buckeye derives the name from its large brown seeds, which resemble the eyes of a deer. **Other Names:** American horse chestnut. **Similar and related species:** The California buckeye (*Aesculus californica*). **Colors:** Young blossoms are yellow, color turns bright crimson as bloom matures. The bottlebrush buckeye (*A. parviflora*) has white flowers and leaves that turn yellow and light orange. **Fragrance:** Young blossoms are honey scented; smell fades as the flowers mature. Leaves smell slightly pleasant when crushed. *Bloom Time*: Midsummer. *Origin:* North America.

Habitat: Slopes. **Earth** (soil type): Slightly acid. **Water** (moisture needs): Moderate, but likes to be kept moist. **Fire** (sun/shade requirements): Sun or part shade. **Air** (climate): US Climate Zones 4–9. Many are heat-resistant.

Tips and Warnings: The bottlebrush buckeye is wonderful for difficult banks and makes an ideal lawn specimen as well. However, it has a big drawback so far as magic is concerned: it does not produce nuts. Buckeye seeds are poisonous.

Magic: Buckeye is one of the premier "hoodhoo" lucky plants, especially for gamblers. Wrap a dollar around a buckeye and carry it for financial luck. More elaborately, drill a hole in the nut, fill it with mercury and seal it with wax. Because of their resemblance to testicles, buckeye is also considered a good luck charm for male potency.

Buckthorn *(Rhamnus* species) This is the herb of **Elven Wishes**.

Horticulture

Description: Spineless, deciduous evergreen shrub. Bark is smooth when plant is young, becomes scaly later. Height 6–15 feet. *Other Names:* Highwaythorn, waythorn, hartsthorn, ramsthorn. *Colors:* Flowers yellow. Small red drupes turn black as they mature.
Fragrance: Flower and freshly cut branches have a rather unpleasant scent. *Bloom Time*: March–May; berries October–November. *Origin:* Mediterranean region, Asia; now common in Britain and the United States. There is also an American variety (*R. purshiana*) native to the northwestern region.

Habitat: Hedgerows, scrub, woodland. **Earth** (soil type): Most species can handle any type, even sandy or clay. **Water** (moisture needs): Moderate. **Fire** (sun/shade requirements): Likes sun.
Air (climate): Can thrive up to US Climate Zone 7. Grows happily near the coast around Britain. Does not like cold winds.

Tips and Warnings: Buckthorn berries attract birds. This plant does well near the sea. Both fruit and bark yields a yellow dye. The fruit and fresh bark are poisonous.

Magic: While buckthorn is most commonly thought of as the herb of legal matters (wear it to court), an older and more magical tradition tells us to sprinkle powdered buckthorn bark in a circle and dance inside it under a full moon. Sooner or later an elf will appear. You must then say, "Stop and grant my wish!" Be quick about it, because the elf will try to escape. But if you catch him before he gets away, he will grant you one wish. Just one. Like fairies, elves can be treacherous. Be careful what you wish for. Buckthorn hung in windows and doors will drive away evil spells and enchantments.

Burdock *(Arctium* species) This is the herb of **Animal Magic**.

Horticulture

Description: Large, bushy biennial herb, broad and furry leaves. The flower heads are spiny balls. During its first year, it produces a basal ring of leaves; the stalk comes up the second year (like mullein).

Common species include the greater burdock (*A. lappa*) and wooly burdock (*A. tomentosum*). Height 3–5 feet. *Other Names:* Buckthorn, clotburr, hardock, batweed, fox's clote, personata, great burdock, bardana, cocklebur, love leaves, or less flatteringly, beggar's buttons, beggar's lice, and hurt burr. *Colors:* Flowers pinkish, lavender, or purple. *Fragrance:* Tart. *Bloom Time*: June or July through September or October. *Origin:* Europe. Grows in most of the temperate climates.

Habitat: Roadsides, waste areas, and fields. **Earth** (soil type): humousy, well-drained soil. **Water** (moisture needs): Burdock is very drought resistant. **Fire** (sun/shade requirements): Prefers sun, although it can tolerate some shade. **Air** (climate): US Climate Zones 3–7.

Tips and Warnings: Gather under a waning moon. It has most magical effects if planted to the south. This is not your typical garden flower, and should not be placed in regular gardens. Still, this deeply rooted plant will help to break up a heavy, clayey soil. Unless you don't mind getting stuck with painful, irritating burrs, you should keep this bush out of your garden. You may collect this plant in the wild where they are more than plentiful. If you decide to plant, the **Earth** Garden is the best choice.

Magic: While noted for its powers in the realm of animal and dog magic, burdock may also be an herb of exorcism, purification rites, and protection. It banishes evil spirits and wards off negative influences. Cut the root in pieces and string it on a red thread hung in the spell-circle for this purpose. This plant is also a traditional ingredient in aphrodisiacal potions. The raw stems increase libido. On a more intellectual level, eating the seed pods help things "stick" in the mind. In ancient times, people believed an oil extract from it helped grow hair. *Call upon Artemis or Diana, the goddesses of wild animals in rites with burdock, if the ritual concerns them. Often used at Beltaine. Leos have an affinity to burdock. Clothe yourself in brown.*

Calendula   (*Calendula officinalis*) This herb is **Proof Against Demons.**

Horticulture

Description: Hardy hairy annual with lanceolate leaves and daisy-like flowers. 12-24 inches. *Name Lore:* The name comes from "Mary's gold", and the flowers were often used to decorate church altars. *Other Names:* Pot marigold, field marigold, golds, ruddes, verrucaria, summer's bride. *Name Lore:* The name "calendula' is related to calendar, and the plant was rumored to bloom every month of the year. The "pot" of pot marigold refers to the plant's being placed in pots, heated, and the yellow color extracted for an inexpensive dye. *Similar and Related Species:* This is not the common annual *Tagetes* that appears in so many parks and gardens. (*Tagetes*, French and African marigolds, have dark green, deeply cut leaves; orange, gold, and/or red flowers and a pungent scent.) *Colors:* Yellow, white, or bright orange. *Fragrance:* Sharp, tangy, grassy. *Bloom Time*: June–September. *Origin:* Southern Europe.

Habitat: Open places. **Earth** (soil type): Average, well drained soil. **Water** (moisture needs): Moderate. **Fire** (sun/shade requirements): Prefers full sun, but can also handle cool shade. **Air** (climate): US Climate Zones 4-10. Can grow all winter in warmer climates.

Tips and Warnings: Easy to grow, and comes in dwarf varieties for the smaller garden. Taller pot marigolds, closer to the original, are also available; these latter are more cold hardy. For best magical

effects, pick in full sun (preferably at noon); it will bring comfort to your heart. Keep calendula sheared to promote re-bloom. Even looking at the flowers is said to be strengthening. Harvest at high noon.

Magic: The calendula enjoys a good reputation in magical circles, being a general all-purpose herb. However, it is most noted for its effectiveness as an anti-demonic, and has some effect, they say, against the Devil himself. This is an herb of love. Carrying calendula into court is said to ensure a favorable verdict. If you put marigold in the mattress or under the bed, it will bring prophetic dreams, especially about a thief. Rubbing your eyelids with calendula water may enable you to see fairies. Hang garlands of the herb around the door to keep evil from entering. If a young woman touches calendula with her feet, she will understand bird language. Calendula is traditionally burned during Beltaine and Mabon (Fall Equinox). *Leos and Arians are the best at dealing with calendula. Calendula may used as an amulet or bathing herb (in which case it will lead to respect and admiration.)*

Camphor Tree *(Cinnamonum camphora)* This herb provides **Release from a Love Affair.**

Horticulture

Description: Subtropical evergreen with clusters of small flowers and leathery leaves. The source of moth-repellent camphor. Camphor trees can live over 900 years. Height up to 100 feet. **Name Lore:** As you can tell by the scientific name, the camphor tree is a relative of the cinnamon tree. **Colors:** Leaves evergreen; flowers white or yellow, berries red. **Fragrance:** Flowers fragrant; foliage is sharply penetrating and aromatic – think mothballs. **Bloom Time:** Spring. **Origin:** Southern Asia, China, Japan.

Habitat: Earth (soil type): Variety of soils. **Water** (moisture needs): Moderate. **Fire** (sun/shade requirements): Full sun to partial shade. **Air** (climate) US Climate Zones 9–10.

Tips and Warnings: This plant has become invasive in many parts of the southeast United States, where it is not native. Camphor is a good tree for a **Water** Garden. Its black berries are messy but attractive to wildlife.

Magic: Camphor is most famous as a psychically cooling herb, bringing release from a painful love affair. Anoint yourself with it after the relationship has run its course (no matter who breaks it off) and you will soon have freedom of mind. Camphor water can also be used to cleanse magical implements and to purify the air; indeed any rite of consecration or purification is strengthened by it use. The use of camphor leads to heightened psychic abilities. At one time, the camphor was reputed to drive away yellow fever from any home near which it was planted. In China, the penalty for a cutting down this tree down was death. *Camphor wood can be burned as incense or worn as an amulet. Camphor is excellent for use during moon rituals and death rites. Rites with camphor are most effective if performed under the full moon, or as close to full as possible. Invoke Diana and the moon. Those born under the sign of Cancer have an affinity to camphor.*

Caraway (*Carum carvi*) Caraway is the herb of **Attachment.**

Horticulture

Description: Biennial or perennial herb with an angular, smooth, branched stem, finely divided leaves (appearing in the second year) and small flowers. Height 2 feet. **Name Lore:** Another Arabic herb, this started as *karawiya* and was taken into Latin as *carvi*. **Other Names:** Kummel. **Colors:** Flowers white, yellow, or faintly pink. **Fragrance:** All parts of the plant are aromatic – nutty and bittersweet. **Bloom Time**: May–July. **Origin:** Europe, North America, and Asia.

Habitat: Meadows and fields; any grassy, sunny areas. **Earth** (soil type): Moist, humous rich soil. **Water** (moisture needs): Moderate. **Fire** (sun/shade requirements): Partial or full sun. **Air** (climate): US Climate Zones 3–7.

Tips and Warnings: Caraway should be planted on Wednesday for the most efficacious magic. Caraway is a good plant for the **Air** Garden. It is most famous for the seeds you find in rye bread, but it has other uses. The fruits and oil are used in flavoring food products, including breads, soups, meats, and cheese. The fleshy root can be eaten as a vegetable. It produces an essential oil, extracted from the ripe seed or fruit. Although caraway is completely safe, its young leaves are very similar to those of several poisonous species like poison hemlock. Use with caution! It can also cause skin irritation in some people.

Magic: As an herb of attachment, caraway works on several levels. Not only does it keep your lover or spouse from straying, but it is also supposed to keep the pets home, and keep your valuables from getting stolen. And there's more; since caraway is associated with the physical aspects of love, it not only keeps your beloved at home, but works as an aphrodisiac as well. It is a standard ingredient in both love potions and wedding cakes; it inspires passion and lust. In addition, it was said that any box containing caraway could never be stolen; so it's a good idea to toss some in with your valuables. Growing caraway in the garden will make sure a would-be thief will be unable to escape. Whoever uses caraway is safe from the wiles of Lilith. *Caraway is used in many rituals including Lughnasa, Mabon (Autumn Equinox), fertility rituals, and most important, handfastings. It also is used to make amulets. Those born under the sign of Cancer have very good luck with caraway in their rites.*

Cassia (*Cinnamonum cassia*) See *Cinnamon*. The two belong to the same family and cassia is very often substituted for true cinnamon.

Catnip (*Nepeta cataria*) This is an herb of **Cat Magic.**

Horticulture

Description: Bushy perennial herb with a tall, hairy, erect, angular stem, and toothed, stalked oval leaves. Flowers in crowded clusters. Height 1-3 feet. **Other Names:** Catmint, catnep, field balm, nip, cat's wort, cat's play. *Colors:* Leaves greenish gray. Flowers whitish-pink, whitish-purple, or lavender with purple spots. *Fragrance:* Leaves herby-grassy smelling and mintily pungent, intoxicating to many cats. *Bloom Time*: June–September. *Origin:* Eurasia, naturalized worldwide.

Habitat: Roadsides, hedge banks. **Earth** (soil type): Chalky, limy, sandy, gravelly soil. **Water** (moisture needs): Catnip is drought resistant, but it doesn't mind a wet summer either. **Fire** (sun/shade requirements): Full sun or light shade. **Air** (climate): US Climate Zones 3–8.

Tips and Warnings: Catnip is suited to the informal garden. It is handsome along a fence or against the house. It also makes a good ground cover. The blue of the flowers provides a nice counterpoint to pinks. Bees like catnip as much as cats do. Catnip leaves and flowering tops can be made into a tea or used as face-wash. It was used to treat colds and bronchitis. At one time it was used to flavor soups and stews.

Magic: This is an herb of all the mystery associated with cats. Catnip is also associated with love (especially when combined with rose petals). If you want someone always to be your friend, hold some catnip in your hand until it is warm, then hold the other person's hand. Keep the catnip in a safe place and your friendship will be secure. In a similar vein, catnip added to a bath will increase a woman's fertility (cats are famously fertile). For a good potion, use in combination with roses. Putting catnip in a pillow facilitates sweet and healing dreams, but if you have a cat, she might keep you from sleeping by attempting to claw out the catnip from the pillowcase.

It is said that executioners used to chew the root to develop the ferocity necessary for their occupation. I am not aware that chewing catnip makes one ferocious, but you never know. Catnip can also be used to summon good spirits. Use catnip leaves to mark sacred texts. Catnip is an important herb for those who need to increase their analytic skills. An incense of catnip and dragon's blood will rid you of unwanted habits. It is used in shape-shifting spells and can be worn as an amulet. *When performing rites with catnip, invoke Bast and Sekhet. Rites with catnip are most efficacious if performed when Venus is visible. People born under the sign of Cancer or Virgo have particular success with it.*

Cedar *(Cedrus* species) This is an herb of **Cleansing.**

Horticulture

Description: Tall coniferous trees noted for the durability and fragrance of their wood. Height 70-130 feet. Many species of cedar are valuable in the garden. Gardening information here is for the cedar of Lebanon (*C. libani*). The famous cedars of Lebanon formed a great forest, which unfortunately was destroyed by over-logging even in biblical times. (The softness and aromatic fragrance of the wood has always been much admired.) Luckily the species is still with us and available in nurseries. Other species of true cedar are the Atlas cedar (*C. atlantica*), which produces an essential oil, and the deodar cedar (*C. deodara*). *Other Names:* Sandarac. *Similar and related species:* The name cedar is vague; arbor vitae and junipers are also frequently called cedar, and share many of the same magical properties. The American red cedar actually belongs to the genus *Juniperus*. (*A true cedar has cones, rather than the berries characteristic of junipers.*) *Colors:* Green needles. *Fragrance:* The wood is famously aromatic (woodsy, evergreen) and moth-repellent, hence its use in closets and clothes chests. *Bloom Time*: Flowers insignificant. *Origin:*

Mountains of the southern and southeastern Mediterranean area and the western Himalayas.

Habitat: Variable, depending on species. **Earth** (soil type): Acid, well-drained, average, loamy soil. Will tolerate even heavy clay if it is not too wet. **Water** (moisture needs): Moderate. **Fire** (sun/shade requirements): Sun. **Air** (climate) US Climate Zones 6–8. Appreciates protection from the wind.

Tips and Warnings: Many cedars come in a dwarf form that is suitable for today's smaller gardens.

Magic: Use cedar any time you wish to clear away negative energy and open your spirit into a higher state of consciousness. Burning cedar wood will protect against bad dreams and provide spiritual protection. *Cedar is an important Yule decoration and can be used as incense or worn as an amulet. Rites involving cedar are efficacious if performed on Tuesday. Sagittarians have good luck with cedar.*

Celandine *(Chelidonium majus)* This is an herb of **Escape.**

Horticulture

Description: Perennial herb with a taproot; erect, branching, leafy stems; four-petalled flowers and a latex-like sap. Height 1–2 feet. *Other Names:* Devil's milk, garden celandine, tetterwort, killwart, swallow herb, swallowwort, greater celandine. The name devil's milk is derived from the plant's habit of exuding a bitter orange latex-like sap. The name swallowwort is derived from the idea that swallows use this same sap to strengthen their nests. *Name Lore:* Celandine comes from *chelidon*, the Greek word for swallow. *Similar and related species:* Greater celandine is not related to the lesser celandine (*Ranunculus ficaria*). *Colors:* Flowers bright yellow, leaves paler on the underside, seeds black with a white appendage. *Fragrance:* Odor of the bruised leaves very unpleasant. *Bloom Time*: April–August. *Origin:* British Isles.

Habitat: Banks, damp places, along fences, walls, roadsides. Often found near houses. **Earth** (soil type): Moist, rich, but can tolerate poor soil. **Water** (moisture needs): High. **Fire** (sun/shade requirements): Partial shade. **Air** (climate): US Climate Zones 4–8.

Tips and Warnings: Celandine can be aggressive, and it has weedy looking foliage. Like many members of the poppy family, celandine will not survive as a cut flower without special treatment (it's the sap, again). The plant stems can stain and irritate the skin. Do not use to remove warts (an old usage). Go to the drugstore.

Magic: Celandine is an herb for the release of those imprisoned physically or mentally. It relieves depression and brings joy. It is also rumored to help those imprisoned escape. Celandine tea can also be used for visionary purposes. One legend says that carrying celandine will vanquish your enemies and allow winning lawsuits; however, you have to carry the heart of a mole at the same time. Fortunately, this is not really necessary. *Rites involving celandine are traditionally burned during Imbolc and Spring Equinox (Ostara). Leos have an affinity to celandine.*

Centaury (*Centaurium umbellatum* or *Erythraea centaurium*) This is the herb of **Chiron the Centaur**.

Horticulture

Description: Annual or biennial herb with a rosette of basal ovate leaves with opposite, sessile, ovate, stem leaves, and cone-shaped flowers. Height 6–18 inches. *Other Names:* Bitter herb, common centaury, European centaury, feverwort, and lesser centaury. *Name Lore:* The name is derived from the centaurs. *Colors:* Flowers often red, depending on species. *Fragrance:* Slight. *Bloom Time*: June–September. *Origin:* Europe.

Habitat: Meadows, forest clearings. **Earth** (soil type): Sandy, but variable, depending on species. **Water** (moisture needs): Moderate. **Fire** (sun/shade requirements): Full sun. **Air** (climate): US Climate Zones 5–8.

Tips and Warnings: Difficult to grow.

Magic: Centaury is very powerful herb of counter-magic; it helps develop psychic awareness when added to incense. Burning centaury drives off snakes. *Invoke the name of Chiron. Sagittarians are best with magic incorporating centaury.*

Chamomile (*Chamamelum nobile,* or its older name *Anthemis nobilis*) This is the herb of **Comfort.**

Horticulture

Description: A low-growing perennial, with a branchy, creeping rhizome, ferny leaves, and hairy stems. Height 7–9 inches. *Name Lore:* Chamomile is Greek for "ground apple," one of its common names. *Other Names:* Roman chamomile, true chamomile, kamai melon, maythen, manzanilla ("little apple"), chamaimelon, ground apple. *Similar and Related Species:* It is sometimes confused with German, or blue chamomile, (*Matricaria chamomilla*), although that plant is in a different genus. Both plants, however, have similar magic powers. There is also "dyer's chamomile" (*Anthemis tincoria*), which blooms a very long time and is taller. *Colors:* Deep yellow flower disk, white or cream petals. *Fragrance:* Strong, pleasantly sweet, fresh, and apple – or honey-like. The very smell has relaxing properties. *Bloom Time*: Spring through summer. *Origin:* Europe and Middle East.

Habitat: Pastures, grassy places. **Earth** (soil type): Sandy, well drained. Not fussy, but the newer cultivars prefer a richer soil. **Water** (moisture needs): Can handle dry conditions, but does much better if soil is kept evenly moist. **Fire** (sun/shade requirements): Filtered light or full sun. **Air** (climate): U.S Climate Zones 5–9.

Tips and Warnings: Chamomile should be planted on Sunday during the first quarter of the moon for utmost magical effect. It can grow in pots (for year-round use), on slopes, just about anywhere. Chamomile is slow to sprout – be patient. This stuff is so tough you can walk on it, and it makes a good ground cover. As a natural insect repellent, it goes well with other plants. It is wonderful in a **Fire** Garden. Not for use with pregnant women. People allergic to ragweed may have a reaction to it.

Magic: An important feature in every medieval herb garden, chamomile produces a sense of calm, peace, comfort, and equilibrium. It can be used as incense, or in an herbal bath to enhance beauty, and is generally considered a money-attractant. It is also used in love potions. Sprinkling it around the house wards off evil spells. The addition of chamomile (either Roman or German chamomile) to almost any beneficent spell empowers the spell by bringing the power and light of the sun with it. Chamomile may also draw fairies. Chamomile may be burned at any blessing, prosperity, or purification rites. It may also be burned during Yule or Litha (Midsummer). *Invoke Woden, or one of many Egyptian gods. Leos have particular affinity to chamomile.*

Cherry *(Prunus* species) This is an herb of **Youth.**

Horticulture

Description: Deciduous tree. Height 90 feet (wild variety); 40–50 feet (orchard type). *Other Names:* The wild cherry is also called the black cherry. *Colors:* Bark dark red-brown, growing gray in maturity. Flowers white in the wild cherry may be clear pink in domestic cultivars. Fruit red or golden, or black in the case of the wild cherry. *Fragrance:* Variable. Some of the most fragrant include *P. avium, P. caroliniana, P. cerasifera, P. mahaleb, P. mume,* and *P. padus.* Most cherries give off a sweet fragrance. *Bloom Time*: April. *Origin:* Wild cherry (*Prunus serotina*) is indigenous to North America. The sweet cherry (*Prunus avium*) is native to Eurasia, but was introduced into Italy in 65 B.C. Both kinds of cherries belong to the rose family.

Habitat: Groves, meadows. **Earth** (soil type): Deep, rich, moist. **Water** (moisture needs): Moderate. **Fire** (sun/shade requirements): Full sun. **Air** (climate): US Climate Zones 4–8.

Tips and Warnings: The wild cherry's fruit can be made into wine or jelly. The wilted (not fresh or completely dried) leaves of the wild cherry are dangerous to livestock, as they contain prussic acid.

Magic: Cherry represents both youth and fertility. It is also associated with female genitalia in both eastern and western culture. Because of its popular associations with both virginity and fertility, it has become known as a bridal flower. To attract a lover, drill holes through 14 cherry stones during the 14 nights of the waxing moon, and string them on a cord around your left thigh. The bark is also used in magical rites to gather energy to finish an old project.

Witches are accustomed to burning cherry chips at their sabbats. The wood drives away bad spirits, so branches were placed in doorways on New Year's Day. One story says that, if you run around a cherry tree three times on Midsummer's Eve, and shake the tree hard, the number of cherries that fall to the ground will reveal the number of years you have left to live or the ultimate age you will attain. It all depends upon whom you ask. You must, of course, recite a spell, which is the following: "Cherry tree, I shaketh thee/ Cherry tree pray tell me/ How many years am I to live?/ By fallen fruit thy answer give." Then start counting.

Chervil (*Anthriscus cerefolium*) This is an herb of **Communication with Departed Spirits**.

Horticulture

Description: Hardy annual with finely divided feathery leaves and flat umbels of small flowers. Chervil looks like a cross between parsley and fern. Height 4 – 24 inches. *Other Names:* French parsley, anise chervil, British myrrh, sweet cicely, and sweet fern. *Similar and Related Species:* At one time both this plant and sweet cicely (*Myrrhis odorata*) were called chervil, so it is sometimes hard to disentangele one from another. *Colors:* Flowers white; leaves bright green. *Fragrance:* Fresh leaves smell like anise. *Bloom Time*: Early summer. *Origin:* Southern Europe and the Middle East.

Habitat **Earth** (soil type): Light, moist. **Water** (moisture needs): Moderate. **Fire** (sun/shade requirements): Prefers full sun, but can handle some shade. **Air** (climate): US Climate Zones 5–9.

Tips and Warnings: Chervil self-seeds and does not transplant well. Flavor reminiscent of anise.

Magic: As an herb of immortality, chervil was used in death rites and to commune with the dead. Pliny said that it stopped the hiccups; it is true that a sudden appearance from Departed Spirits will scare most people enough to stop their hiccups. Boiling the roots was said to prevent plague. Considering the number of plants presumed to prevent plague, it's rather surprising that anyone caught the disease. *Clothe yourself in black.*

Chestnut See Buckeye

Chickweed (*Stellaria media* and S. *pubera*) This is the herb of **Bird Magic.**

Horticulture

Description: Hardy small annual, biennial, or perennial with small, ovate, star-like flowers in loose branching clusters, and weak, reclining stems. May form dense mats. Some sticky to the touch. *Other Names:* Starwort, birdseed, passerina, starweed, winterweed, adder's mouth, satin flower. *Similar and Related Species:* There are several varieties, star chickweed, the field chickweed, hairy chickweed, the common chickweed, smooth chickweed, and the mouse-ear chickweed. *Colors:* Flowers white. Leaves bright green. *Fragrance:* Bitter or sour. *Bloom Time*: March–September. *Origin:* Eurasia; now found over most of the world, even very cold places.

Habitat: Yards, gardens, grasslands, waste places. Some species found in woods. **Earth** (soil type): Prefers humous, well drained, but not particular. **Water** (moisture needs): Moderate. **Fire** (sun/shade requirements): Full sun. **Air** (climate): US Climate Zones 3–9

Tips and Warnings: Chickweed can be an annoying, although rather handsome weed in the garden. It has most magic if planted to the south. It is sometimes eaten as a substitute for spinach.

Magic: Chickweed was once used as a tonic for caged birds, and can be carried or used in a potion to attract love; it can attract love even when simply worn. It is said that if the chickweed blossoms fully, the rest of the day will be fine, but if the blossoms close up, expect rain within a few hour. Chickweed can also be used to stop gossip. *When working magic with chickweed, invoke the moon.*

Chicory *(Cichorium intybus)* This is an herb of **Overcoming Obstacles.**

Horticulture

Description: This is a perennial, stiff, bristly-stemmed herb with a long taproot, and angular, narrow, dandelion-like leaves. The flowers, each lasting only a day, are fringed and ray-like. Height 1–4 feet. *Other Names:* Wild succory, succory, blue sailors. *Similar and Related Species:* The plant is closely related to dandelions and endive (*C. endiva*). Endive, however, has curly leaves. *Colors:* Flowers are bright sky-blue or violet.
Fragrance: Subtle. *Bloom Time*: June-October. *Origin:* Europe and North America.

Habitat: Fields, hedgerows, roadsides. **Earth** (soil type): Prefers lime rich, deep soil. **Water** (moisture needs): Chicory can withstand drought. **Fire** (sun/shade requirements): Sunny. **Air** (climate): US Climate Zones 4–7.

Tips and Warnings: People usually just find chicory, but if you plant it, the best time is the third quarter of the moon. To use its magical powers, harvest on Midsummer's Eve (if it's out) or more reliably on July 25 (St. James' Day) with a golden knife at noon or the witching hour, and don't speak to anyone while you're doing it. The Egyptians ate chicory as a vegetable. The young roots can be boiled and eaten, and are also a famous coffee substitute. Chicory can be used in salads.

Magic: Chicory is said to remove all obstacles from your path. In the same vein, chicory's lock-opening abilities are renowned. The catch (to use a pun) is that the chicory must be correctly harvested. see above. Then simply rub it against the lock. The same ritual may make you invisible, which is why chicory is known as the herb of secrets. In the same way, chicory removes all obstacles that life sets before you.

It has wonderful power over the more worldly aspects of life; wearing it will help you cultivate thriftiness and win the favor of influential people. It will also improve your sense of humor. Chicory can make one forget a lover (that alone is enough to improve your sense of humor) and can be worn as an amulet. *Virgos have an especial affinity for chicory.*

Cinnamon *(Cinnamonum zeylanicum; Cinnamonum aromaticum)* This is the herb of **Energy.**

Horticulture

Description: Evergreen tree with oval or lance-shaped leaves and small flowers. Height 25 feet. *Other Names:* Sweet wood, cassia. *Similar and Related Species:* Most of the "cinnamon" marketed in the United States is not true cinnamon, but derives from the bark of the related cassia tree (*C. cassia*), which has a similar flavor and magical uses. *Colors:* Bark reddish-brown; flowers white or yellow, fruit bluish with white spots. *Fragrance:* Spicy, mild, warm, woody. *Bloom Time*: Spring. *Origin:* Asia.

Habitat: Moist maritime climates.h **Earth** (soil type): Variable. **Water** (moisture needs): Moderate. **Fire** (sun/shade requirements): Full sun. **Air** (climate): Tropical.

Tips and Warnings "And lucent drops, tinct with cinnamon" (Keats, "The Eve of St. Agnes"). Nobody ever gave a sweeter description of candy. Pure cinnamon oil extracted from the bark can cause nausea and vomiting. Applied to the skin it can cause burning and irritation. The essential oil from the leaf is a bit safer, but should still be diluted. Used in toothpaste, as it has anti-cavity properties. Cinnamon sticks can be used to flavor hot drinks like mulled wine, cider, chocolate, or coffee. The ancient Egyptians used it both as an offering and as embalming oil. Perfumes incorporating cinnamon should be worn on Wednesday.

Magic: Cinnamon is an extremely self-assertive herb! Cinnamon empowers all rites, particularly those designed to provide spiritual insight and illumination. It is also an herb of protection, prosperity, and clairvoyance. And it is famous as aphrodisiac. The idea of cinnamon as a life-giving tree pervades the western religious tradition; it is supposed to have been one of the trees in the Garden of Eden, perhaps the Tree of Life itself. Cinnamon is frequently burned in order to develop spiritual and psychic abilities. On a physical energy level, cinnamon stimulates sexual fervor and desire. It draws money. On a more spiritual level (and usually combined with sandalwood) it inspires insightful, illuminating meditation. In medieval days, it was especially popular as love charm or potion. Cinnamon is often used as a bathing herb, incense, or amulet. *Magical working with cinnamon is more efficacious if done in the autumn and during the day rather than in the evening. When working magic with cinnamon, invoke Mercury, Aphrodite, or Venus. Those born under the sign of Aries have very good luck using cinnamon in their rites. Clothe yourself in red.*

Cinquefoil See Potentilla.

Clover (*Trefolium* species) This is the herb of **Good Luck**.

Horticulture

Description: Clover is one of several plants (wood sorrel is another) that are sometimes referred to as shamrock, a plant strongly associated with Ireland and Celtic national consciousness. Height 4–10 inches. *Other Names:* Trefoil, honeystalks. It is sometimes called St. Patrick's leaves or "little clover" (*seamrog* in Gaelic from which come the name shamrock.) *Similar and related species:* Red clover (*T. pratense*) and white clover (*T.repens*) share most of the same magical powers. The true shamrock is the *Oxalis acetosella*, a part of Irish culture from time immemorial *Colors:* White, or purplish pink, depending on whether the species is white or red clover. *Fragrance:* Warm and dry.
Bloom Time: April–October. *Origin:* Europe.

Habitat: Grassy places, fields. **Earth** (soil type): Tolerant; white clover is fond of clay. **Water** (moisture needs): Moderate. **Fire** (sun/shade requirements): Full sun, tolerates some shade. **Air** (climate): US Climate Zones 3–9.

Tips and Warnings: Unfortunately, people who desire a uniform, monoculture lawn consider clover a weed. That's too bad since they are missing out on one of the great glories of nature. You don't need to garden for it, it will appear almost "magically" in the average lawn. And far from being a weed, planting a whole crop of clover is a wonderful way to protect the soil from winter erosion and compaction. If you do plant it, plant it on Sunday for the best magic. Clover is pollinated by bees, and is in fact an important source of nectar.

Magic: This simple plant is one of the most magical of all! The Druids considered it sacred. Any kind of clover (shamrock) brings good luck, especially when carried, either in a red flannel bag or in your purse or pocket or as an amulet. The three-leaf clover is supposed to keep you young and beautiful, but the four-leaf clover is especially lucky. (You have to be lucky to find one!) Each leaf brings a different sort of luck. Beginning at the left, the first leaf brings fame, the second wealth, the third love, and the fourth health. Another formulation has a slightly different list: peace of mind, psychic powers, money, and treasure. The size and quality of each leaf determines the amount of the blessing. A girl who finds a four-leaf clover and puts it in her shoe will marry the first man she sees. It also keeps one from going mad, which is even more important. Clover draws fairies and if you put a four-leaf clover in your hat, you'll be sure to see a fairy, even ones that are normally invisible. Fairies, however, can be dangerous, so be careful. The Christian church also used it as an emblem of the Trinity. Clover is also an herb against evil spirits; soak clover in vinegar for three days and sprinkle the vinegar in each corner of the house, and you'll banish them. *Clothe yourself in green. Invoke Blodewedd* (Celtic goddess of spring).

Coltsfoot (*Tussilago farfara*) This is the herb of **Horse Magic**.

Horticulture

Description: Perennial herb with a branchy stem and large flowers and leaves. *Name Lore:* The leaves are shaped like the hoof of a horse. *Other Names:* British tobacco, butterbur, donnhove, fieldhove, coughwort, horse hoof, clayweed, dummyweed, gowan, and son-before-the-father. *Colors:* Flowers yellow, appearing before leaves in the early spring. *Fragrance:* Strong and bitter. *Bloom Time*: February–April. *Origin:* Europe and Asia.

Habitat: Wasteland, roadsides, banks and damp places, dunes. **Earth** (soil type): Moist. **Water** (moisture needs): Moderate. **Fire** (sun/shade requirements): Full sun to partial shade. **Air** (climate): US Climate Zones 4–8.

Tips and Warnings: The flower heads of coltsfoot can be made into a wine.

Magic: In addition to being magical for horses, coltsfoot is an herb of peacefulness, love and calm. It is frequently included in love spells, and when smoked it invokes visions. It is especially useful to protect horses from sorcery and is an important herb for anyone working with horses or cattle. *When doing coltsfoot magic, invoke Brighid, Etain (Celtic goddess of horses) or Poseidon. Taurians have very good luck with coltsfoot.*

Columbine (*Aquilegia vulgaris* and cultivars) Columbine is **Proof against Envy**.

Horticulture

Description: Perennial. The columbine flower is famous for its spurs. Height 2–3 feet. *Name Lore:*

"Columbine" comes from the Latin word for doves, *columba*, which the Romans thought it resembled. The columbine got its scientific name *Aquila* ("eagle") in reference to its flower spurs resembling eagle claws. *Other Names:* Lion's herb. *Colors:* Various, including red, purple, yellow, and white. The *A. canadensis* is yellow and black. Many are multi-colored. *Fragrance:* Subtle. *Bloom Time*: April–July, depending on cultivar. *Origin:* Widespread over the northern hemisphere.

Habitat: Steep rocky slopes, damp woodlands. **Earth** (soil type): Prefers average or good soil, but most can tolerate sandy or poor soils, or any well-drained soil. The *A. canadensis* needs a richer soil. All columbines prefer a slightly acid soil. **Water** (moisture needs): Moderate. **Fire** (sun/shade requirements): Partial shade to full sun. Needs protection from the sun in hot climates. **Air** (climate): US Climate Zone 3–9, depending on variety.

Tips and Warnings: Columbine was an important feature in every medieval herb garden. It has most magic if planted to the south. There are wonderful hybrids of this flower. However, while it sets seeds easily, the daughter plants become progressively less interesting in color. Cut them back after flowering to get new leaves. Columbine looks beautiful with astilbe, alyssum, forget-me-nots, and flax. Columbine is attractive to hummingbirds and butterflies.

Magic: Many minor magical properties are attributed to the columbine; it is noted as an antidote against envy and covetousness, and as an herb of courage and resolve (blue columbine). It is attractive to fairies. Native Americans made a potion that included columbine to attract a mate. It can also be used to find a lost lover. However, in the European tradition, columbine is the wrong plant to give as a present as it implies a woman will be faithless and a man be cuckolded. It was at one time thought to cure measles and smallpox. However, the real reason to grow columbines in the garden is because of their singular and versatile beauty. *When doing magic with columbine, invoke Freya.*

Comfrey *(Symphytum officinale)* Comfrey is an herb of **Safe Travel**.

Horticulture

Description: Square-stemmed perennial with large, bristly, veined leaves and flowers shaped like the fingers of a glove. *Other Names:* Bone-knit (because of its reputed ability to heal fractures), yalluc, boneset, bruisewort, consolida, gum plant, knitbone, slippery root, consound, salsify. *Colors:* Flowers purple to white. *Fragrance:* Subtle.
Bloom Time: May–July. *Origin*: Europe. Early colonists brought the plant to America.

Habitat: Grassy, damp, marshy places. **Earth** (soil type): Moist, rich. Can tolerate a heavy clay soil. **Water** (moisture needs): High. **Fire** (sun/shade requirements): Filtered sunlight or shade. **Air** (climate): US Climate Zones 5–10.

Tip and Warnings: For best magical results, plant comfrey on Saturday. This deeply rooted plant will help to break up a heavy, clayey soil. Harvest frequently. Overdosing with comfrey can cause liver damage. Comfrey can be confused with the poisonous foxglove when not in bloom.

Magic: This practical herb is good for all rites of a practical nature, especially those concerning land and travel. Place comfrey root in the bottom of luggage for safe travel, at least safe for the luggage.

If you want to be safe as well, better carry some as an amulet. It is also used for rites involving land. Comfrey incense restores a sense of balance and equilibrium. *Capricorns have a special affinity to comfrey. Choose a time to perform the rite when Saturn is visible.*

Coriander *(Coriandrum sativum)* This is the herb of **Physical Love**.

Horticulture

Description: Annual with an erect stem, alternate, deeply cut leaves, and tiny flowers. Cultivated mainly for seeds. Height 12–30 inches. *Other Names:* Cilantro, Chinese parsley. *Colors:* Flowers pink, red, or white. Foliage bright green. Fruit red-brown. *Fragrance:* Strong. Coriander is said by some to smell like bedbugs. However, I have no idea what bedbugs smell like, so I cannot confirm this. Others say the seeds have a sharp (though pleasant) smell. The fruits, as they ripen, become aromatic and spicy. Some liken it to a lemon smell. This is something we must each judge for ourselves. *Bloom Time*: June–July. *Origin:* Eastern Mediterranean.

Habitat: Waste places, roadsides (in the Middle East) as a garden escape. **Earth** (soil type): Moderately rich, light, and well-drained. **Water** (moisture needs): Moderate. **Fire** (sun/shade requirements): Prefers sun, can tolerate partial shade. **Air** (climate): US Climate Zones 2–9. Needs protection from wind.

Tips and Warnings: Coriander is a good container plant; it also grows well near dill, basil, lemon balm, oregano, and caraway. Coriander flowers attract bees, ladybugs, and lacewings (all beneficial). Some writers believe that coriander ought not to be used as incense, as it may intensify negative feelings, although others use it for clairvoyant workings. Spicy coriander can be used to flavor soups. The roots can be cooked and eaten.

Magic: Coriander's use as a love potion traces back all the way to *One Thousand and One Arabian Nights.* The ancient Chinese thought it had the power to make one immortal, while the Egyptians used it as funeral offerings. Its oil is used to anoint candles at Handfastings. Fresh coriander may be tied with a ribbon and hung in the home to bring peace and protection to the house. Used as an amulet, it is especially useful for people who can't seem to get along with others, or for those who need to preserve their freedom from undue outside pressure. *Arians have a special affinity for coriander.*

Cowbane See **Water** Hemlock

Crocus See Saffron

Cumin *(Nigella sativa, Cuminum cyminum)* This is the herb of a **Domestic Harmony.**

Horticulture

Description: Low-growing plant with slender branches, finely cut, feathery leaves, and clusters of small flowers. The seeds, which are really fruit in this case, are oblong in shape. Height 1 foot. **Other Names:** Black cumin, fitches. **Colors:** Flowers white to rose. **Fragrance:** Odor of fruits similar to caraway. **Bloom Time**: June–July. **Origin:** Egypt and Turkey, now throughout Mediterranean.

Habitat: Earth (soil type): Loamy, light, well-drained, and fertile. **Water** (moisture needs): Moderate. **Fire** (sun/shade requirements): Sunny. **Air** (climate) US Climate Zones 8–10.

Tips and Warnings: Crushed and ground it is used to flavor meats and fish. It is also an ingredient in curry powder. The essential oil has been used for perfumes.

Magic: Cumin seed brings harmony, luck, and peace to the home. To insure domestic tranquility, sprinkle the seeds on the doorstep once a week at dawn. The idea behind the rite is that if you begin each day early with the idea of keeping a happy home, you'll be more likely to succeed. If burned as incense or worn as an amulet, cumin provides protection. Cumin also prevents theft and has many of the same magical attributes as coriander. *Arians make excellent magic with cumin.*

Cypress *(Cupressus* and *Chamaecyparis* species) This is the herb of **Eternal Life.**

Horticulture

Description: True cypresses (*Cupressus*) and False cypress (*Chamaecyparis*) are coniferous, evergreen trees and shrubs with small scale like leaves; belonging to the same family (*Cupressaceae*). For magical purposes the two genera and hybrids bred from them are interchangeable. True cypresses include Italian cypress (*Cupressus sempervirens*) and the Monteray cypress (*C. macrocarpa*). *Chamaecypares* species include the Nootka cypress (*Chamaecypares Nookatensis*) and the white cypress (*C. thyoides*). The Leyland cypress (x Cupressocypans) is a hybrid and unknown in the wild. **Name Lore:** In Greek myth, the young man Cyparissus was transformed into a cypress tree. **Other Names:** Tree of death. **Similar and related species:** The bald cypress is of a different genus. Many cedars are also referred to as cypress. **Colors:** Green. **Fragrance:** Aromatic wood. The fragrance is most noticeable on warm days. **Bloom Time**: Flowers insignificant. **Origin:** Europe and North America, depending on species.

Habitat: Cultivated. One of the most common species, the Leyland cypress (*x Cupressocyparis*), is not known in the wild. **Earth** (soil type): Moist and fertile, but tolerates sandy, peaty, and clayey soils. **Water** (moisture needs): Moderate. **Fire** (sun/shade requirements): Prefers full sun. **Air** (climate): US Climate Zones 4–8.

Tips and Warnings: According to Scott Cunningham, cypress, if planted, should be situated on the north. Perfumes incorporating cypress should be worn on Tuesday. Not all species of cypress are suitable for planting where heavy snows are common; the narrow tops tend to split under the weight.

Magic: Cypress wood is extremely resistant to rot, which may have engendered the first association with immortality. (In fact, it was often used for coffins in Greece and Egypt.) The Italian Cypress (*C. sempervirens*) is frequently mentioned in the Bible (It was used to build Noah's ark), sometimes under the confusing name of gopherwood. (So far as I know gophers are not common in the Holy Land.) Cypress smoke incense consecrates magical implements. Some folks hang cypress in the home for protection or wear it as an amulet. *When doing rites with cypress, invoke Hercules, Saturn, Apollo, or Pluto. Fairies are attracted to cypress. Cypress oil can be worn at Samhain and used during death rites.*

Daffodil (*Narcissus* species) This is the herb of **Ostara**.

Horticulture

Description: Bulb flower with long, slender leaves. There are twelve divisions of daffodils, based upon flower types, but most look pretty similar. *Other Names*: Narcissus, Lent lily, jonquil. *Similar and Related Species:* All daffodils are narcissi, but not all narcissi are daffodils. *Name Lore:* Daffodils derive their scientific name Narcissus, from the Greek *Narke*, which means "numbness". This may be why we call some numb-in-the-head people "daffy." (The bulb contains toxic alkaloids that can paralyze the central nervous system.) Daffodils are, of course, associated with the Greek Narcissus, who drowned himself by staring overlong at his beautiful reflection in a pool. He was turned into the flower. *Colors:* Yellow, orange, white. *Fragrance:* Some hybrids very sweet. *Bloom Time*: March–April. *Origin:* Europe.

Habitat: Meadows. **Earth** (soil type): Well-drained and enriched with compost. **Water** (moisture needs): Moderate. **Fire** (sun/shade requirements): Full sun to partial shade. **Air** (climate): US Climate Zones 3–6.

Tips and Warnings: For best magical results, plant on Thursday. Daffodils have the most magic if planted in the south of the garden. There seems to be an argument as to precisely the right time; it apparently doesn't make any difference so long as it is not the fourth quarter of the moon. The best time to pick daffodils for magic is on the night of the full, or at least waxing, moon. Yellow daffodils are best cut on Tuesday, white daffodils, which are excellent for a moon garden, are best picked on Friday. Daffodils partner very well with forget-me-nots and tulips. Daffodils are glorious, but can present a very ragged appearance in the garden after they have finished blooming. The foliage can't be cut back for 6–8 weeks (it's needed in order for the bulb to flower the following season.) So you have two choices – plant the daffodils away from the main garden, or attempt to disguise the old foliage with another plant (like peonies, which are just coming into bloom as the daffodils are fading). Late-blooming varieties of daffodils are probably not the best choice in the Southern US – it's too hot for them. Daffodils exude a substance that may kill off other flowers in an arrangement. They are best placed in a vase by themselves. If you must mix them with other flowers, soak them for an hour alone, rinse, and then add the other blooms. The bulbs are poisonous.

Magic: No other plant speaks so strongly of the new season as this classical favorite. Of course, the daffodil has other powers as well. It can be used in rites of counter-magic, exorcism, and purification. Just growing it in the garden is powerful protector. Generally, it is good luck, but it is *unlucky* to bring daffodils into a home unless the bunch totals more than thirteen; it can also have a bad effect on the laying hens. A large bunch of daffodils is effective in banishing evil sprits. However, it's bad luck if the first daffodil you see in the spring hangs its head in your direction. The Romans thought that daffodil sap healed wounds, but this is not true. (The Romans were in the habits of believing many untrue things, just like the rest of us.) In China, it symbolizes marriage and good luck in the coming year. Carry a daffodil bulb in your pocket and you'll be safe at night. *When doing magic with Daffodils, invoke, the name of Ostara, the Germanic Goddess of Spring, or her Roman equivalent, Flora. Leos have particular luck with daffodils.*

Daisy (*Bellis* species, *Chrysanthemum leucanthemum*) This is the herb of **Love Divination**.

Horticulture

Description: The common daisy (*Bellis perennis*) is a short-lived perennial (often grown as a hardy annual) with a rosette of oval green leaves and short, thick stems. Height up to 6 inches. *Chrysanthemum leucanthemum*, the ox-eye daisy, is also a perennial with a rosette of leaves. Its leaves are dark green, and spoon-shaped. Its flowers are long-stalked and 8–24 inches in height. *Name Lore:* Daisy comes from "day's eye," since the flower closes at night. *Other Names:* Moondaisy, moonflower, bairnwort, thunderflower, bruisewort. *Colors:* Rays white or pink; centers yellow. *Fragrance:* Subtle. *Bloom Time*: April–August. *Origin:* Worldwide, depending on cultivar.

Habitat: Fields, meadows, waste places, roadsides. **Earth** (soil type): Well-drained. **Water** (moisture needs): Does best in moist conditions. **Fire** (sun/shade requirements): Full sun best for most varieties; some can handle partial shade. **Air** (climate): US Climate Zones 5–9.

Tips and Warnings: Daisies are an excellent plant for the **Earth** Garden. Daisies, however, are slightly poisonous so don't eat them.

Magic: The familiar "he-loves-me-he-loves-me-not" charm has devolved from more ancient and powerful rites, many of which have unfortunately long been forgotten. It is rumored to keep away lightning; when worn as an amulet, it is especially protective for children and babies. For some, daisies signify rebirth. Daisies are attractive to fairies. *In rites involving daisies, invoke the names of Balder, Jupiter, Freya, or St. John. People born under the sign of Cancer have a special affinity to daisies.*

Damiana (*Turnera diffusa* or *T. aphrodisiaca*) This is an herb of **Sexual Attachment**.

Horticulture

Description: Small shrub with smooth inch-long, serrated leaves that have dense hairs on the underside. It has been used for thousands of years by the Mayas of Central America. *Other Names:* Loveleaf, Venus tonic. *Colors:* Flowers yellow; leaves pale green. *Fragrance:* Bittersweet. *Bloom Time*: Summer. *Origin:* Gulf of Mexico and Caribbean.

Habitat: Open places. **Earth** (soil type): Any good garden soil. **Water** (moisture needs): High in summer, low in fall. **Fire** (sun/shade requirements): Full sun. **Air** (climate): Tropical.

Tips and Warnings: This herb is a hallucinogen.

Magic: Damiana is famous as both an aphrodisiac and a hallucinogenic herb. To regain your wandering lover, soak damiana in wine for three hours and sprinkle it on the front and back door steps. Do this every day for 21 days, and your beloved will return. This is also a good herb for love potions, and can increase the power of other spells. It is used as incense and worn as amulet. This herb should be stored in a quartz crystal container. *Invoke Aprodite in rituals involving damiana.*

Dandelion (*Taraxacum officinale*) This is an herb of **Prevision**.

Horticulture

Description: Hardy herbaceous perennial with a long, thin milky taproot, a hollow stem, and 1–2 inch blossoms with no central disk. The flowers open in the morning and close in the evening. The number of incisions in the edges of the leaves reveals how much light the plant gets; more notches mean more sunlight. Height 6–12 inches. *Name Lore:* The name refers to the shape of the leaves, bearing a supposed resemblance to lion's teeth. (According to an alternate explanation, the name comes from the stamina one gets from drinking dandelion tea.) *Other Names:* Blowball, lion's tooth, swine's snout, pissenlit, cankerwort, Irish daisy, priest's crown, telltime, puffball, white endive, wild endive. *Colors:* Flowers are brilliant yellow; leaves dark green. *Fragrance:* Bittersweet. *Bloom Time*: March–September. *Origin:* Eurasia, now worldwide in temperate regions.

Habitat: Yards, waste places. **Earth** (soil type): Prefers heavy, rich, well-drained soil; tolerates poor soil. **Water** (moisture needs): Moderate. **Fire** (sun/shade requirements): Sun or part shade. **Air** (climate): US Climate Zones 2–10.

Tips and Warnings: For the best magic, dandelions are gathered ritually at midsummer (this is true of many yellow flowers). The roots, however, are best gathered when they are most bitter – that's in the fall. For most culinary use, pick the leaves early – before the flowers form. The leaves can be included raw in salads, or blanched and added to salt pork. Dandelion salads are supposed be very healthy, especially if eaten on Mondays and Thursdays. Although older leaves have a bitter taste, you can buy dandelion seeds that produce plants with a milder flavor. The roots can be roasted and used as a coffee substitute, and the flowers can be made into a wine. It has been used as a source of latex. Native Americans made a yellow dye from the roots and flowers. And while most people don't welcome dandelions into the garden, this deep-rooted plant does help break up a heavy, clayey soil. Dandelions help fruit trees become more productive. Dandelion is best in an **Air** (the seeds sail beautifully upon the wind) or **Earth** Garden (most appropriate for perhaps the most widely spread plant on the planet).

Magic: How fitting that the age-old, bittersweet trinity–time, longing, and love–are linked forever in this most common of herbs. If you pick a dandelion puffball on the night of the full moon and blow the seeds to each of the four winds, your wish will come true. Your wish will also come true if you can blow all the seeds off in one breath. If you can't blow them all off, the number of seeds left will indicate how many children you will have. (That could be a lot, so blow hard!) Or if you blow on a dandelion puff one time, the number of seeds left equals the number of years that will pass before your handfasting. Or if you murmur words of love and blow the seeds gently in the direction of your lover, the seeds will carry your words to him or her. Dandelion tea increases psychic abilities.

Dandelions are also used to summon spirits and control the winds. (Bury a dandelion at the northwest corner of the house for favorable winds.) One rather overstated tradition says they constitute the body of God. (I suppose if this means that, like dandelions, God is everywhere, it may be true!) *Rites with dandelion seem to work best on nights when Jupiter is visible. When working with dandelion, invoke Belenos or Hecate. Librans have good luck with dandelions.*

Deadly Nightshade See Belladonna

Delphinium See Larkspur.

Dill (*Anethum gravolens*) This is the herb of **Discernment**.

Horticulture

Description: Hardy annual with narrow, feathery, fernlike leaves, and smooth, shiny, hollow stems. Height 2–3 feet. *Name Lore:* The word dill is said to come from an old Norse word *dylla* that means "soothing." *Other Names:* Devil-away, dill weed (applied to the foliage), aneton, anethum, meeting house seed, anetom dill seed. *Colors:* Stems and leaves blue-green; flowers yellowish. *Fragrance:* All parts of the plant are nuttily aromatic, especially the fruits and seeds. *Bloom Time*: July–September. *Origin:* Native to eastern Mediterranean and western Asia, including Russia.

Habitat: Open places. **Earth** (soil type): Well-drained, moderately rich. **Water** (moisture needs): Needs to be well-watered. **Fire** (sun/shade requirements): Sunny. **Air** (climate): US climate zones 6–10. These tall herbs should be planted away from wind.

Tips and Warnings: Easy to grow, but a slow starter (later it takes off). Dill reseeds itself. For best magical results, plant dill on Wednesday, during the first quarter of the moon. This plant draws the larvae of the monarch butterfly, a very desirable insect; it also attracts beneficial wasps. Dill does not transplant easily. Do not plant near fennel, angelica, or caraway; they cross-pollinate and taste funny. Harvest when the seeds have turned brown. Widely used for pickling. Roasted dill seeds can even be used as a coffee substitute, while the fresh leaves can be used to flavor cream cheese. The leaves can be used in salads and soups and to spice up new potatoes. Dill seeds have been used as breath fresheners. Dill causes dermatitis in some people.

Magic: Dill has the remarkable power to comfort and to keep one awake. It has been used for everything from good luck to banishment. It gets rid of malign spirits (put some in the windows), but it is good luck for a bride (put some in your shoe). Sprinkle some dill seed in your bath before a date for a romantic evening; the flowers can be used in love potions. Dill seeds attract money. (The Greeks were quite sure of it.) In Roman times, flowering dill wreaths crowned war heroes. Hang dill over a cradle to protect and soothe a baby. Dill protects against the evil eye and witchcraft. Hang it over a door and you'll avert the envy of others. Puritans reportedly chewed dill seeds to keep them awake and suppress hunger pangs during their interminable church services. They also used the seeds to banish hiccups, which they believed were sent by the devil to distract them during church meetings. Greeks and Romans used dill as a perfume and incense. Rubbing a newborn calf with dill and salt will protect it from evil influences. However, the most unique quality of dill is that it "strengthens the brain," enabling the practitioner to discern between true magic and superstition.

Interestingly, fairies cannot bear dill and will not venture near a garden where it grows, no matter what else you may plant there. Although it is quite trendy to invite fairies into one's garden, I wouldn't attempt it myself. You never know how fairies are going to act from one minute to the next. *People born under the sign of Cancer have the best luck with dill.*

Dittany *(Dictamnus albus)* This is an herb of **Spiritual Manifestation**.

Horticulture

Description: Tender bushy perennial with fibrous roots, fuzzy leaves, and square erect stem. Height 2.5 feet. *Other Names:* Burning bush, dittany of Crete, gas plant. *Colors:* Flowers pinkish or white. Leaves are silvery, dark green. *Fragrance:* Strong, herby, lemon or orange-like fragrance from both leaves and flowers, especially when the sun is hot. (The sun draws the volatile oils into the air.) The very smell is said to drive away venomous animals. *Bloom Time*: Late May–June. Blooming period is short. *Origin:* Europe, Mediterranean area, and Asia.

Habitat: Edges of meadows. **Earth** (soil type): Lime-rich, well-drained soil. **Water** (moisture needs): Moderate. **Fire** (sun/shade requirements): Prefers full sun, but can handle part shade. **Air** (climate): Likes heat, but does well in US Climate Zones 3–8.

Tips and Warnings: The vapor this plant produces is flammable – hence the name burning bush or gas plant. Needs winter protection, but the foliage is pretty all year round. Dittany is hard to transplant, because of the long tap root. The plant can be toxic in large doses.

Magic: This is an herb of spiritual manifestation, and can be used for divination and to encourage sprits to incarnate themselves. Another use of dittany is to aid out-of-body experiences. That's one reason it was used to ease the pains of childbirth. There are those who suggest that dittany was the original burning bush of the Bible, but, of course, no one can sure. *Capricorns have a special affinity to dittany. Use dittany during Samhain.*

Dogwood *(Cornus florida)* This is the herb of **Dog Magic**.

Horticulture

Description: Deciduous broadleaf tree with oval leaves and insignificant flowers. The famous blooms are composed mostly of bracts. Height 10–20 feet. *Other Names:* Squawbush. *Name Lore:* The scientific name *cornus* means "horn" and perhaps refers to the hard wood of the tree. *Colors:* The actual flowers are tiny yellow things, but the brilliant bracts give the flower-like appearance; these can be white or pink, as there are both red and white flowering varieties. Leaves dark green, turning red, brown, or yellow in autumn. Twigs are often reddish. Berries can be red (*C. florida*), orange-red, or black. *Similar and Related Species:* There is also a Chinese dogwood (*C. kousa*) that blooms several weeks after the *C. florida*. *Fragrance:* Subtle. *Bloom Time*: May. *Origin:* Europe and America.

Habitat: Edges of woods. **Earth** (soil type): Organically rich, well-drained, acid. Cannot handle wet or alkaline soils. **Water** (moisture needs): Moderate. **Fire** (sun/shade requirements): Part-sun to light shade. **Air** (climate): US Climate Zones 4–9.

Tips and Warnings: Plant in mid-fall or early spring. The dogwood flowers most spectacularly after a cold winter, although late frost can be harmful. Both the summer and fall foliage is striking. Dogwood also attracts wildlife, particularly birds, which love the fruit. In old days, dogwood twigs were used as toothbrushes. Be careful not to nick your dogwood with the lawnmower – or you'll kill it easily.

Magic: Dogwood, if only because of its name, symbolizes dog magic; from ancient times the trees were considered protective of dogs. But it has other virtues as well. On Midsummer's Eve, carry a bit of cloth dampened by the sap of a flowering dogwood and your wishes will come true. Dogwood helps people to attain self-confidence and to keep an open mind. Oil of dogwood helps keep writings secret. Odysseus' men fed upon dogwood berries after Circe had turned them into pigs. One legend credits the flowering dogwood as the tree upon which Jesus was crucified; however, this cultivar (*C. florida*) is native to the eastern United States and doesn't grow in the Middle East. Another story says that the Trojan horse was built of dogwood, and indeed its wood is extremely hard. *Use dogwood for help in healing, protecting, or training dogs, or for general protection rites. Use the blossoms for spring festivals and the wood during Mabon or Lughnasa. Invoke Mars. The four sepals of the flower represent both the four directions and the four elements, so include a bow to each direction while performing dogwood rites.*

Dragon's Blood *(Daemonorops draco; Dracaena draco)* This is the herb of **Empowerment**.

Horticulture

Description: Dragon's blood is a slender, climbing rattan palm tree, with prickly stalks and cherry sized, pointy berries; the resin extracted from the immature fruits (dragon's blood) has special use in magic workings. *Name Lore: Daemonorops* means "demon shrub," from the Greek. *Other Names:* Blood, blume, calamus draco, socotrine, Zanzibar drop, draconis resina, sanguis draconis, dragon's blood palm, HiraDukhi. *Colors:* Resin dark red. *Fragrance:* The resin is almost odorless, but when burned smells like frankincense. Some find it vaguely sweet. *Bloom time:* Flowers spring; fruits, summer. *Origin:* Malaysia and Indonesia.

Habitat: Forest edges. **Earth** (soil type): Ordinary garden soil. **Water** (moisture needs): Moderate. **Fire** (sun/shade requirements): Full sun. **Air** (climate): Tropical.

Tips and Warnings: Dragon's blood does not grow well in temperate climates; it is extremely demanding. You'll probably have to purchase commercial resin for use. Dragon's blood is also used as a varnish for violins.

Magic: Dragon's blood is a general energy source; adding this resin to any magical working or incense increases its efficacy. You may also use it as incense by itself. In addition, it works for protection, exorcism, or banishment, and for love magic. If a woman burns the resin it will entice her errant lover to return; just burn the incense by a window and wait. It also is said to restore potency when placed under a mattress. Dragon's blood ink is extremely efficacious for writing out love spells. *People born under the sign of Aries are particularly successful using drangon's blood. Rites with dragon's blood are most effective when Mars is visible.*

Echinacea *(Echinacea augustifolia* or *E. purpurea)* This is the herb of **Strength**.

Horticulture

Description: Hairy perennial with narrow leaves and large daisylike flowers. Height 2–4 feet. *Other Names:* Coneflower, rudbeckia. *Colors:* Flowers purplish or pink; stem purplish; leaves dark green. *Fragrance:* Some cultivars like Echinacea Ruby Giant are delightfully fragrant. *Bloom Time*: July–September. *Origin:* North America, prairie region.

Habitat: Fields, roadsides. **Earth** (soil type): Well-composted, sandy, rich, well-drained; it adapts to many different soil types. **Water** (moisture needs): Drought tolerant. **Fire** (sun/shade requirements): Full sun. **Air** (climate): US Climate Zones 3–9.

Tips and Warnings: Easy to grow and long-lived. Seed can be sown in spring or fall. This tough, deeply rooted plant will help to break up a heavy, clayey soil. It draws butterflies and goldfinch. On the other hand, deer hate echinacea, so it is safe to grow outside fenced areas. It contains a compound toxic to flies and mosquitoes.

Magic: The famous immune-boosting power of echinacea makes it a natural for strengthening the practitioner and her spells and potions, especially money magic. The dried flowers can be used for incense. Some people believe *E. augustifolia* is the superior magical plant. I have not found this to be true; anyway, the *E. purpurea* is a more colorful garden flower. Plains Indians held it in great esteem and believed it effective against snakebite. *Rites using coneflower are most efficacious in midsummer. Clothe yourself in red.*

Elder *(Sambucus nigra; S. canadensis; S. mexicana)* This is the herb of **Cursing and Blessing**.

Horticulture

Description: Deciduous shrub or small tree with saw-toothed pointy leaflets, and clusters of flowers. *Name Lore:* "Elder" stems from the Anglo-Saxon word *aeld*, or *eldrun*, which means fire; its hollow twigs were commonly used for kindling. *Other Names:* Devil's eye, lady elder, bat tree, ellhorn, pipe tree, sureau, rob elder, European elder, boretree, burtree, hollunder, sweet elder, tree of doom, old lady, elderberry. *Similar and Related Species:* Although several species of elder exist, the *S. nigra,* or black elder, is most closely associated with the magical tradition. *Colors:* Bark grayish-brown. Flowers white, creamy, or yellow, depending on cultivar. Some have yellow leaves. Black, blue, or red fruits, depending on cultivar. *Fragrance:* Fruity or bittersweet, sophisticated. Fragrance is often stronger in the evening. Some species gives off a strong odor when the leaves are crushed. *Bloom Time*: June–July. *Origin:* Europe.

Habitat: Woods, damp areas, and waste places. **Earth** (soil type): Nitrogen-rich. **Water** (moisture needs): Moderate. **Fire** (sun/shade requirements): Best color in the sun; some species tolerate light shade. **Air** (climate): US Climate Zones 3–10.

Tips and Warnings: Best for informal gardens. It has most magic if planted in the south or east of the garden. One horrid old tradition says that elder will grow only where blood has been shed. A carefree plant, most species are fast growing and graceful. The seeds are poisonous, but the berries are edible if cooked properly. Because of the ambivalence surrounding this plant, it's safer to perform elder-magic only outside. Medieval monks used elderberries to create purple ink for their illustrated manuscripts. It also provides the famous elderberry wine, made famous in *Arsenic and Old Lace*, and can be made into an oddly flavored jelly. Be sure you truly want an elder tree before you plant one. There is a tale of a dryad, the Elder Mother, who reportedly lives in the tree and will kill anyone who cuts it down.

Magic: Elder is a paradoxical herb, which like its patron deity, Hecate, has the power to curse and to bless. In general, it is an herb of protection, love, and energy. A grove of elders is holy ground. The Druids used the powerful elder for blessing, cursing, and breaking curses. But it has a darker side. It is believed in Germany that the plant can induce ghosts to come into a house, and it has traditionally been used to summon spirits. The stakes were once even higher in England: to be safe, some say it should never be brought into the home. There's an old English saying, "Hawthorn blooms and elder flowers/Fill the home with evil powers." Some say it's the elder flowers that cause the trouble. Others claim that burning the wood in the house is dangerous; such activity can summon the Devil or the wrath of Hecate. The Scots, however, take a cheerier view of the plant: an elderberry branch gathered on May Eve hung over doors and windows banishes spirits and all hostile magic; a branch buried with a corpse will keep away witches. Elder wood protects against lightning. The flowers can be used in wish-fulfillment charms, while flowers, leaves, and berries are all used for personal or residential blessings, as well as for protection. Elder wood makes a good all-around magic wand, one particularly efficacious for exorcisms and other types of cleansing.

The knotted twigs are efficacious against arthritis, if carried in the pocket. (They also get rid of warts. During the waning moon, you must cut the twig with a silver blade, rub the wart with the twig, and then bury the twig in some mud – at midnight. When the twig has rotted away, the troublesome wart will be gone. This may take some time.) The Roman statesman Pliny said that elderberry leaves in wine cured snakebite. Some people weave elder branches into pentagrams for protection of their altars. Fairies (especially the Scandinavian Hydermolder) are quite attracted to elder. If you stand under an elder tree on Midsummer's Eve, you may see the King of Fairies pass. Rites involving elder are traditional on Midsummer's Eve, or Litha, when the flowers may be burned as incense. At Beltaine drink some elderberry wine! Elder may also be used at blessings, handfastings, healings, prosperity rituals, exorcisms, and death rites (when a sprig of elder is traditionally put into the coffin; indeed the entire coffin may be made of elder wood). The last three days of October are also sacred to elder. *Invoke Hecate when performing magic with elder; wear green or red. Sagittarians and Scorpios work the best magic with elder. The most auspicious date is November 25.*

Elecampane *(Inula helenium)* This is the herb of **Psychic Powers.**

Horticulture

Description: Perennial herb with several erect, softly hairy stems and large, ovate, toothed, pointed leaves. Flowers in large, terminal heads, 3–4 inches in diameter, on long stalks. It grows into a large clump. Height 4–5 feet. ***Name Lore:*** The specific scientific name *helenium* is derived from Helen of Troy, who took some of the plant with her when she eloped with Paris. ***Other Names:*** Elfwort, scabwort, nurse-heal, yellow starwort, elf dock, wild sunflower, horseheal, velvet dock. *Colors:* Flowers bright yellow. Leaves olive colored and veined white. *Fragrance:* Bittersweet. Dried roots have an unusual, pungent smell. ***Bloom Time***: July–August. ***Origin:*** Asia and Europe, but naturalized in eastern North America.

Habitat: Fields, open woods, damp pastures, roadsides, marshy places. **Earth** (soil type): Ordinary garden soil, though it prefers a damp loamy soil. Can tolerate heavy clay. **Water** (moisture needs): Elecampane is quite drought resistant. **Fire** (sun/shade requirements): Likes shade. **Air** (climate): US Climate Zones 5–9.

Tips and Warnings: At one time elecampane root was candied and eaten. A cordial was made from it by infusing elecampane roots with sugar and currants in white port.

Magic: This is an herb of consecration, joy, nature magic, and purification. It is frequently used in incense to strengthen clairvoyant powers. and is sometimes used as a love-attractant. Pliny declared it was good for the digestion and imparted mirth. Most famously, though, it is said that smoldering the herb on charcoal will sharpen psychic powers, particularly when scrying (using a crystal ball). Elecampane has long been associated with elves and fairies. *Clothe yourself in white. Those born under the sign of Virgo have a special affinity to elecampane.*

Elm *(Ulmus* species) This is the tree of **Shadows.**

Horticulture

Description: Deciduous tree with saw-toothed leaves and clusters of small flowers. Over 25 species. Alas, the great old American elms (*U. Americana*) and English elms (*U. procera*) are mostly gone now, killed off by Dutch elm disease (which arrived from Holland in the twentieth century) carried by the nicely named but horrible ambrosia beetle. Today these elm trees die when they are about 30 years old; formerly they lived to be about 400. Height up to 150 feet. Other species of elm include the small-leaved elm (*U. alata*) slippery elm (*U. fulva*), the common, or field elm (*U. campestris*), and the wych elm (*U. glabra*). *Colors:* Reddish stamens with purple heads. Light gold leaves in the fall. *Fragrance:* Subtle. ***Bloom Time***: Various, often March–April. Leaves come out in May. ***Origin:*** Europe and America.

Habitat: Variable depending on the species. Often open places, meadows. **Earth** (soil type): Any ordinary soil. Tolerates salty soil. **Water** (moisture needs): Moderate. **Fire** (sun/shade requirements): Full sun. **Air** (climate) US Zones 2–9. Can handle cold, exposed sites.

Tips and Warnings: If possible, plant to the east. It is possible to find species of elm resistant (but not immune) to Dutch elm disease, including the Wych elm. It used to be said that when the elm leaves are as big as a mouse's ear, it was time to sow barley.

Magic: The elm is a tree of death, elves, and shadows. While some modern formularies ascribe love to elm, that is not my experience. Elm is said to attract elves, but many traditions say it has an animosity toward humans (so do elves). There is a terrifying saying about elm: "Elm hateth man, and waiteth." Read *Desire Under the Elms* and you might agree! At any rate, elm leaves and branches are helpful in making contact with the fairy folk, if that is your desire. In olden days it was said that when the leaves fell out of season, it foretold a plague affecting cattle.

The slippery elm has a more cheerful reputation. Its inner bark can be hung around a child's neck as an amulet to insure good speaking skills. And if the bark and leaves of the slippery elm are burned and worn in a bag about the neck, it is said that your friends will stop gossiping about you. Of course, you might give them something new to talk about. Legend says that a fairy hides under every elm leaf, although I can't stress often enough what a bad idea I think this is. The first elm grove sprang into being when Orpheus played a love song to Eurydice, and has ever since been associated with that unlucky pair. Eurydice, if you recall, was unable to escape the realm of shadows when Orpheus looked back upon her. Elm works well in spells dealing with shadows, death rites and the shadow realm. (Elves once guarded the burial mounds of the dead and elm was once a common wood for coffins.) At one time it was often planted in tainted or uncleansable areas to warn off others. The young branches make an excellent magic wand. Elm has been used in sorcery in dark spells that cause depression or gloom; it is said to dull the senses. *Rites involving elm are most efficacious when performed on Tuesday. Invoke Odin. Summer and autumn are the best times. Capricorns have special affinity to elm.*

Evening Primrose *(Oenothera biennis, O. caespitosa, O. pallida)* This is the herb of **Hunting Magic**.

Horticulture

Description: Biennial and perennial species. Pointed, alternate leaves and large, four-petalled, cup-shaped flowers borne in a dense terminal spike. Flowers open in the evening. Height 18–48 inches, depending on variety. *Other Names:* King's cure-all, sand lily, German rampion, fever plant, scabish, gumbo lily (*O. caespitosa*). *Similar and Related Species:* Some member of this genus open during daylight hours, others wait until evening. It is difficult to distinguish between species, as this plant hybridizes rather freely. *Colors:* Flowers yellow for *O. biennis*, white for *O. caespitosa* and *O. pallida. Fragrance:* Sweet, especially in the evening. (They are pollinated by night-flying insects). If they are not pollinated in the evening, some may stay open for a while in the morning, hoping for better luck. *Bloom Time*: June–September. *Origin:* North American prairies, now found over the world.

Habitat: Dry open spaces, roadsides, waste places, and fields. **Earth** (soil type): Ordinary garden soil. **Water** (moisture needs): Prefers to be well watered. **Fire** (sun/shade requirements): Prefers shade. **Air** (climate): US climate Zones 5–8.

Tips and Warnings: The evening primrose is an excellent choice for a moon garden. This plant draws deer, rodents, bees, butterflies, birds, and caterpillars. The young root is edible and can be added to soup and stews. The leaves can be put into salads.

Magic: Native Americans used to rub evening primrose on the soles of their moccasins to bring luck. By analogy, the herb can also be used for luck in hunting any item of value. It is unlucky to bring primroses into the house. Some believe that the evening primrose increases one's desire for drink.

Eyebright *(Euphrasia officinalis)* This is the herb of **Cheerfulness.**

Horticulture

Description: Annual semi-parasitic herb with short, branched, square, leafy stems, and tiny, bristle-toothed leaves. The roots attach to grasses. Height 4–8 inches. *Name Lore:* The scientific name *Euphrasia*, is the Greek word for merriment. *Other Names:* Red eyebright, euphronsyne, meadow eyebright, *Colors:* White, yellowish, red, or violet-tinged, with a bright orange spot at the entrance to the flower-throat. *Fragrance:* Subtle.
Bloom Time: June–September. *Origin:* Europe.

Habitat: Meadows, grassy places, roadsides, and damp pastures. **Earth** (soil type): chalky. **Water** (moisture needs): Moderate. **Fire** (sun/shade requirements): Prefers semi-shade. **Air** (climate): US Climate Zones 5–8.

Tips and Warnings: Sow in spring among grass in a moist location. All else being equal, plant to the east, the direction of sunrise. These plants attract bees.

Magic: Eyebright is best known for its magical mood enhancement and banishment of depression. It also helps to enhance mental acuity, with additional benefit in aiding insight, clairvoyance, and stimulating the intellect. As an amulet, it is said to protect against eye diseases, and may also be used in the bath. *Invoke Brighid during rites with eyebright. Leos have a particular affinity to this herb.*

Fennel *(Foeniculum vulgare)* This is the herb of **Persuasion**.

Horticulture

Description: A delicate perennial, annual, or biennial with a straight sturdy stem, feathery leaves, and small flowers blooming in large umbels. Height 2–6 feet. *Name Lore:* From Latin *fæniculum*, a diminutive of *fænum,* or "hay." The Greek word for fennel is Marathon, so-named because the place was apparently overgrown with the stuff. Marathon may be related to a Greek verb meaning "to waste away," or at least to get thin; the herb was used as a dietary aid for centuries. Another way to get thin is to start running marathons. *Colors:* Flowers yellow, leaves dark green. Stems blue-green. *Fragrance:* Strong, licorice-like, hay-like, bittersweet. *Bloom Time*: July–November. *Origin:* Mediterranean but naturalized throughout Europe.

Habitat: Wastelands, coastal areas. **Earth** (soil type): Well-drained sandy or loamy. Tolerates poor soil. **Water** (moisture needs): Moderate. **Fire** (sun/shade requirements): Sun. **Air** (climate): US Climate Zones 5–8.

Tips and Warnings: Fennel is best suited to an informal garden. For best magical results, plant fennel on Wednesday or Sunday, and gather on Midsummer's Eve. Fennel does well in a **Fire** Garden as it attracts butterflies, birds, and beneficial insects. The Romans were extremely fond of licorice-tasting fennel and ate the entire plants from seed to root. It is considered good raw with salad dressing and can also be used to flavor fish. Today fennel remains more popular in Europe than in the United States. I must also warn you, that according to some traditions, it is bad luck to *grow* fennel at all, although the herb itself is valuable. Handling fennel causes skin irritation in some people. An old rhyme says "Sow fennel, sow sorrow." Pliny claimed that snakes ate fennel just before shedding their skins. I am afraid this is another of his little fibs. Snakes don't eat vegetables under any circumstance whatever.

Magic: Fennel is one of those all-purpose herbs that combine well with others, especially with St. John's wort for protection against evil witches. It can also undo ill effects of witchcraft. But it does have special power all its own: it is said that merely carrying fennel on your person will convince others to believe your words; it is suspected that many politicians carry a bit of fennel at all times.

In addition, fennel is an herb of success, fertility, healing, and purification, imparting courage in the face of danger. Greek legend says that knowledge came to human beings in the form of a burning stalk, symbolic of Prometheus, inside a fennel stem. Traditionally this energizing herb cures demonic possession if tied around the neck or carried in a small bag. Likewise, if hung over a door along with St. John's wort on Midsummer's Eve (or on the Solstice), it will keep evil spirits away from the house insects too. Or stuff your keyholes with it. If you have keyholes (most people don't, nowadays). *Fennel may be used in consecrations, counter-magic, and protection rites, as well as in rites aimed at business success. Fennel may be worn as an amulet. Invoke Diana, Aine, Adonis, or Dionysus, whose devotees carried wands of fennel topped with a pine cone for fertility. St John's Eve is the most propitious time for rites with fennel, and it is particularly auspicious when Mercury is visible. Clothe yourself in yellow. Those born under the sign of Virgo can make very efficacious magic with fennel.*

Fern See particular variety: Bracken fern, Moonwort, or Male fern.

Fig (*Ficus carica* or *F. religiosa*) This is the herb of **Enlightenment**.

Horticulture

Description: Deciduous subtropical tree with soft, pithy wood, large petiolate leaves and generally smooth bark. Height 30 feet. ***Colors:*** Greenish. ***Fragrance:*** Subtle. ***Bloom Time***: Twice a year. ***Origin:*** Southern Arabia and similar places. In Britain they can be grown in the south and west of the country in a protected spot – or elsewhere under glass.

Habitat: In the wild, often found near wells. In the US, figs can be grown in California, Texas, and the Gulf states. **Earth** (soil type): Sandy. **Water** (moisture needs): Moderate. **Fire** (sun/shade requirements): Full, intense sun. **Air** (climate): Cannot handle frost or cold winters. Spring winds interfere with wasp pollination and produce scarred fruit.

Tips and Warnings: The fig is a wonderful shade tree, but only a few species bear edible fruits. Even of these, many will not bear unless the climate is just right. Those that do produce bear fruit twice yearly, with the heavier crop occurring in the fall. The fig has been used as a sweetener by desert communities for millennia. It has also been used as a coffee substitute, not to mention appearing as the famous Fig Newton. A perfume has been made from its essential oil.

Magic: The Buddha sat under *Ficus religiosa* when he achieved his Enlightenment. The fig is also mentioned in the Bible more than any other plant, possibly because of its great economic importance.

Adam and Eve made their first garments from this plant. According to Islamic and Gnostic tradition, a fig tree was one of the two forbidden trees in the Garden of Eden. (The other was the olive.) "Sitting under one's own fig tree" was representative of peace and prosperity, and that is the symbolism it carries even into today's garden – places fortunate enough to be able to grow figs. Supposedly the prophet Isaiah, who practiced medicine in addition to his prophetic function, cured King Hezekiah's "swelling" with a poultice made of figs. Figs have a strong association with fertility, the fruit being female, and the leaf male. The fig was also a symbol of the Great Mother in Indo-Iranian myth. Figs have traditionally been used in rites of spring – and all romantic spring picnics should include a few figs to munch on. *Invoke: Dionysus (or Bacchus), Venus, Poseidon, Saturn, or Priapus. For more spiritual purposes, sit beneath a fig tree and mediate in the manner of Siddhartha Buddha. The fig may be worn as an amulet.*

Figwort *(Scrophularia nodosa)* This is the herb of **Health**.

Horticulture

Description: Perennial herb with a tall square stem, oval to lanceolate leaves. Height 16–32 inches. *Name Lore:* Some liken the resemblance of the roots swellings to figs. *Other Names:* Throatwort. *Colors:* Flowers purple or brownish-red. *Fragrance:* Unpleasant. *Bloom Time*: June–August. *Origin:* Europe.

Habitat: Damp woods and other wet areas. **Earth** (soil type): Ordinary soil. **Water** (moisture needs): Moderate. **Fire** (sun/shade requirements): Partial shade. **Air** (climate): US Climate Zones 5–9.

Tips and Warnings: Figwort is attractive to wildlife, especially hummingbirds. It can also be made into a tea.

Magic: This is a general herb of health as well as protection. Pass a figwort plant through a Midsummer's Eve fire and hang the plant from doors and windows. That will keep away evil spirits, protects against the evil eye, and will bring health, joy, and peace to the occupants of the home.

Fir *(Abies* species, especially *A. balsamea)* This is the tree of **Winter**.

Horticulture

Description: Coniferous resinous trees with flat evergreen needles. Height 25–50 feet. *Colors:* Needles green, cones purplish. *Fragrance:* In some species, like the balsam (*A. balsamea*) all parts of the tree are fragrant. *Bloom Time*: Flowers, insignificant. *Origin:* Eastern United States, other species of fir worldwide.

Habitat: Coniferous forests, often found in pure stands. **Earth** (soil type): Acid. **Water** (moisture needs): Moderate. **Fire** (sun/shade requirements): Grows best in full sun. **Air** (climate): US Climate Zones 2–6.

Tips and Warnings: Perfumes incorporating balsam should be worn on Tuesday. Deer and moose browse the foliage in winter.

Magic: For Saint Boniface, the balsam fir was the ideal emblem of Christmas and a symbol of everlasting life, joy, birth and rebirth. The fir serves as a symbol of life in darkest hours of winter, and literally provides food to starving animals. For that reason, many consider it a tree of great mystery. It has a practical magical use as well: lay a green branch across a bed to prevent nightmares, and hang it over the barn door to keep spirits from stealing the grain. Balsam is also used to invoke spirits. Magic wands made from fir are considered especially efficacious in spells involving prosperity. When topped with a cone, fir wands are also powerful in rites of sexual magic. *Magic with fir is most efficacious when the moon is as near full as possible. Wear black and white.*

Flax *(Linum usitatissimum)* This is the herb of **Beauty**.

Horticulture

Description: Slender, erect annual, biennial, or perennial herb with narrow, pointed, alternate leaves and five-petalled flowers. Height 1–3 feet. ***Other Names:*** Linseed.

Colors: Flowers white to pale blue. Wild species may have pink or yellow flowers. Seeds brown and glossy. Blue-flowered flax tends to have bluish foliage. ***Fragrance:*** Subtle.

Bloom Time: May–August, depending on the cultivar. ***Origin:*** Europe, Asia, and Mediterranean. Found widely.

Habitat: Roadsides, waste places. **Earth** (soil type): Light, well-drained, average. **Water** (moisture needs): Moderate. **Fire** (sun/shade requirements): Full sun. **Air** (climate): US Climate Zones 5–9.

Tips and Warnings: Flax was an important feature in every medieval herb garden. Flax use dates back 10,000 years, and is the source of linen, one of the oldest textiles in the world. Linseed oil is also obtained from flax. The seeds have broad medicinal use; indeed the word "liniment" comes form "linen." Crushed flaxseed is considered to make a good poultice for colds.

Magic: From days of old, it has been said that a child who plays or sleeps in a field of flax will grow up beautiful. Just as the flax has both outward good looks and inner usefulness, it reminds us of the nature of true beauty. In addition, flax is an herb of protection, the flowering agents are used in charms against sorcery. *Flax is frequently used as a decoration at Samhain.*

Forget-Me-Not *(Mysotis sylvatica)* This is an herb of **Remembrance**.

Horticulture

Description: Annual. Several cultivars, some sprawling (Height 3-8 inches), some more erect (Height 15-23 inches). Five blue petals with a yellow "eye." ***Name Lore:*** The name "forget-me-not" supposedly derives from the last words a German knight shrieked to his ladylove as he tumbled into a river, from whose banks he had gathered the blossoms. ***Other Names:*** Also called mouse-ear, which is what the genus name actually means in Greek. ***Colors:*** Sky blue. ***Bloom Time***: May–October, depending on the cultivar. Origin: Europe.

Habitat: Stream banks, moist areas. **Earth** (soil type): Moist, humus rich soil. **Water** (moisture needs): High. **Fire** (sun/shade requirements): Prefers partial shade, but can handle a lot of shade. **Air** (climate): US Climate Zones 3–8 for most species.

Tips and Warnings: The forget-me-not combines well with many spring flowers. It also makes an excellent choice for a moon garden. These hardy annuals can be sown early in the spring, or, in mild areas, even in the preceding fall. The leaves of this plant are extremely bitter.

Magic: This is an herb of minor magic; it is symbolic of devoted remembrance. It is said to have one additional virtue, though: boil the bitter leaves in wine to palliate the effects of adder or scorpion venom. The origin of this story probably derives from the tightly curled root, which resembles a scorpion.

European folklore notes that this flower asks us never to forget, although the message is carried in a variety of stories. In Egyptian tales, placing the leaves over the eyes during the month of Thoth will enable one to have visions. Literary people might (or might not) recall that the Lady Chatterley's lover put forget-me-nots in her pubic hair. The plant has always been associated with lovers.

Foxglove (*Digitalis purpurea* and *D. lanata*) This is the herb of the **Fairy Folk**.

Horticulture

Description: Reseeding biennial with large, wavy leaves; straight, un-branched stems; and large, bell-shaped flowers. Height 2 feet. **Name Lore:** *Digitalis* means "finger," and both the common name and the Latin refer to its glove-like appearance. "Fox" may refer to real foxes, as some think, or to "folk" meaning the fairy folk. Fairies are probably more likely than foxes to wear gloves, but not much. **Other Names:** Fairy bells, fairy's glove, fairy caps, deadman's bells, fox's claws, fairy thimbles, witch's bells, witches' glove, folk's glove, fox bell. **Colors:** Often purple or pink with spots, but other colors such as white, yellow, or strawberry are also seen. **Fragrance:** Subtle. **Bloom Time**: June–August. **Origin:** Europe; has naturalized to the United States.

Habitat: Woodlands. **Earth** (soil type): Woody slopes and clearings. Prefers rich, well-drained, acid soil. **Water** (moisture needs): Prefers to be well watered. **Fire** (sun/shade requirements): Dappled sunshine or partial shade. **Air** (climate): US Climate Zones 4–8.

Tips and Warnings: These tall plants must be staked or planted against a wall to stay upright. They are good at stimulating the growth of nearby plants and helping their resistance to disease. They also improve the storage qualities of potatoes and tomatoes grown near them. Even flower arrangements last longer if foxglove is included. An excellent plant for the **Fire** Garden. Digitalis, a cardiovascular drug, is extracted from the leaves. All parts of the plants are very poisonous.

Magic: Foxglove is primarily used to commune with the sprits of the Otherworld, particularly the Netherworld and the Fairy Folk, and to protect against ghosts and sorcery. Foxglove, however, is a notoriously tricky herb to deal with in the magical realm. Don't pick it – just plant it and let it do its magic by itself. *If you are brave enough to use foxglove, use it in rites of vision, immortality, and nature magic. Foxglove may be worn as an amulet. Librans have a special affinity to foxglove.*

Frankincense (*Boswellia thurifera* and *B. sacra*) This is the herb of **Consecration.**

Horticulture

Description: *Boswellia* is a small tree with leaves divided into narrow leaflets and star-shaped flowers. (It is related to the tree that produces myrrh.) Technically, frankincense is not an herb, but a white or colorless resin produced by several species of Boswellia. The sap is "bled" from the trees, the "tears" scraped off and collected in baskets. It is later burned as incense. **Name Lore:** The word *frankincense* means "free-burning." **Other Names:** Olibanum, gum thus, luban, incense. **Colors:** Flowers white with rose tints. **Fragrance:** Pungent, strong. **Bloom Time**: Harvesting of the resin is from May–September. **Origin:** Middle East, India, and desert Africa.

Habitat: Often found on slopes. **Earth** (soil type): Limey. **Water** (moisture needs): Low. **Fire** (sun/shade requirements): Full sun. **Air** (climate): Subtropical.

Tips and Warnings: Boswellia makes a handsome landscape or specimen tree, looking somewhat like the mountain ash. The aromatic gum was used for everything from perfumes to fumigants (sometimes much the same thing). The Roman Catholic Church still uses it as incense. The ancient Egyptians made their famous eye-makeup (kohl) from it. If you are able to plant frankincense, the west is the most propitious direction.

Magic: A plant of almost unlimited power, this wonderful substance is able to bring consecrating and spiritual element even to material endeavors. Frankincense is reputed to rid a person and their home of malign influences, including evil spirits. It helps divinity become manifest and aids the practitioner in contacting other planes of existence. Used as an incense or placed under the pillow it will help produce prophetic dreams. It is said that 35 grains of frankincense will improve the memory. It is associated with self-discipline and self-control. Pliny believed that frankincense acted as a powerful antidote to poisoning from hemlock. *The resin may be used to consecrate magic wands. Frankincense is suitable for almost any ceremony or celebration: all Sun festivals (Beltaine, Lughnasa, Yule) and rites of purification, spiritual growth, blessing, exorcisms, divination, and protection. (For protective magic incense, combine with cumin). Invoke Ra, Bel, Baal, Isis, Yahweh, or the Christ-Child. Aquarians have a special affinity to frankincense. Frankincense may be worn as an amulet as well as used in incense.*

Fumitory *(Fumaria officinalis)* This is the herb of **Samhain**.

Horticulture

Description: Annual herb with a low-branching, leafy stem and tubular flowers. Height 30 inches. **Name Lore:** The Greek name was *Kapnos*, which means "smoke." It was once sold in apothecary shops under the Latin name *Fumus Terrae*, or smoke of the earth. **Other Names:** **Earth**-smoke, erdrauch, hedge fumitory, wax dolls. **Colors:** Flower petals pink or purple with dark red tips; leaves gray-green. **Fragrance:** Unpleasant and smoke-like. **Bloom Time**: May–September. **Origin:** Europe and North Africa.

Habitat: Roadsides, cultivated ground. **Earth** (soil type): Ordinary. **Water** (moisture needs): Moderate. **Fire** (sun/shade requirements): Prefers sun. **Air** (climate): US Climate Zones 5–9.

Tips and Warnings: All else being equal, plant fumitory in the north of the garden. All parts of the plant are poisonous.

Magic: This herb has been strongly linked to the Underworld and all its powers. Throw it into a fire to become invisible. It is primarily used at Samhain, where it banishes negative energies. It may also be used in purifications; burn the stem and leaf to banish evil spirits. *Fumitory may be carried as an amulet, used as incense, or in the ritual bath, or as a wash to consecrate magical implements. Invoke Apollo. Capricorns have good luck with fumitory.*

Garlic *(Allium sativum)* This is the herb of **Defense against Vampires**.

Horticulture

Description: Perennial herb with small flowers, grass-like leaves, and a bulb divided in 12-18 bulblets or cloves. Height 1-2 feet. *Other Names:* Suan, poor man's treacle. *Colors:* Blooms purplish or pinkish white. *Fragrance:* Characteristic. *Bloom Time*: July–September. *Origin:* Originally India or Central Asia, now worldwide._

Habitat: Fields, roadsides. **Earth** (soil type): Rich, sandy for preference, but can handle many different types, including clay. **Water** (moisture needs): Moderate. **Fire** (sun/shade requirements): Full sun. **Air** (climate): US Climates Zones 2–10.

Tips and Warnings: Best planted during the third or fourth quarter of the moon. It is said that bruising the cloves slightly before planting will increase the savor of garlic; to the same purpose, it is suggested that olive stones be buried close by. Garlic plants cannot tolerate weeds growing near them. Harvest in fall when the tops begin to turn brown. One exception: while almost any kind of garlic is beneficial for health treatments, make sure the garlic you use for vampire-repulsion is harvested in May. Other kinds aren't as good. The essential oil extracted from garlic can be irritating. Since the characteristic odor of garlic gets right down into the lungs, it has to wear away by itself – just brushing your teeth won't do the trick. An excellent plant for the **Fire** Garden.

Magic: Garlic is a powerful herb of endurance and good fortune. It prevents storms at sea, protects against death by drowning and the evil eye, and guards against jealousy as well. When hung in the bedroom it is especially protective of sleeping children. In Greek lore, chewing garlic assures victory in competition. In Chinese lore it assures that one will have many children. Ancient Egyptians used garlic as a medium of exchange; a slave cost about 15 pounds of garlic. They also used it as an aphrodisiac. (I have my own theories about this; the smell covered up any body odor.) Rubbing the lips with garlic is supposed to be cooling during hot weather. Garlic can be used whenever energy is needed for conflict. Just eating it makes you stronger. Its most famous use, however, is as protection from vampires. Luckily you don't have to eat it: simply hang it on the doors and windows. One story, shared by Christians and Muslims, is that garlic sprang up where the Devil's left foot stepped when he left the Garden of Eden. (The onion sprang from the right foot.) Cybele, however, dislikes garlic and refused to allow it in her temples. *Garlic may be carried as an amulet. Invoke Hecate when doing magic with garlic. Arians have good luck with garlic.*

German Chamomile *(Chamomilla recutita,* or *Matricaria recutita)* This is the herb of **Comfort** (See also Chamomile).

Horticulture

Description: Annual herb with a downy, erect stem, ferny leaves, and daisy-like flowers. Height 1–2 feet. *Other Names:* Scented mayweed, wild chamomile, Hungarian chamomile. *Similar and Related Species:* The Roman chamomile is a perennial; the German variety is an annual and grows taller. Both share the same magical powers. *Colors:* Both species have yellow-centered flowers with white petals. *Fragrance:* All parts of the plant are aromatic: apple-scented, sweet, or woodsy. Some liken it to the scent of green tea. The German variety is less fragrant than the Roman version, however. *Bloom Time*: May–August. *Origin:* Europe.

Habitat: Roadsides, fields, wastelands. **Earth** (soil type): Light, moist, well-drained. **Water** (moisture needs): Needs to be well watered. **Fire** (sun/shade requirements): Part shade or full sun. **Air** (climate): US climate zones 5–9. Cannot handle heat.

Tips and Warnings: German chamomile should be planted on Sunday, during the first quarter of the moon. It does well in a fall garden. This is a great plant for a container. Planting chamomile will help ailing plants regain their strength (and improve their flavor), but don't allow the chamomile to stay there long. When you see an improvement in the ailing plants, yank out the chamomile from that section, otherwise the other plants will return to ill health. It has an especially good effect on cabbages, mints, and onions, although don't plant it too close to the last. People allergic to ragweed may also have problems with German chamomile.

Magic: German chamomile has the same magical properties as Roman Chamomile.

Ginger *(Zingiber officinalis)* This is the herb of **Success.**

Horticulture

Description: Herb with several stems, long, narrow leaves and spiky flowers. Height 4 feet. *Other Names:* Shringara and gingerroot. *Colors:* Flowers purple and white. *Fragrance:* Subtle. *Bloom Time*: Spring. *Origin:* South Asia, now grown worldwide in warm climates.

Habitat: Open places. **Earth** (soil type): Average. **Water** (moisture needs): Low–moderate. **Fire** (sun/shade requirements): Sunny. **Air** (climate): Tropical.

Tips and Warnings: Ginger should be planted during the third quarter of the moon. Excellent for the **Fire** Garden. A healthy ginger plant is said to indicate a healthy gardener.

Magic: The magical power of ginger comes from the essential oil extracted from the whole or powdered root. This is an herb for great success in all endeavors; it also works as an enhancer for magical spells, particularly those involving protection rites or passionate love. *Ginger may be carried as an amulet, used as incense, or taken as a potion. Arians have special luck with ginger.*

Ginseng *(Panax ginseng, P. quinquefolium)* This is the herb of **Fertility** (see Mandrake).

Horticulture

Description: Small five-petalled flowers, seedy berries, fleshy root resembling a human form. *Colors:* Flowers whitish, berries red. *Fragrance:* Similar to lily of the valley. *Bloom Time*: Flowers May–August; fruits July–August. *Origin:* China and North America.

Habitat: Rich, deciduous woods. **Earth** (soil type): Rich, moist. **Water** (moisture needs): Moderate. **Fire** (sun/shade requirements): Partial shade. **Air** (climate): US Climate Zones 5–9.

Tips and Warnings: While cultivated ginseng does not seem to have the same medicinal powers as the wild type, for magical purposes they are equally efficacious. Ginseng is difficult to grow; it does best when planted during the third quarter of the moon. Large doses raise the blood pressure.

Magic: American (*P. quinquefolium*) and Chinese (*P. ginseng*) are the equivalent of mandrake; ginseng and mandrake, although not related, have identical magical properties. (See mandrake.) The root of the ginseng protects against illness. In China ginseng root is said to be a dose of immortality. And at one time only members of the nobility were allowed to use it.

Grape *(Vitis vinifera)* This is the herb of **Celebration.**

Horticulture

Description: Deciduous vine with inconspicuous flowers and heart-shaped leaves. Height 20 feet. *Colors:* Greenish. *Fragrance:* Intense. *Bloom Time*: Spring. *Origin* Eastern Mediterranean, but grapes can be grown in all but the coldest areas.

Habitat: Sloping ground. The wild vine grows in forests. **Earth** (soil type): Average. **Water** (moisture needs): Moderate. **Fire** (sun/shade requirements): Sun or partial shade. **Air** (climate): US Climate Zone 4–10 for most species.

Tips and Warnings: Harvest grapes as close to the full moon as possible. Grapes are excellent for an **Air** Garden.

Magic: Everyone is acquainted with the magical powers of wine, but the entire plant is important in all love magic and other workings. The grape vine stands for joy, fertility, happiness, inspiration, prosperity, and vitality. *Invoke Bacchus and Dionysus when working with grape. The most auspicious date is March 16 (in honor of Dionysus); August 19 is also auspicious. Wear variegated clothing. Grape may also be carried as an amulet. Those born under the sign of Pisces have a particular affinity for grape.*

Hawthorn (*Crataegus monogyna* and *C. oxyacantha*) This is the herb of **Beltaine**.

Horticulture

Description: Deciduous broadleaf tree with thorny twigs, and small, five-petalled flowers. Over 1000 species, some living over 400 years. Almost as if it knows how important it is in the western magical tradition, the hawthorn prefers to grow near people rather than in the forest. When growing in hedgerows, it frequently accompanies blackthorn; however, unlike blackthorn, hawthorn has a rather slight root system and is not greedy of soil nutrients. Height 12–30 feet. *Other Names:* May, maybush, hagthorn, haws, mayblossom, huath, motherdie, bread-and-cheese, tree of chastity, or whitethorn. *Name Lore:* The name "hawthorn" is a corruption of "hedge-thorn." *Similar and Related Species:* The single-flowered white variety has the strongest magical power, as opposed to the double form or pink varieties. *Colors:* Flowers are white (common hawthorn) or pink (English hawthorn, *C. momgyna*); bright red berries. Leaves shiny green above and gray-green below. Deep red foliage in the fall. *Fragrance:* Very strong, almost to the point of rankness. Some say it combines the odors of bitter almond, coumarin, and fish. Others consider the scent erotic. *Bloom Time*: Flowers in May–June. Some can blossom twice in a year, depending on conditions. Berries September–November. *Origin:* Europe and Britain.

Habitat: Hedgerows, scrub, woods. **Earth** (soil type): Ordinary well-drained garden soil.
Water (moisture needs): Low. **Fire** (sun/shade requirements): Sunny, but will tolerate some shade.
Air (climate): US Climate Zones 3–8. It can handle wind and air pollution.

Tips and Warnings: Plant in early spring or late fall. An accommodating, easy-to-grow plant, although it is subject to a rather alarming number of bacterial and fungal diseases. Since the hawthorn is frequently wider than it is high, it can easily be encouraged to form a hedge. It is thornier when grown as a hedge than when cultivated as a small tree. It also withstands pollution well. It is fertilized by species of flies, not by moths or butterflies. More than 50 species of insects gain sustenance from it. Birds will eat the berries. It makes a great barbed wire replacement. Cutting hawthorn carelessly for magical purposes can put one in magical danger; novices should attempt it only under supervision of a magical practitioner.

Magic: This is an herb of protection, fertility, and acute perception, very strongly associated with Beltaine. It symbolizes hope, fertility, prosperity, purity, and joy. Hawthorn is also reputed to have power over storms at sea and lightning. It brings luck to fishermen, and is a traditional guardian of wells. It may also protect the house against ghosts. One legend names hawthorn as the plant of the crown of thorns. The relationship between hawthorns and witches is ambiguous; some say that hawthorn gives power over witches. However, some modern day witches claim hawthorn for their own; one ancient story says that witches can transform themselves into hawthorn. Cutting down any thorn bush is unlucky, but cutting down a hawthorn is worst of all, especially in Ireland. The Romans attached hawthorn sprigs to the cradle of a newborn baby to protect it from sickness and evil. However, some folks maintain that hawthorn is unlucky to bring into a house, possibly even causing a death in the family. Magic wands made of hawthorn are among the most powerful of all. The wild white forms are reputed to be much more powerful than common garden cultivars, however.

Hawthorn is holy to the fairy folk (some of them actually live in hawthorn), and sitting beneath a hawthorn on Samhain Eve will bring you under a fairy enchantment. If a young woman bathes her faces in hawthorn blossom water at dawn on May Day (while wearing a sprig from the rowan tree), her beauty will be assured forever. The Maypole should be crowned with a hawthorn garland and decorating one's barn on May Day will insure good milk all summer. It is also lucky at handfastings, and the ancient Celts traditionally married when the hawthorn was in blossom. At the New Year, it was believed in some communities that hanging a globe made of hawthorn in the kitchen would protect the house from fire for another year.

Magical rites performed with hawthorn are most efficacious at Beltaine, but May 4 and 13 are also auspicious, with Saturday and Sunday being the best days. Sagittarians have good luck with it. When working magic with hawthorn, invoke Blodewedd, Cardea, Flora, Hymen, and Olwen. Hawthorn may also be carried as an amulet.

Hazel *(Corylus avellana)* This is the herb of **Insight**.

Horticulture

Description: Tall deciduous shrub or very small tree with tiny flowers in catkins and smooth, peeling-bark. Produces filberts or hazelnuts. **Other Names:** Coll. **Colors:** Bark light reddish or brown, leaves lime green, nuts brown, flowers red. **Fragrance:** Subtle. **Bloom Time**: January–April. Fruits ripe in September. **Origin:** Common throughout Europe, America, Africa, and western Asia.

Habitat: Damp woods, scrub, and hedges. Often found near ponds. **Earth** (soil type): Well-drained. **Water** (moisture needs): Average. **Fire** (sun/shade requirements): Full sun to partial shade. **Air** (climate): US Climate Zones 4–8. Needs shelter from cold winds.

Tips and Warnings: For most magical effects, plant on Wednesday, Thursday, or Sunday. Best harvested at Samhain (at night) or Palm Sunday.

Magic: Hazel is an herb of great powers, bringing luck, protection, and wisdom. The Celts tell stories about various fish swallowing hazelnuts and then becoming all-wise. The European variety of hazel was reputed to protect pilgrims from thieves, if they bound hazel branches to their walking staffs. Wearing a woven hazel crown around the forehead will grant wishes or make you invisible. If worn at sea, hazel protects against shipwreck. At home, it protects against thunder and lightning – if gathered on Palm Sunday and kept alive indoors in water. The hazelnut is especially lucky for poets and other artists; once it was known as the food of the gods. However, hazel's prime use is as a diviner of hidden knowledge and secret treasures. Diviners often eat hazelnuts to enhance their visionary powers, and to this day, dowsers favor hazel twigs. They are reputed to find lost objects as well as water. The wood from the hazel tree makes one of the all-around best magic wands, and is especially efficacious in performing love spells. The wand must be from a tree that has not yet borne fruit, and cut with a single stroke of a magical sickle. Don't cut down the whole tree; in ancient Ireland it is said that the cutting of a hazel earned the death penalty. Older formulas talk about using magpie blood to complete the magical empowerment, but this is wrong. No true magic comes from the pain of others. Hazelnuts insure fertility. Folklore says you can name two hazelnuts after two lovers and put them side-by-side in a fire. If they burn quietly together, the lovers are faithful, but if one moves apart, the relationship is doomed.

Rites involving hazel wood are most efficacious when performed in very early spring (Imbolc); those using the nuts are most efficacious in autumn. The best day for performing rites with hazel is Wednesday, and the most auspicious date of the year is August 5. The entire month of July is also excellent. Stringing hazelnuts around will invite the help of fairies in your workings. Hazel may also be carried as an amulet. Those born under the sign of Virgo or Cancer have a special affinity to hazel. Invoke Artemis, Diana, Mercury, or Thor. Wear brown.

Heal-All *(Prunella vulgaris)* This is the herb of **Bewitchment Protection**.

Horticulture

Description: Low, stumpy perennial herb, with freely branching, slightly hairy, square stems and large, lanceolate leaves. Small, almost stalk-less tubular flowers. Height 1 foot. ***Other Names:*** All-heal, heart-of-the-earth, self-heal, hook heal, panay, Hercules' woundwort. ***Similar and Related Species:*** Bugles and skullcaps are frequently mistaken for true heal-all. ***Colors:*** Flowers bluish or purplish. ***Fragrance:*** Subtle. ***Bloom Time***: May–October. ***Origin:*** Eurasia, now found throughout the world.

Habitat: Grassy meadows, woodland clearings, fields, roadsides, lawns. **Earth** (soil type): Good garden soil. **Water** (moisture needs): Keep moist. **Fire** (sun/shade requirements): Full sun in cooler climates, part shade elsewhere. **Air** (climate): Grows in a wide variety of climates.

Tips and Warnings: Harvest at night when Sirius (the Dog Star) rises in the summer. For magical uses, the whole plants, roots and all should be dug out with a golden (or something symbolically gold) implement; there should be no moon. Although heal-all is a wild flower, you should grow your own. It is unethical to despoil the natural gifts of the earth for your own ends. Bees are attracted to heal-all. The young leaves are edible, although bitter.

Magic: As an herb against bewitchment, heal-all works on several levels. It not only keeps the practitioner safe from hostile spells, but also from enthrallment by one's own desires and uncontrolled passions. It used to be said that if anyone picked this plant, the devil would carry him away. To pick safely, follow the tips already mentioned.

Heather *(Calluna vulgaris)* This is the herb of **Imbolc**.

Horticulture

Description: A low, straggling, evergreen shrub with needle-like leaves. ***Name Lore:*** The name Calluna derives from the Greek verb *kallunein*, which means, "to make beautiful. Well-named. ***Other Names:*** Ling, Scottish heather. ***Similar and Related Species:*** Both heaths and heathers belong to the *Ericaceae* family, grow in similar conditions and are quite similar in appearance. Most heaths belong to the genus *Erica* and most heathers to the genus *Calluna*. For magical purposes they can be regarded as interchangeable. ***Colors:*** Flowers pale pink, white or purplish." ***Fragrance:*** Subtle. ***Bloom Time***: Almost constant, at least in my garden. Some varieties bloom in early spring, other August–September. ***Origin:*** Europe.

Habitat: Bogs, heaths, and moors. **Earth** (soil type): Barren, acidic soils. **Water** (moisture needs): Moderate. **Fire** (sun/shade requirements): Full sun to part shade. **Air** (climate): US Climate Zones 4–7.

Tips and Warnings: For most magical results, plant on Thursday. Heather is attractive to bees. Heather lasts a very long time in a flower arrangement and is traditionally used as brush or sweeper. It is also a good bathing herb, providing great energy.

Magic: Heather is an herb of immortality, blossoming at the most impossible times. White heather is especially lucky to bring into the home, but other kinds of heather should be left outside. White heather is also a protecting plant when worn, especially against rape. It is said that if heather and fern are dipped in water and waved about, the rain will come. Red heather can be used for beginning or ending an affair. Purple heather is used in rituals that promote spiritual growth; it is also used for encouragement. *Heather is used at important festivals such as Midsummer's Eve, Lughnasa, Imbolc, and at handfastings (tuck some in the bridal bouquet). Invoke Venus, Isis, Osiris, or Adonis. (This has always puzzled me. Heather doesn't grow anywhere near Egypt.) While Imbolc is the best time to perform rites with heather, purple heather can be also burned to summon spirits during Samhain. Heather also works very well during daylight hours. Taurians work powerful magic with heather. Wear black.*

Hellebore *(Helleborus officinalis)*

H. officinalis is, perhaps, the hellebore of the ancient Greeks. But it is difficult to be sure which type of hellebore the ancients used. The important thing to remember about hellebores is that they are very poisonous. The name itself indicates this, coming from the Greek *elein* "to injur" and *bora* meaning "food." See Black Hellebore and Lenten Rose.

Hemp *(Cannabis sativa)* This is the herb of **Visions.**

Horticulture

Description: Annual or biennial, with small flowers and erect, hairy stem. Height 10-15 feet. *Other Names:* Marijuana, cannabis, hashish, gallowgrass, ganja, neckweed. *Colors:* Flowers greenish. *Fragrance:* Subtle, except when it's burning. *Bloom Time*: August. *Origin:* Central Asia and India, now worldwide.

Habitat: Waste places, prairies. **Earth** (soil type): Ordinary garden soil. **Water** (moisture needs): Moderate. **Fire** (sun/shade requirements): Full sun. **Air** (climate): US Climate Zones 4–9.

Warnings: Although hemp was once an important feature in every medieval herb garden, today it is illegal in most places, even for harmless magical purposes. It has most magic if grown in the south of the garden.

Magic: Hemp is a famous although mild hallucinogen and allows the experienced and well-balanced practitioner an alternate reality. Its use has been debased by teenagers who thought they discovered it in the 1960s, but that need not concern us here. If hemp and mugwort are burned together, psychic powers will be unleashed. It is also used in love potions, as well as in ancient flying and invisibility ointments. People in Africa also believed it was a gift from the gods. There are several European rites involving hemp seed that enable the diviner to see one's future husband. Sow hemp seeds at midnight on the eve of the Midsummer Solstice; you'll have a vision of your future mate. Or throw the hemp seeds over the right shoulder and chant the proper incantation. Of course, the rite must be performed at night when the inquirer is alone. Indian legend says that the god Shiva brought a plant sometimes identified as hemp down from the Himalayas for the enjoyment of the people; he should be invoked during magical rites using this herb. It is sometimes used as decoration at Litha. *Hemp is most successfully used by those born under the sign of Pisces or Aries. For magical purposes, hemp may be used as incense or amulet.*

Henbane   (*Hyoscyamus niger*) This is the herb of the **Damned.**

Horticulture

Description: Annual or biannual downy herb with an erect stem, bell-shaped flowers, and sticky leaves. *Name Lore:* It's scientific name means "hog-bean," indicating that hogs can eat it. The English "henbane" tells us, however, it is toxic to poultry. *Other Names:* Devil's eye, black nightshade, henballs, hog's bean, Jupiter's bean, poison tobacco, gabhann, bazar bang, banj barry, henbells, sukran. *Colors:* Leaves gray-green. Flowers gray-yellow with violet veins. *Fragrance:* Fetid and just plain nasty. Ugh. *Bloom Time*: June–September. *Origin:* Mediterranean. Now widely distributed.

Habitat: Waste places, roadsides, often found near the sea. **Earth** (soil type): Sandy or stony. **Water** (moisture needs): Low to moderate. **Fire** (sun/shade requirements): Tolerates some shade. **Air** (climate): Grows in a variety of climates.

Tips and Warnings: Older plants are hard to transplant. For magical rites, henbane must be harvested at dawn, and according to master magician Scott Cunningham, be gathered while standing naked on one foot. This is one reason why the magical garden should be well hidden. Henbane is extremely poisonous. That's another reason it should be well hidden. Henbane is a notable poison, especially in literature. Do you remember *Hamlet?* "Sleeping within my orchard/My custom always of the afternoon,/Upon my secure hour thy uncle stole,/With juice of cursed hebenon [henbane] in a vial,/And in the porches of my ears did pour,/The leprous distilment; whose effect/Holds such an enmity with blood of man." *Hamlet*, Act I, Scene v.

Magic: They say the dead in Hades are crowned with henbane, which, considering how bad it smells is punishment enough. Despite its rather unsavory reputation, henbane is frequently used to consecrate magical implements (although not by me!) It is strongly associated with sorcery. It is a typical ingredient in the old "flying ointments" of witches. It was also used for general divination and prophecy, and is used to attract the love of women when carried along with cinnamon in a bag. It is said that throwing it on the water may bring rain. But don't drink the water afterward. *Although it is poisonous, henbane may be safely used in a sachet to attract the opposite sex, add bachelor buttons, coriander, elecampane, and periwinkle. Henbane may also be carried as an amulet. Aquarians have a special affinity with it.*

Holly *(Ilex species)* This is the herb of **Yule.**

Horticulture

Description: Evergreen shrub or small tree. The English holly is *Ilex aquifolium,* and is probably the most commonly referred to. Most are bushy evergreens with tough, leathery, toothed leaves and very small flowers. The English holly has very shiny, light-reflecting leaves, the American holly (*Ilex opaca*) less so. Height 45 feet. *Name Lore:* A corruption of "holy tree." The scientific name *Ilex* means evergreen; *aquifolium* means "spiky leaves." *Other Names:* Holy bush, holy tree, hulver bush, tinne, holme, hulm, hulm chase, holme chaste, bat's wing, or Christ's thorn. *Similar and Related Species:* There are three genera and over 300 species of holly, and it is often impossible to know which kind of holly is referred to in the old charms and books. Most magical texts refer to the *Ilex aquifolium.* *Colors:* Bark ashen; leaves dark green, berries bright or dark red; flowers usually white inside, with a pink outside. *Fragrance:* Green. *Bloom Time*: May. Both male and female hollies have flowers, but those on the female will turn to berries if fertilized by a nearby male. (Some varieties self-pollinate.) The flowers on the female tree are somewhat larger. *Origin:* Europe, North Africa, and Western Asia.

Habitat: Oak and beech woods, hedgerows. **Earth** (soil type): Most prefer a well-drained, clayey, moisture-retentive soil. **Water** (moisture needs): Medium. **Fire** (sun/shade requirements): Full sun or partial shade. Some can thrive and even produces fruit in shady conditions. **Air** (climate): US Climate Zones 5–9. Dislikes the drying winds of winter.

Tips and Warnings: For most magical results, plant on Thursday. Prefers a sheltered position. Plant hollies near your home; your house will shelter it, and it in turn provides magical protection. Holly is a slow grower, and resents transplanting. Rabbits devour the lower leaves of the plants during hard winters, so keep them protected. Provide the rabbits alternative food. Despite its preferences, hollies are adaptable plants and can adjust to a wide variety of climates and soils. Most hollies have poisonous berries, although birds can eat them with impunity. In folk medicine, scratching one's feet or legs with a holly branch and then walking barefoot in the snow will prevent fever and chilblains. This doesn't sound likely to me, although I have never tried it. On the other hand I have never had chilblains. Holly wood bowls are healthful, and drinking milk from them will cure a cough. It is unlucky to crush a holly berry with one's foot, to cut down a holly, or to sweep a fireplace with a holly branch (not that anyone would, anyway.)

Magic: "Of all the trees that are in the wood,/The holly bears the crown," says the carol. This is a tree of death, regeneration, protection, animal magic, counter-magic, and luck. In ancient days, tales were told of the Holly King, a giant clothed in shining holly branches. He is a rather ferocious figure, but represents the power of life even in the dark of winter at Yule. The branches of the female holly are lucky for women, and those of male for men. It's not always easy to tell them apart unless berries are present. Only the female has berries. To see one's future husband in a dream, pick nine female holly leaves, tie them in nine knots in a three-cornered kerchief, lay them on a pillow and go to sleep. Utter no words before dawn. Planting holly near a graveyard keeps the devil away. In some places, holly collars were placed around horses' necks to protect them from witches. Holly can be used to empower all magical rites. In some circles, thee stiff, prickly holly is traditionally considered a "man's plant," and twining ivy a "woman's plant."

You may take a sprig of the Yule holly and tie it outside the door to protect the home from lightning. For added effect, plant a whole bush. That not only takes care of the lightning problem, but also black magic, evil beings, and animals being a nuisance. Pliny says that tossing a bit of holly wood in the direction of a recalcitrant or wild animal will cause it to obey you instantly. Pliny obviously never owned a basset hound.

Holly tied to the bedpost will prevent women from turning into witches, always a useful precaution. Holly wreaths may be worn by the groom at a wedding. To protect a baby, soak some holly leaves in water, leave overnight under a full moon, and sprinkle on the newborn. Supposedly holly can predict the weather, too. If the holly bush has few or no berries, expect a pleasant summer. If there are many berries, the weather will be bad.

Some say the cross of Christ was made of holly, that prickles sprang up where he walked during the Passion, and that his blood stained the berries red. Holly makes excellent magic wands and walking sticks, and is protective in both roles. (This is suggested by the sharp edges of the leaves.)

Fairies and elves are quite fond of holly, and take refuge in it. Bringing holly into the home during Yule to consecrate the home will allow the household to interact with fairies safely (for once). In fact, *not* having holly in the home at Yule brings awful luck for the entire family; Yule holly left over will bring good luck for the following year. However, holly should not be brought into the home *before* Christmas Eve and it must be removed on Twelfth Night or in the Celtic tradition by January 31 (Imbolc Eve). Bad luck (or goblins) will strike for each leaf left after that time. *Rites involving holly are most efficacious if performed on Tuesday and in mid-winter (Yuletide) or midsummer, (June 21 or 24) or July 8. Invoke the thunder lords Thor, Taranis, or Tannus; wear dark gray. Holly may be carried as an amulet. Leos and Gemini have a special affinity with it.*

Hollyhock (*Althaea rosa*) This is the herb of **Prosperity**.

Horticulture

Description: Biennial or short-lived but treated as a self-sowing annual with tall, erect, leafy stems and flowers arranged in a spiky cluster. Height 4–6 feet. ***Name Lore:*** *Althaea* comes from the Greek and means "heal." ***Other Names:*** Alcea. ***Similar and Related Species:*** *A. officinalis* (marshmallow). ***Colors:*** Blooms white, yellow, pink, red, or almost black; a huge range of colors. ***Fragrance:*** Subtle. ***Bloom Time:*** July–September. ***Origin:*** China and Central Europe.

Habitat: Along fences. **Earth** (soil type): Moist, fertile, and well-drained. **Water** (moisture needs): High. **Fire** (sun/shade requirements): Sun to part shade. **Air** (climate): US Climate Zones 3–9.

Tips and Warnings: Easy to grow. Hollyhocks are attractive to hummingbirds.

Magic: Hollyhocks are lucky for attracting material wealth and happiness. They also draw fairies to the garden (who may hide under them) and can summon good spirits. Hollyhocks are also often used in amulets to ward off evil influences and sorcery. They help develop psychic abilities. It is magically quite similar to its relative the marshmallow plant, and (as a better garden plant) can be used for the same rites. *Magic with hollyhock is usually performed at Lughnasa or during rites of prosperity. Clothe yourself in green.*

Honeysuckle *(Lonicera species)* This is the herb of **Balance**.

Horticulture

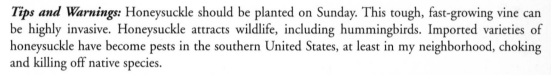

Description: Deciduous or semi-evergreen shrub with yellow or red flowers. There are over 150 species. Height 2–30 feet. *Other Names:* Woodbine, eglantine, goat's leaf. *Colors:* Flowers yellow or crimson; semi-evergreen in milder climates. *Fragrance:* Fruity, strong, sweet. Most smell strongest in the evening. *Bloom Time*: Late–mid- spring.
Origin: Europe and North America.

Habitat: Woods, along fences. **Earth** (soil type): Well-drained, fertile, **Water** (moisture needs): Moderate. **Fire** (sun/shade requirements): Best in full sun, but honeysuckle can tolerate partial shade. **Air** (climate): US Climate Zones 4–9.

Tips and Warnings: Honeysuckle should be planted on Sunday. This tough, fast-growing vine can be highly invasive. Honeysuckle attracts wildlife, including hummingbirds. Imported varieties of honeysuckle have become pests in the southern United States, at least in my neighborhood, choking and killing off native species.

Magic: The honeysuckle provides a nice minor-magic note to so many spells that I call it the herb of balance. While not a player in complex magic, it is such a delight that no garden can afford to be without it. Honeysuckle improves psychic powers, it is said, if you rub the leaves against your forehead. Rubbing your temples with its oil is supposed to help the memory, although it can make one forget a lover. It also brings wealth and improves the temper. It is a plant of general protection, riches, prosperity, and rebirth. *Clothe yourself in brown.*

Horehound *(Marrubium vulgare)* This is an herb of **Spell-breaking**.

Horticulture

Description: Perennial with toothed, wrinkled, oval opposite leaves and square stems. Flowers grow in whirls. *Name Lore:* The name should be spelled "hoarhound," since hoar is an old word denoting a gray color. The "hound" part of the name tells us that the plant was once believed to protect people from the bite of rabid dogs. **Other Names:** White horehound, marrob, eye of the star, hoarhound, seed of Horus, eye of the star, bull's blood, and haran haran. **Similar and Related Species:** There is also a black horehound *(Ballota nigra)*. *Colors*: Leaves blue-green, calyx white. *Fragrance:* Rank, bitter. *Bloom Time:* May–September. *Origin:* Eurasia, North Africa.

Habitat: Waste places. **Earth** (soil type): Dry, sandy. Tolerates poor soil. **Water** (moisture needs): Moderate. **Fire** (sun/shade requirements): Sunny, although the black horehound can tolerate some shade. **Air**: US Climate Zones 4–9.

Tips and Warnings: For best gardening results, plant horehound on Wednesday. Horehound candy can be given to bless guests. Horehound needs lots of room, but if you have the space, it makes a wonderful choice for a moon garden. Plant juice may cause dermatitis.

Magic: This is an herb of protection and vision. Horehound is a notable spell-breaker and hex cracker and banishes evil spirits from the home. *Bind the horehound in a ribbon and hang it. It may also be carried as an amulet. When working with horehound, invoke Saturn, Horus, Isis, or Osiris. Scorpios have a special affinity to horehound.*

Houseleek (*Sempervivum triste*; *Sempervivum tectorum*) This is an herb of **Safety**.

Horticulture

Description: Perennial herb. Spread 3-8 inches. *Other Names:* Devil's beard. *Colors:* Leaves reddish or bluish-green; flowers dull red. *Fragrance:* Subtle. *Bloom Time*: July. *Origin:* Central and southern Europe.

Habitat: Weathered rocks and screes. **Earth** (soil type): Rocky. **Water** (moisture needs): Low. **Fire** (sun/shade requirements): Sun. **Air** (climate): US Climate Zones 5–9.

Tips and Warnings: For best magical results houseleek should be planted on Thursday. Bees are attracted to houseleek.

Magic: Houseleek makes your home a truly safe haven, and especially when it grows on the outside of walls brings general good luck to all the inhabitants. It also protects houses against fire, lightning, and storm, so it's considered good luck to plant one as close to the house as possible. If you're lucky enough to have a thatched roof – well, just plant one into the thatch. If you cut it down – bad luck to the house will follow. Houseleek can also be used in charms to attract a lover. *Sagittarians have especiallly good luck with houseleek. Invoke Jupiter.*

Hyacinth (*Hyacinthus orientalis*) This is the herb of **Relaxation**.

Horticulture

Description: Bulb flower with narrow, basal leaves and showy flowers. Height 5–6 inches. *Colors:* Purple, white, pink, yellow. *Fragrance:* Heavy. *Bloom Time*: Early spring. *Origin:* Mediterranean. *Name Lore:* Hyacinth was a youth loved by both Apollo and Zephyr (the west wind). He preferred Apollo (ho wouldn't?) and was killed by the jealous Zephyr. His blood became the flower, whose petals are supposedly inscribed with the word *AI* meaning "woe."

Habitat: Edges of woods. **Earth** (soil type): Good, rich. **Water** (moisture needs): Moderate. **Fire** (sun/shade requirements): Full or partial sun. **Air** (climate): US Climate Zones 3–6

Tips and Warnings: Hyacinths should be planted in the third quarter of the waning moon. It has most magic if planted in the south of the garden.

Magic: Hyacinth is an herb of peace, love, and relaxation. The scent of the flowers relieves grief. A living hyacinth kept near your bed will provide spiritual protection during sleep, guarding against nightmares. Hyacinth is also reputed to protect against the evil eye. *Hyacinth may also be carried as an amulet. Invoke Apollo. Sagittarians have a special affinity to it.*

Hydrangea *(Hydrangea macrophylla)* This is the herb of **Spinsterhood.**

Horticulture

Description: Deciduous bushy shrub reaching up to 12 feet in height. *Other Names:* Hortensia. *Colors:* Flowers blue in acid soil (if aluminum is available), pink in basic soil. There are also white varieties. *Fragrance:* Soft, with a hint of Gardenia. *Bloom Time*: June–November, depending on the variety. *Origin:* Japan.

Habitat **Earth** (soil type): Damp and rich, well-drained enriched with organics. **Water** (moisture needs): High. **Fire** (sun/shade requirements): Semi-shade or shade to avoid scorching. **Air** (climate): US Climate Zones 6–10. Need some protection (hilling or mulching) in places with very long or hard winters.

Tips and Warnings: Acid soil produces flowers in shades of blue, alkaline (basic) soil yields pink tones. Apply aluminum sulfate for blue or lime for pink every other year to correct the soil. These plants do best if sheltered from the wind, and can be easily grown on the shady sides of buildings or under trees. Prune immediately after blooming. Easy to grow, at least for most people. For some unknown reason, I have never had any luck with them.

Magic: Hydrangea planted near the house (especially the front door) or brought into the home is supposed to doom female occupants to spinsterhood. The powdered bark is considered a very powerful hex breaker.

Hyssop *(Hyssopus officinalis)* This is the Herb of **Purification.**

Horticulture

Description: Deciduous perennial culinary and medicinal shrub. It has square, many-branched stems and opposite leaves. It attains a height of 1–2 feet. *Other Names:* Ysopo, holy herb. *Similar and related species:* This may not be the "hyssop" mentioned in the Bible. It probably isn't; the plant called hyssop in most translations of the Bible may in fact be marjoram. Here's another problem the Middle East plant we call hyssop *(Origanum syriacum)* is not related to the *Hyssopus officinalis*, which is native to Europe, and with which we are presently concerned. *Colors:* Bright blue or purple flower with violet stamens. There are also red and white cultivars. *Fragrance:* Pleasantly but subtly aromatic, with medicinal-smelling leaves. *Bloom Time*: July–October. *Origin:* Italy, now naturalized everywhere.

Habitat: Dry banks, old walls. **Earth** (soil type): Well-drained. **Water** (moisture needs): Low. Hyssop is drought resistant. **Fire** (sun/shade requirements): Full sun preferred but can tolerate partial sun. **Air**(climate):US Climate Zones 6–9.

Tips and Warnings: Easy to grow. Hyssop was an important feature in the medieval herb garden. Hyssop should be harvested during the full moon of Cancer. It is quite attractive to bees, butterflies, and hummingbirds, and it is not so invasive as mint. Pesky insects don't seem to like hyssop much, so it can be planted among vegetables to help foil them. It can be used to flavor salads, although it is slightly bitter. It can also be made into a tea, and is also used to flavor Chartreuse. When left in a drawer it gives clothes and linen a fresh scent. Beekeepers once rubbed hyssop leaves on hives to calm the bees. So they say.

Magic: "Purge me with hyssop, and I shall be clean..." Psalm 51. Hyssop was sacred to both the ancient Israelites and Greeks, and for the same reason: it purifies. If hung at doors and windows, it also protects the home, especially against burglars. It protects against all negative influences. The oil is supposed to increase finances. Fairies are also very fond of hyssop. Hyssop can be used during Yule and at rites of counter-magic, protection, consecration, and purification. *It may be used to consecrate magical implements. It can be burned as incense or worn as an amulet. Those born under the sign of Cancer have a special affinity for hyssop.*

Iris *(Iris species, especially I. florentina)* This is the herb of **Spring.**

Horticulture

Description: Perennial herb with a thickened rhizome and sword-shaped leaves. There are over 500 species of iris. Most magical purposes require orris root from *I. florentina.* **Name Lore:** The iris was named after the goddess Iris, the Lady of the Rainbow. *Other Names:* Flag, flag lily, poison flag, water flag, fleur-de-lis, Florentine iris, iris root, love root, Queen Elizabeth root, and liver lily. *Similar and Related Species:* Common irises include the bearded iris (many different species), the Japanese iris (*I. ensata*), and the Siberian iris (*I. sibirica*). *Colors:* Like the rainbow, irises come in many colors, most commonly yellow and purple. *Iris florentina* is blue and white. Leaves grayish-green. *Fragrance:* Semi-sweet. There is definitely something magical about the fragrances of the iris. Purple irises have a definite purple smell, and I don't know how else to explain it. The root of *I. florentina* orris is fragrant. *Bloom Time*: May–June for most cultivars. *Origin:* Originally, the Mediterranean, but now all over the world in temperate regions.

Habitat: Waste places. **Earth** (soil type): Moist, rich, acid (especially for Japanese irises). **Water** (moisture needs): From arid to dry, depending on species. **Fire** (sun/shade requirements): Full sun, although in hot climates some shade is a good idea. **Air** (climate): US Climate Zones 3–8, depending on species.

Tips and Warnings: Irises should be planted during the third quarter of the moon. Each cultivar of iris has a short blooming season, but if you plant several varieties, you can extend the blooming season for weeks. Iris is attractive to birds (including hummingbirds) and bumblebees. The iris is an excellent plant for the **Earth** Garden. Although generally safe, orris roots, consumed in large quantities, can cause breathing problems and inflammation of the bowel. It is not legal to sell pure orris root in the United States. The splendid iris will bloom from early to late spring, if you are wise in your choice of cultivars.

Magic: One story says that the iris saved the life of Clovis, the leader of the Franks. He was trying to escape across a river and noted the flowers growing in the shallow water. He correctly figured it was safe to cross at that point. He took his coat of arms from the iris, believing that one petal represented faith, another courage, and the third wisdom. (The iris is the inspiration for the *Fleur de Lys*.) The actual name *Fleur de Lys* means "flower of Louis," referring to Louis VII, who copied Clovis's. He adopted the iris as a symbol of victory; Charles IV later used it on the national banner. The Egyptians also had a nationalistic interpretation of the iris using one to adorn the royal scepter (and the Sphinx's forehead).

As the flower of the rainbow, the iris reminds us just how important those spring showers are, for they produce the glorious scented palette of spring. It is an herb of protection, purification, knowledge, baby blessings, and death rites. If it seems odd that the same plant serves to honor babies and the deceased, we should remember that the rainbow has one foot in heaven, and one on earth. Indeed, the goddess Iris often served as messenger for the other gods. For this reason, the ancient Greeks put iris on the graves of young women, so that the goddess might lead them into the Otherworld. (Iris is famous as "margin" plant, partly on water, partly on land.) *The root of I. florentina or orris, is carried to promote love or used in love potions. Invoke Iris, Juno, or the Virgin Mary. Iris may also be used as incense. Aquarians have a special affinity to iris.*

Ivy (*Hedera helix*) This is an herb of **Ecstasy**.

Horticulture

Description: Evergreen woody climber. Other Names: Gort. ***Colors:*** Green. ***Fragrance:*** Subtle. ***Bloom Time***: September–frost. ***Origin:*** Europe and Asia.

Habitat: Woods, hedges, walls. **Earth** (soil type): Ordinary garden soil. **Water** (moisture needs): Moderate. **Fire** (sun/shade requirements): Variable. Some types like sun, others shade. **Air** (climate): US Climate Zones 3–8.

Tips and Warnings: In the garden, ivy adds a cooling note, and since it is said to inspire deep thoughts, is an excellent choice for a mediation garden. It was formerly believed that a garland of ivy, bound about the head with a light-blue thread would relieve headaches. All parts of the plant are poisonous.

Magic: Cooperation, humility, fertility, love, sexual enjoyment, faithfulness are the attributes of ivy. Many people have tried to tame the ivy, and there is a long tradition of its being a gentle, feminine herb, a symbol of devotion. Some claim its humble gracefulness is a complement to the more masculine holly. But there is another tradition, equally old, equally strong which identified ivy as a wild and exultant herb that crowned the fiercely beautiful head of Dionysus. (Ultimately, this gave ivy a rather demonic reputation in the Christian church and its use was forbidden.) As an evergreen, it has overtones of immortality. If ivy planted on a grave will not grow, the deceased is unhappy in the Other World. But if it flourishes on a young woman's grave, it means that her death was caused by unrequited love. Sometimes you just can't win. Others suggest that ivy planted on graves represents a love that endures beyond death.

The connection of ivy and love is undoubtedly inspired by the "clinging" nature of ivy. If a maiden places an ivy leaf against her heart and recites: "Ivy, ivy, I love you/In my bosom I place you/The first young man who speaks to me/My future husband he will be," it will happen as spoken. Some believe bringing an ivy plant into the house is bad luck. Ivy can be used at all rites of love, sexuality, and feasting. *Invoke Attis, Dionysus, Thalia, Osiris, or Bacchus. The most propitious date is September 30. Wear blue. Ivy may be carried as an amulet. Scorpios have a special affinity to ivy.*

Jasmine *(Jasminum officinale)* This is the herb of the **Moon**.

Horticulture

Description: Deciduous or semi-evergreen vine with small flowers. Sprawling plant, can reach 40 feet if given support. *Other Names:* Tore, sambac, chameli. *Colors:* Blossoms white. Some varieties tinged with pink. *Fragrance:* Heavy, semi-sweet, to some overpowering. Possibly the most richly scented of all flowers. *Bloom Time:* Midsummer–early fall. *Origin:* Persia.

Habitat: Open areas. **Earth** (soil type): Moist, humus-rich. **Water** (moisture needs): High. **Fire** (sun/shade requirements): Full sun. **Air** (climate): US Zones 7–10. Jasmines enjoy humidity.

Tips and Warnings: Try placing your jasmine in a container that you can bring inside when it gets too cold. It has most magic if placed in the south of the garden. Another advantage of containers is that you can move the plant about to be as close to or far from as you wish. Keep pruning for continued bloom and scent. The berries are poisonous.

Magic: Jasmine is an herb of love, especially spiritual love, although at the same time, jasmine is reported to be a powerful aphrodisiac and to attract money and other material objects. "The Isis of flowers." (Dickens). It brings on prophetic dreams and helps people develop new ideas. It is associated with happiness and prosperity, but to dream *about* jasmine means a transitory success. Jasmine is connected to the moon, night, and sleep. It is helpful for relaxation and meditation. To increase the power of jasmine, store with quartz. Jasmine ointment may be used in handfasting rites to symbolize permanent love. *It is also burned during Ostara. Rites with jasmine are most effective at night when Mercury is visible. Jasmine may also be carried as an amulet. Invoke Diana, Aphrodite, or Vishnu. Those born under the sign of Cancer have the best luck in working with jasmine.*

Juniper *(Juniperus communis)* This herb is **Proof against Witches**.

Horticulture

Description: Evergreen tree (rare) or sprawling shrub with tangled branches, and needle or scale-like leaves. Height 6–20 feet. *Other Names:* Genevrier. *Colors:* Bark and twigs reddish brown. Needles sea green. Females flowers greenish; male flowers yellowish. Cones red or blue. *Fragrance:* Resinous, mild, most noticeable on warm days. *Bloom Time:* May–June. *Origin:* Found widely in temperate climates around the world.

Habitat: Edges of woods. **Earth** (soil type): Lime-rich. Tolerant, can handle dry soil and drought. **Water** (moisture needs): Moderate. **Fire** (sun/shade requirements): Full sun to light shade.

Air (climate): US Climate Zones 3–8.

Tips and Warnings: Juniper should be planted on Sunday during the second quarter of the moon. Creeping juniper attracts many kinds of small wildlife.

Magic: This is an herb of love and counter-magic, important in both ancient European and Native American religious rites. Its most specific use was as a witch-preventative. Plant a juniper outside your door; any witch trying to get in will be forced to count the needles first and so be stymied. It also banishes evil spirits and breaks curses. It was said that one who cuts down a juniper tree would die within the year. Carry a juniper amulet to avert accidents. Juniper increases psychic powers and attracts love. At one time, it was believed that eating juniper berries was believed to protect against plague, and to prevent and cure snakebite. Burning juniper would make sure the fairies did not come and snatch away a child. Men chewing upon the berries are supposed to become more potent. Some believe that wearing a sprig of juniper keeps one safe from accidents. Juniper is attractive to fairies, except when you burn it; that keeps them away. *Juniper may be used at consecrations, exorcisms, protection and purifications rites. It is most effectively used by Arians.*

Lamb's Ears See Betony.

Larkspur or Delphinium *(Delphinium species)* This is the herb of **Leadership.**

Horticulture

Description: Annual or biennial herb, with an erect, leafy stem and showy blooms borne on a terminal spike. Several species exist; the usual garden species are *D. ajacis* and *D. consolida*. Although magic texts generally refer to larkspur, it is most often the delphinium hybrids, developed from *D. elata*, that are grown in gardens. Height 3–4 feet. *Name Lore:* The word delphinium derives from the Greek word for dolphins, under the notion that the flowers resemble the heads of dolphins. This requires some imagination, which the Greeks had, probably accounting for much of their success.
Other Names: Forking larkspur, field larkspur, stavesacre, lousewort. *Colors:* Flowers blue, or blue/violet. Some varieties can be white, purple, or bi-colored. *Fragrance:* Subtle. *Bloom Time*: June–July for most cultivars. *Origin:* Mediterranean region.

Habitat **Earth** (soil type): Needs a deep, nutrient-rich, well-composted soil. Slightly alkaline preferred. **Water** (moisture needs): Cannot handle drought, but doesn't want to stand around in water either. **Fire** (sun/shade requirements): Full sun. **Air** (climate): Flourishes in US Climate Zones 3–8. Prefers cool moist areas. This plant is subject to wind damage.

Tips and Warnings: Plant in a sheltered location. This handsome architectural plant must be planted against a wall or staked and given plenty of growing room. Altogether a rather difficult plant (but worth it). It is not long-lived, and many gardeners don't even bother with trying to nurse them through the winter. While it is growing, keep trimming out the weak growth. All parts of the plant except the flower are toxic, especially to cattle. This is a beautiful plant to grow near roses.

Magic: This is really a plant of minor magic, but it is so beautiful we shouldn't neglect to include it in our garden. Its main attribute is that is inspires leaders to altruistic and generous actions. *There is also a wonderful bit of folklore attached to the plant. On Midsummer Eve take a bunch of larkspur and gaze through it while looking at the Midsummer's fire. It will prevent blindness and eye disease for a year. Repeat every year for full effect. Invoke Ajax.*

LAVENDER (*Lavandula angustifolia* and others) This is the herb of **Refreshment**.

Horticulture

Description: Small, perennial evergreen "subshrub" (a word I love), with a branched, woody stem. Height 20–30 inches. ***Name Lore:*** The word *lavender* comes from the Latin word meaning "to wash." ***Other Names:*** Elf leaf, English lavender, asarum, nard, spike. ***Colors:*** Flowers are lavender, bluish, or mauve; leaves are first whitish, then turn gray-green. ***Fragrance:*** All parts of the plant are aromatic, with a fresh, bittersweet, clean scent. Flowers and foliage have the same scent, but the flower fragrance is much the stronger. ***Bloom Time***: June–August. ***Origin:*** Western Mediterranean or possibly India.

Habitat: **Earth** (soil type): Soil should be well-drained, but lavender thrives even in poor soil. It can handle dry, alkaline, chalky, or sandy soil very easily. **Water** (moisture needs): Low. Drought tolerant, but can also handle a lot of moisture. **Fire** (sun/shade requirements): Full sun or part shade. **Air** (climate): US Climate Zones 5–9 for most varieties. Some are more resistant to cold than others.

Tips and Warnings: For best magical results, plant lavender on Wednesday, during the first quarter of the moon. Lavender is an undemanding plant, and there is a variety for almost every garden and use; it was an important feature in every medieval herb garden, and is a perfect choice for a moon garden. Don't water until the tips of the top branch begin to droop. If the tips are brown, the plants are too wet. Can be cut back hard after flowering. The flowers attract butterflies and bees. Lavender retains its fragrance after drying. Leaving lavender in a drawer or hanging it upside down in closets repels moths. Perfume is also made from its flowers. The Romans (and everyone since) made a strong, clean-smelling soap from it. A lavender herbal bath evokes peacefulness. Save some lavender to throw on the fire on a winter's night to remind you of summer. Externally it is used as a skin freshener.

Magic: Lavender brings calmness, peace, healing (especially from depression), happiness, and joy. Lavender's most important magical use is to help control anger, especially in an abusive relationship. It brings refreshment on both a physical, mental, and emotional level.

It also helps psychic awareness. It said that smelling lavender gives the ability to see ghosts. Place some under your pillow, wish hard, and dream. If the dream concerns your wish, the wish will come true (even if the dream indicates otherwise). It also protects against the evil eye. The smell is supposed to attract the opposite sex, and is often used in cachets for that effect. But it is also known as the herb of chastity, since chastity and cleanliness have traditional associations. It's best carried as an amulet with rosemary for this purpose. Lavender draws fairies and elves, hence the name "elf leaf."

It can be burned at Litha (Midsummer). It can also be used in a bath before almost any magical rite: healing, fertility, protection (especially against abuse in a relationship), success, and purification rituals; handfastings (use in a bridal crown); and love magic (use the oil to anoint love-candles). May be brought into a room to honor a new baby and keep it safe. *Rites involving lavender are most effective if performed on Wednesday; an East Wind is most auspicious. Beltaine is also auspicious. Those born under the sign of Virgo or Leo are best able to work magic with lavender.*

Lemon Balm *(Melissa officinalis)* This is the herb of **Compassion**.

Horticulture

Description: Perennial herb with opposite leaves, inconspicuous flowers and oval leaves. This was favorite herb of the ancient Greeks. Height 12–18 inches. ***Other Names:*** Bee plant, balm, bee balm, honey plant, garden balm, sweet-mary, balm Melissa, sweet balm, pimentary, goose tongue. ***Name Lore:*** The Greek word *Melissa* means "bee." ***Similar and Related Species:*** Here is another case where the common names can be deceiving. The true bee balm is monarda, also called bergamot. See Bergamot. ***Colors:*** Flowers whitish. ***Fragrance:*** Leaves strongly lemon-scented. ***Bloom Time***: May–September. ***Origin:*** Mediterranean.

Habitat: Mountainsides, barnyards, old house sites, open woods. **Earth** (soil type): Prefers a moist, sandy, alkaline soil. **Water** (moisture needs): Moderate. **Fire** (sun/shade requirements): Likes full sun, but is fine with dappled or part shade. **Air** (climate) US Climate Zones 4–9.

Tips and Warnings: This deeply rooted plant will help to break up a heavy, clayey soil. One old story says that lemon balm should be picked only when someone is playing music to distract the snakes that constantly guard it. This plant is attractive to hummingbirds. Balm can be added to soup and stews, fish, lamb, and dressing. It makes a good tea and when added to wine, it is supposed to drive away sadness.

Magic: Lemon Balm is an herb of compassion, healing, and justice (which is sometimes compassionate and sometimes not). It also serves in love charms. It is said that if the leaves are rubbed on beehives, it will keep the bees together. The same is said about some other herbs. (Although not a beekeeper myself, I wouldn't advise anyone to go about rubbing leaves of any sort on beehives.) Lemon balm may draw fairies as well as bees. If you put the entire plant into a piece of linen with a silk thread, and wear it under your clothes you'll be happy and have your wishes fulfilled. Discorides claimed that it healed wounds, and Pliny went a step further (as is his wont), saying that simply tying a sprig of the stuff to a sword would staunch the blood of whomever the sword pierced. This seems at cross-purposes. The purpose of a sword is not to staunch wounds. Perhaps, however, that is why it is truly the herb of compassion. *When doing magic with lemon balm, invoke Diana. Those born under the sign of Cancer have particular luck with lemon balm.*

Lenten Rose *(Helleborus orientalis)* This is the herb of **Mental Clarity**.
See also Black Hellebore, Hellebore.

Horticulture

Description: Perennial, self-seeder with evergreen foliage and large blooms. All parts of the plant are poisonous. *Similar and Species:* Black hellebore *(Helleborus niger)*, green hellebore *(H. viridis)*. White hellebore or false helleborine *(Veratrum album* and its variants) is really a member of the lily family. *Colors:* The *H. orientalis,* or Lenten rose has pink, cream or dusty rose flowers *Fragrance:* Subtle. *Bloom Time*: February–March. *Origin:* Southern and central Europe

Habitat: Woodlands. **Earth** (soil type): Calcareous, moist, rich, moisture retentive. **Water** (moisture needs): High. **Fire** (sun/shade requirements): Prefers shade, but can handle partial sun. **Air** (climate): US Climate Zones 4–8.

Tips and Warnings: The Lenten rose is easier to grow than *H. niger.* (It is sometimes unclear from old texts as to which variety of hellebore was efficacious for magical purposes.) This plant like all the hellebores is highly poisonous.

Magic: The Lenten Rose is believed to increase mental powers and cure insanity, rather the opposite magical signature from black hellebore. Hellebores generally are supposed to confer invisibility if the magic-worker walks upon the powdered plant. If the plant was dried and burned, it would banish ghosts and possessed creatures. The Lenten rose was grown to remind monks of the purity of Jesus. It was also used for astral projections.

Lilac *(Syringa* species) This is the herb of **Recollection of Past Lives**.

Horticulture

Description: Deciduous shrubs and small trees. **Height** 8–15 feet. *Name Lore:* The word "lilac" comes from the Arabic *laylak*, meaning "blue." *Other Names:* Nila, syringia. *Colors:* Usually purple, but blue, white, and even yellow cultivars exist. Leaves mid-green. *Fragrance:* Heavy but gentle, cloying to some, heavenly to others. Not all species are fragrant. *Bloom Time*: May. *Origin:* Middle East.

Habitat: Open places. **Earth** (soil type): Well-drained, enriched with well-composted manure. **Water** (moisture needs): Moderate. **Fire** (sun/shade requirements): Open sunlight. **Air** (climate): US Climate Zones 3–8. Prefers an airy location.

Tips and Warnings: The lilac is a very long-lived plant – and will outlive you. A yearly top dressing of manure is valuable.

Magic: Lilac and oil of lilac symbolize the beauty of the soul. They represent forgiveness and prestore peace and harmony. Lilac is an herb of love and can be used an an amulet to banish evil spirits. Oil can also be used to recall past lives and increase pyshcic powers. Burning lilac wood gives the same scent as the flowers. Lilac draws fairies.

Lily (*Lilium species*) This is the herb of **Purity of Heart**.

Horticulture

Description: This is a very large family of plants indeed; there are over 4000 different species, usually with bulbs or tubers. Most are perennial. Flower types include the familiar trumpet, but also upward-facing and downward-turning flowers. Height 3–7 feet. **Colors:** One Christian legend states that lilies were first yellow, but turned white at the touch of the Virgin Mary. The Oriental, or Asiatic, lily (one of several known as the Easter Lily) comes in many colors, including white. No lily is pure blue. **Fragrance:** The Asiatic hybrids are very fragrant. Interestingly, the scent of the lily cannot be extracted as an essential oil, unlike the scent of most flowers, adding to its mystique. **Bloom Time**: June–July or July–August, depending upon the variety. **Origin:** Asia.

Habitat: Fields. **Earth** (soil type): Humus rich, average, well-drained. **Water** (moisture needs): Moderate. **Fire** (sun/shade requirements): Prefers full sun, but can tolerate light shade. **Air** (climate): US Climate Zones 3–8. Needs a cold dormant period.

Tips and Warnings: Easy to grow and makes a nice match with azaleas. The so-called Madonna lily (*L. candidium*) looks lovely with delphiniums. For the best new varieties, check with the North American Lily Society and the Royal Horticultural Society Lily Group.

Magic: "Who can describe the exceeding whiteness of the lily?" murmured Walafrid Strabo, some time in the ninth century. From ancient times, the lily was a favorite choice in the decorative arts, all around the Mediterranean. In magic, the lily is supposed to drive away snakes. The lily may (or may not) be the flower Jesus referred to as "the lily of the field" in Matthew 6:28.

One myth states that the lily was born from drops of Hera's (the goddess in charge of marriage and childbirth) milk. Apparently, Hera's rival, the sensual Aphrodite, hated the pure look of the flower, and so added its pistil, which according to the story resembles a donkey's penis. (I have no idea, really.) Another legend says that the lily sprang from Eve's tears when she found she was going to become a mother. Lilies can be used as an amulet to break evil love spells. Because it also symbolizes resurrection, the lily can be used in death rites as well as at Ostara (Easter for Christians). *Rites with lily are most effective when the moon is visible. Clothe yourself in white. Those born under the sign of Scorpio and Pisces have a special affinity. Invoke Hera or Juno.*

Linden, or Lime (*Tilia* species) This is a tree of **Soothsaying**.

Horticulture

Description: Tall deciduous tree with small flowers and dense foliage. About 60 species. Height 50–90 feet. **Other Names:** Spoonwood and wycopy. The American Linden (*T. Americana*) is also called the basswood. ***Similar and Related Species:*** In Britain, most *Tilia* species are known as "lime trees," although there is no connection between the linden and the citrus tree (*Citrus aurantifolia*) except the scent. ***Colors:*** Flowers creamy white (European) or greenish-yellow (American). ***Fragrance:*** Many varieties sweetly scented, especially the European linden. Scent is heavy, with a slight spicy tang. ***Bloom Time:*** June. ***Origin:*** Europe, North America.

Habitat: Deciduous woods or woodland margins. **Earth** (soil type): Average. **Water** (moisture needs): Moderate. **Fire** (sun/shade requirements): Full sun to light shade. **Air** (climate): US Climate Zones 3–9.

Tips and Warnings: These trees make excellent specimens for urban areas, as they can withstand pollution. The blossoms are reputed to produce an especially delicious honey, and can also make a tea.

Magic: This is a traditional tree of judgment and soothsaying. The soothsayer would twine the leaves around her fingers, and allow the tree to "talk" to her. Consequently, in days of old a linden tree was placed at the center of town, and used as a meeting place for town authorities; the tree came to represent the whole community. Even today, they say, mysterious white ladies with crowns of gentian and edelweiss may frequent a grove of linden trees. These are the fairy "white ladies" and must be treated with respect. This is a tree of general good luck and encouragement; the bark is used for protection, while the flowers and leaves are used for rites of immortality. Linden twigs protect against the evil eye. The mystic nun Hildegard of Bingen (1098–1179) believed that covering the eyes with linden leaves would induce sleep. *When performing magic with Linden, invoke Freya, to whom the tree is sacred. Taurians have a special affinity to linden magic.*

Lotus (*Nelumbo* species) This is the herb of **Spiritual Truth**.

Horticulture

Description: The beautiful leaves of the true lotus are round (as opposed to the notched leaf of the water lily) and flowers are held well above the water, rather than resting on it. The lotus has been called the "eternal flower." The leaves of this plant can exceed two feet, so it is suitable only for a largish body of water. However, there is a dwarf variety more appropriate for a small pond. ***Colors:*** Flowers blue, white, and red. The last color was considered the most sacred by the ancient Egyptians, although they generally disliked red. ***Fragrance:*** Fragrant. ***Bloom Time:*** Each bloom lasts for about three days. In Beijing, it used to be said that the lotus bloomed on eighth day of the fourth month, the birthday of the Buddha. ***Origin:*** Southern Mediterranean, Asia.

Habitat: Quiet waters. **Earth** (soil type): Good mud on the bottom. **Water** (moisture needs): High. **Fire** (sun/shade requirements): Prefers full sun. **Air** (climate): Tropical but can be over-wintered with care.

Tips and Warnings: The roots and seeds of the lotus can be eaten. Homer and Tennyson even wrote about a land of Lotus-eaters, whose dietary habits made them dreamy and intoxicated. The rhizomes of lotus should be dug up in the autumn and stored in their original soil, covered with 2–8 inches of water. They should be kept cool (41°–50°F, 5°–10°C) and not allowed to freeze.

Magic: In Asia, the lotus has much the same power as the rose in Europe. The sacred lotus is the symbol of the Buddha, as well as of many Hindu gods and goddesses, primarily Brahma and Lakshmi.

(The goddess of the Lotus was Padma, also the name of the flower in Sanskrit.) The Buddha or a Hindu deity is often depicting as sitting or lying upon the lotus. The Buddha himself is described as having "lotus eyes, lotus feet, and lotus thighs." Perhaps because of this, oil of lotus is considered an ideal meditation aid.

In Hindu thought, the pink blossom represents the *yoni*, or female sexual organ. In Chinese Buddhism, while all lotuses represent spirituality, the blue lotus is particularly associated with cleanliness and modesty, as well as the Buddhist concept of *sunyata* or emptiness. The lotus also represents summer in Chinese culture, and its seeds represent fertility. In China, the day of the lotus is the eighth day of the first month – if a woman sews on this day, it is said she will have menstrual problems.

The lotus was also sacred to the ancient Egyptians. The lotus, in fact, is said to have originated from the primordial ooze, it therefore symbolizes life and creation. The Mayans too venerated a variety of lotus. Because of its spiritual powers, lotus can be used as an antidote to love spells. Lotus oil brings healing, blessing, luck and happiness. Wearing lotus oil is associated with luck and happiness.

Because the lotus is sacred to so many cultures, it is considered a particularly appropriate offering to many deities. The Egyptian god Horus is frequently depicted as sitting upon the lotus, while Osiris wore a lotus headdress when he rose from the dead. The blue lotus was associated with Nefertum, the god of Memphis, who was known as "the lord of sweet fragrances." It also signified fertility. In Tibetan Buddhist thought, the lotus is associated with purity. And the famous Tibetan prayer is couched in lotus symbolism: *Om mani padme hum* – "All hail to the jewel in the lotus." The blossom symbolizes the compassion of the Bodhisattva. Because the lotus opens at sunrise and closes at sundown, it is closely associated with the power of the sun. The lotus also symbolizes the growth of the spirit from the mud of the earth, through the water, until it reaches the spiritual air, when it opens and reveals its fire. It is the symbol of non-attachment to material things, *Avalokiteshvara*. The lotus may be used in rites of consecration, fertility (blue lotus), protection, purification, and death rites After all, the mummy of Ramses II was found with a necklace of lotus petals. *Clothe yourself in white and yellow. Invoke the names of Brahma, Hermes, Horus, Isis, Lakshmi, Mithra, Osiris, or Vishnu.*

Lovage (*Levisticum officinalis*) This is an herb of **Legal Victory**.

Horticulture

Description: Perennial herb with a hollow, branched stem. It can grow very large. *Other Names:* Love root, sea parsley, love stem, nine-stem, love parsley, loving herbs, lavose. *Colors:* Flowers greenish-yellow. *Fragrance:* Rich. *Bloom Time*: July–August. *Origin:* Mediterranean region but naturalized throughout Europe.

Habitat: Meadows and grassy places. **Earth** (soil type): Fertile moist, well-drained. **Water** (moisture needs): Moderate. **Fire** (sun/shade requirements): Prefers full sun, but will tolerate partial shade. **Air** (climate): US Climate Zones 5–8.

Tips and Warnings: Lovage should be planted on Sunday. Lovage, whose height makes it an excellent choice for a focal point in a small-herb bed, is most suitable for informal gardens. A cordial by the same name was made from it. Lovage was also be used in salads and to flavor soups. At one time it was used as bath cologne. Culpeper insisted it removed freckles. The hollow stems can be used as straws.

Magic: Bathing in lovage root is supposed to help assure victory in court cases, attract lovers, and provide psychic protection and cleansing. It is also considered an aphrodisiac, possibly because of its English name, which, however, is probably derived from Liguria, where the herb is common. *Clothe yourself in orange. Taurians have a special affinity to lovage.*

Lupin, or Lupine   (*Lupinus* species) This is the herb **Wolf Magic.**

Horticulture

Description: The lupine is a leguminous plant; some varieties are annuals, some perennials, and some are actually small evergreen shrubs. All varieties have palmately compound leaves, meaning that the leaves resemble outspread fingers, and flowers borne on spikes. In some varieties, the leaves are covered with white hairs. The leaves (not the flower) follow the sun's path from morning to evening, and fold up at night. Hybrid lupins are large and showy plants frequently grown in gardens. Height 8–48 inches. *Name Lore:* The word "lupine" derives from the Latin word for wolf, and there was a false report that the lupine ravaged the soil as a wolf does its prey. Just the opposite is true. *Other Names:* Wild lupine, sundial plant, bluebonnet. *Colors:* All colors, including cream, white, yellow, and bicolors. Blue predominates, however. *Fragrance:* Subtle. *Bloom Time*: May-June. *Origin:* Europe; Mediterranean; North America.

Habitat: Dry clearings, open woodland. **Earth** (soil type): Deep, sandy, acid, rich, well-drained. **Water** (moisture needs): Low–moderate, but can handle a wide variety. Meadow lupine (*L. polyphyllus*) needs a moister soil than others. **Fire** (sun/shade requirements): Full sun for most species. Some can handle partial shade. **Air** (climate): US Climate Zones 3–8 for most. Likes cool, damp areas, and dislike the hot summer winds; best in areas with cool summers.

Tips and Warnings: Easy to grow, but difficult to transplant because of the long taproot. This important plant (like most members of the pea family) fixes nitrogen in the soil. Lupine seeds can be sown directly into the ground during the fall. Mulch to keep roots cool, and do not add lime or manure to this plant. Some, especially hybrid lupins, need to be staked. If you choose various species judiciously, you'll have color all season long. Lupine is attractive to hummingbirds, bumblebees, and many butterflies.

Magic: Lupine is an excellent herb for all magic involving wolves and the spirit of the wild. Seers of the ancient oracle of Epiros ate the bitter lupine peas to help them communicate with the dead and in all celebrations of the imagination. However, in an opposing tradition, the lupine stands for voraciousness (note the resemblance to *lupus* or "wolf" hidden in the name).

Male Fern   (*Dryoperis filix-mas*) This herb is the **Rainbringer.**

Horticulture

Description: Large, herbaceous perennial fern, with narrow, fringed leaves. Height 2–4 feet. *Name Lore:* There is no such thing as male versus a female fern, but this herb was given that name because of its upright, tough appearance, as opposed to the female, or bracken fern. *Other Names:* Devil's bush, apsidium, bear fern, basket fern, knotty brake, bear's paw root, shield fern, sweet brake. *Colors:* Leaves pale green. Rhizomes are reddish. *Fragrance:* Ferny. *Bloom Time*: Ferns do not flower. *Origin:* All parts of Europe and temperate zones in Asia and North America.

Habitat: Shady woods, on rocks, by streams. **Earth** (soil type): Dry, fertile, rocky slopes. **Water** (moisture needs): High. **Water** lightly but frequently. **Fire** (sun/shade requirements): Shade to part–shade. **Air** (climate): US Climate Zones 3–7.

Tips and Warnings: For magical rites, the roots should be gathered on Midsummer's Eve. The roots can be boiled and eaten as a vegetable, although large amounts may be toxic.

Magic: Male fern and bracken fern share most magical affinities, the two most marked being invisibility and the power to bring rain, with perhaps the bracken fern a bit more famous for the former and the male fern for the latter. This is a general good luck plant guaranteed to attract both women and wealth. According to Russian folklore, anyone who catches a fern blooming on Midsummer's Eve and throws it into the air will find treasure where it lands. Since ferns don't bloom, this is a pretty safe prediction. The Syrian Christians used to say that gathering fern spores on Christmas night will make the devil give up his money. If burned outdoors, it will bring rain, and if dried over the Midsummer's Eve fire, it will serve as a protective amulet. Its spores could render the wearer invisible. Since the spores are practically invisible themselves, there seems to be a connection here. It is also said that the spores can be put into a love philter or tea to attract love. The plant was traditionally dug up and all but five coiled fronds removed, so that the root resembled a human hand, the coiled fiddleheads being the fingers. This was then smoked in the midsummer bonfire, and the preserved charm hung as protection.

Mandrake *(Mandragora officinarum)* This is the herb of **Fertility**.

Horticulture

Description: A Mediterranean herb of the nightshade family, with ovately pointed leaves and bell-shaped flowers. The root may be forked and famously was said to resemble a person. *Name Lore:* The mandrake is also referred to as mandragora, reflecting the ancient belief that mandrakes were inhabited by "man-dragons." *Other Names:* Satan's apple, alraun, brain thief, gallows, devil's apples, baaras, duck's foot, ground lemon, warlock weed, devil's candle (on account of the lurid glow the leaves were said emit by night). *Similar and Related Species:* In the United States, the May Apple *(Podophyllum peltatum)* is also referred to as a mandrake, although it is an entirely different plant. *Colors:* Purple or whitish flowers. Orange/yellow fruit. *Fragrance:* Mature leaves have an unpleasant smell. Fruit has a mild, apple-like smell. *Bloom Time*: Spring. *Origin:* Eurasia.

Habitat: Waste areas. **Earth** (soil type): Ordinary. **Water** (moisture needs): Moderate. **Fire** (sun/shade requirements): Shade. **Air** (climate): US Climate Zones 4–7.

Tips and Warnings: Harvest only when the moon is full. For best results it has to be gathered beneath a gallows and in the company of a black dog. (In fact, some legends say the plant develops from the sperm of a hanged man. Only the person who wants to use it should uproot it. If that's you, stuff your ears with cotton. Legend says that the roots scream when being pulled from the earth. Supposedly you need the help of black dogs to pull out the root, who, unfortunately will be either (a) poisoned by the scent or (2) die from the noise of the screaming plant. The plants are supposed to sweat blood, too. The plant does contain poisonous tropane alkaloids with narcotic or hallucinogenic properties. The root and fruit are both poisonous. According to James Duke, "The fruit, eaten in quantity, produces dizziness and may cause insanity."

Magic: Although the forked mandrake root is preeminently and famously an herb of fertility, its other powers are legion. It is also an herb of love spells, demon banishment, home protection, exorcisms, purifications, curses, divinations, and prosperity. Genesis tells of its use by Leah and Rachel in their attempts to become pregnant. It is said to attract money and lead its possessors to treasure. Any money left near it will double overnight, at least metaphorically. For magical use, some say the mandrake root should be soaked in white wine on Saturday and kept wrapped in red silk, and no one but the harvester-owner should touch or even look at it. A competing theory suggests the dry root must be prominently displayed for three days on the mantel before it is activated. It repels disease and confers invisibility (or at least keeps you from being noticed). Mandrake increases clairvoyance and leads to occult knowledge. It was also used in the traditional witches' flying ointment. In the west, it is supposed to increase passion, but in China (the plant was introduced there by Muslim traders in the Middle Ages) it was reported that a bit of mandrake rubbed on the body of a man would deprive him of all sensation for three days. In some cases a towel was merely soaked in an herbal preparation. For purification purposes, the root should be soaked in water for a lunar cycle, and then sprinkled on the celebrants. *Although formerly used as a drug or potion, mandrake is most safely used as an amulet. When working magic with mandrake, invoke Circe, Diana, Hecate, Hathor, and the Germanic Alrauna Maiden. Clothe yourself in green. Taurians have a special affinity to mandrake.*

Marigold   (*Tagetes* species) This herb is **Proof Against Minor Demons**.

Horticulture

Description: This is the New World marigold, not to be confused with *calendula*, although for magical purposes they may sometimes be switched.
Name Lore: The name *Tagetes* is from *Tagetes*, Jupiter's grandson, a god of the Underworld. ***Other Names:*** French marigold, African marigold. ***Colors:*** Flowers yellow or red and yellow. ***Fragrance:*** Some find the scent distinctly unpleasing, but the so-called signet marigold, or *Tagetes tenuifolia,* has a wonderful lemon-like scent in the foliage. ***Bloom Time***: Summer. ***Origin:*** South America.

Habitat: Open places. **Earth** (soil type): Ordinary. **Water** (moisture needs): Moderate. **Fire** (sun/shade requirements) Full Sun. **Air** (climate) US Climates 4–10. Grown as an annual in the northern zones.

Tips and Warnings: Marigolds are a superior plant in the garden; they kill nematodes in the soil that harm tomatoes and potatoes.

Magic: This plant is not the same as the more magically powerful calendula, but can be used for many of the same purposes. (See also *Calendula*.)

Marijuana See Hemp.

Marjoram (*Origanum marjorana*, or *Marjorana hortensis*) This is the herb of **Joy**.

Horticulture

Description: Annual or biennial culinary mint, with erect, branchy, square, hairy stems, tiny flowers, and thick textured leaves. Height 1–3 feet. ***Other Names:*** Sweet marjoram, amaracus, knotted marjoram, joy of the mountains. ***Similar and related species:*** Wild marjoram or oregano (*Orignanum vulgare*) flowers later than the garden variety and has different magical properties (see Oregano). ***Colors:*** Leaves grayish. Flowers white or purplish. ***Fragrance:*** All parts of the plant have a sweet or bittersweet aroma, especially noticeable in warm weather. Some compare the scent to that of oregano. ***Bloom Time***: June. ***Origin:*** North Africa, Asia. Naturalized throughout the Mediterranean and widely cultivated in North America and Britain.

Habitat: Dry slopes, among rocks, hillsides, and mountains. **Earth** (soil type): Well-drained, somewhat alkaline soil. **Water** (moisture needs): Marjoram can handle drought. **Fire** (sun/shade requirements): Sunny. **Air** (climate): US Climate Zones 5–8

Tips and Warnings: Marjoram was traditionally added to lamb and fish. Can also be added to soups and stews, ideally just before they are served. In former times, marjoram was used as a strewing herb on floors to keep the house sweet and collect the dust. It was all swept out together during housecleaning. Marjoram makes a wonderful container plant. It grows well with bee balm (*Monarda*), oregano, and thyme. Prune frequently to keep this plant sweet. If your soil is acid, sweeten it with lime.

Magic: Marjoram is indeed the most joyful of herbs. It brings joy and happiness to every aspect of life, and has absolutely no downside. The Greeks even sprinkled it on graves to bring contentment and blessing to the dead. Sprinkling it about the home is sure to attract a husband and repel snakes at the same time. The wonderful thing here is that it assures a woman that she won't get a snake for a husband. Rub it on your body, and you dream of a future spouse. It will also improve happiness in marriage. Marjoram is useful in all love charms and is good herb to use at handfastings. It also brings wealth and banishes grief. It aids psychic development. Marjoram is sacred to Aphrodite, or Venus, who was the first to cultivate it. It is also sacred to Shiva and Vishnu. According to Greek myth, a man named Amarakos in service to the king dropped a precious bottle of perfume and broke it. He was so terrified he fell down in a swoon; the gods turned him into marjoram. It is not clear if this was a reward or punishment. *Marjoram may be carried as an amulet. Invoke Aphrodite or Venus.*

Meadowsweet (*Spiraea ulmaria*, syn. *Filipendula ulmaria*) This is the herb of **Summer.**

Horticulture.

Description: Perennial herb with a tough, erect, leafy stem and clustered flowers. Height 4 feet. ***Other Names:*** Queen of the meadow, bridewort, gravel root, trumpet weed, bride of the meadow, little queen. *Colors:* Flowers creamy-white. Leaves dark green on top and white underneath. Stems may be purple. *Fragrance:* Mild or strongly fragrant, with an unusual aroma. ***Bloom Time***: June–September. *Origin:* Europe.

Habitat: Damp woods, marshy meadows. **Earth** (soil type): rich. **Water** (moisture needs): high. **Fire** (sun/shade requirements): Sun to part shade. **Air** (climate): US climate zone 2–7.

Tips and Warnings: Traditionally harvested at Midsummer. Once used to flavor mead. It was from meadowsweet flower heads that salicyclic acid was first isolated in 1839, ultimately giving birth to aspirin.

Magic: Nothing sings summer so wonderfully as meadowsweet. It is an herb of happiness and love, and sacred to the Druids. Meadowsweet is useful in love charms. It can also be used to discern the gender of a thief. *Use in all joyful summer charms, beginning at Beltaine.*

Mint *(Mentha* species) See also individual species for special magical affinities.

Horticulture

Description: Perennial. Most mints range from 14–36 inches in height. ***Name Lore:*** There was an unfortunate Greek nymph named Minte who attracted the unwelcome attentions of Pluto. The jealous Persephone turned her into a plant, but a nice plant. *Colors:* Variable. *Fragrance:* Clean. Greeks used to rub mint on their arms as a deodorant. ***Bloom Time***: Variable. *Origin:* Almost every continent has a native variety. Originally mints may be from India or other parts of Asia.

Habitat: Streambeds, riverbanks, swampy places. **Earth** (soil type): Tolerates poor soil, but enriching your soils gives you better results. Mints prefer well-drained soils. **Water** (moisture needs): High. **Fire** (sun/shade requirements): Can handle partial shade. **Air** (climate): Variable, depending on species.

Tips and Warnings: Easy to grow. For best magical results, plant most mints on Friday. Most varieties are most magical when planted in the east of the garden. All varieties of mints are invasive so be careful where you plant it. Mints are also tough. You can plant them under the garden gate; as you enter the garden and step on the herbs the fresh sweet smell will be released. Keep pruning the plants to keep them from flowering and to force a solid, bushy growth. Do not plant mint near chamomile or parsley. Although using bonfire ash to enrich the soil is good for many plants, it has a bad effect on mints. Mints are beneficial to cabbage. They are attractive to butterflies, as well. Various mints are widely used in candy and gum. The Romans rubbed their tables down with mint to prepare for feasts. It was also considered a valuable strewing herb. Baths can be scented with mint, and it is a common ingredient in toothpaste.

Magic: All mints are protective; most can be used to invoke and banish spirits. Drinking mint tea before going to bed may bring on dreams that provide spiritual guidance. The Druids were also very fond of mint. Mint attracts money, business, and prosperity. It is a good plant for the traveler. Most mints are wonderful at blessings. *Mint may be used as an amulet. Invoke Pluto.*

Mistletoe *(Viscum album)* This is the herb of the **Druids**.

Horticulture

Description: This is an evergreen semi-parasitic plant, drawing both water and mineral from its host tree, usually a hardwood. *Other Names:* Devil's fuge, all-heal, holy wood, golden bough, birdlime, Druid's herb, donnerbesen, loranthus, and witches' broom. *Similar and Related Species:* American mistletoe *(Phoradendron flavescens)* is similar in appearance but lacks the extensive magical tradition of *V. album*. *Colors:* Berries are white. *Fragrance:* Some have described it as "ethereal." Others can't smell a thing. *Bloom Time*: The berries ripen in midwinter. Flowers in February. *Origin:* Northern Europe and east to Asia.

Habitat: Found hanging on trees, usually the apple, but most famously the oak. It also can be found on elm, ash, spruce, poplar, and pine. **Earth** (soil type): Depends on source tree. **Water** (moisture needs): Low. **Fire** (sun/shade requirements): Sun. **Air** (climate) US Climate Zones 4–8.

Tips and Warnings: Mistletoe is not a garden plant, of course. It must be found in the wild or obtained from a commercial source. The plant has a two-year growing cycle. According to one ancient tradition, mistletoe must be cut on the first day of the new moon. The gardener must wear all white. A competing source states that the sixth day of the new moon is better. Still another legend insists that mistletoe's powers peak on St. *John's Eve* (Midsummer's Eve) and should be picked then. The Winter Solstice is another choice. It *cannot* be touched with iron or steel implements, only silver or gold, preferably the latter. One problem here, of course, is that golden or even silver knives are pretty hard to come by. In addition, gold is too soft to harvest mistletoe. Some writers suggest that the ancient Druids just gilded a regular knife to harvest the stuff, but I suspect that's cheating. The right magic should enable the practitioner to use real gold. Be sure to cut the plant with a single stroke. The ancient Druids were supposed to have sacrifice as pair of white bulls while cutting the mistletoe, but you can omit that step. If the mistletoe touches the earth, the spirit leaves it. The mistletoe, being an aerial plant, should never be permitted to touch the ground, but placed upon a white cloth. The berries of this plant are poisonous. Cutting down any tree bearing mistletoe is extremely unlucky.

Magic: This is an herb of protection. Because of its unusual growing habits, it is considered a plant beyond all boundaries. "The Druids are wont to sing to the mistletoe" (Ovid). According to legend, it springs up where lightning has struck a tree. Possibly as a result, it is believed to repel lightning when hung around the neck or placed on the doors, chimney, or windows. It strengthens all magical spells, and protects against evil spirits and witches, especially if you gather it on Midsummer's Day and hang around your neck (which may also make you invisible). It can open locks, and used to be carried by women who wanted to conceive.

Mistletoe is associated with the sun; it was the most holy plant for the Druids, especially when growing upon an oak (which is not common). Mistletoe berries were said to contain the sperm of the oak. The mistletoe enables one to experience aspects of the Otherworld. Mistletoe can be used to fashion a magic wand that has great power in this regard. Mistletoe placed beneath the pillow at night insures spiritual protection during sleep. It brings luck to hunters. Mistletoe outside the doorstep means welcome, except to fairies. Fairies can't stand the stuff, and so it was traditionally placed in a cradle to keep them from stealing a baby, as is immemorial fairy custom. (There is, however, an alternate Italian tale that implies that mistletoe keeps fairies eternally young. Perhaps only Italian fairies.)

We are all acquainted with kissing beneath the Mistletoe during Yule/Winter Solstice. In ancient days, foes meeting in its presence suppressed their animosity and exchanged the kiss of peace beneath it. The ancient pagan kissing tradition continues into Christianity. The mythical story is this: Mistletoe was unwittingly responsible for the death of the Norse god Balder. Luckily, Freya, the goddess of love, restored him to life; she then pronounced herself protectoress of the plant, ordering that those who passed beneath it must kiss to show their peaceful intentions. That custom is, of course, still with us. Young men and women must also kiss beneath the plant before their wedding day – or they will never be able to have children. A somewhat gentler story claims that un-kissed maidens will not marry during the upcoming year. It is customary to pluck a berry from the mistletoe with each kiss. The mistletoe should not be taken down until January 6 (Epiphany) and should be kept until the following year. In addition, it can be used at any consecrating, purification, and protection rites. *When working with mistletoe, invoke Apollo, Venus, Freya, Frigga, and Odin. Mistletoe may be carried as an amulet. Leos have a special affinity to mistletoe.*

Monkshood *(Aconitum napellus* and *A. carmichaelii)* This is the plant of **Astral Projection**.

Horticulture

Description: Perennial herb or shrub, growing from 2–5 feet high. Flowers are helmet-shaped, thus accounting for a couple of its common names. There are 100 species of Aconitum. The flower had five large purple sepals and four to six small petals. *Name Lore:* Greek myth says that aconite grew from the foam that dripped from the mouth of Cerberus, when Hercules dragged him up from hell, on the hill Aconitum, hence its Greek name *Other Names:* Aconite, wolfbane, soldier's cap. The name wolfbane refers to the story that in days of old, arrows were tipped with monkshood to kill wolves. (The word akon means, "dart".) Or alternatively, wolf bait was poisoned with the stuff. *Colors:* Glossy leaves dark green above, lighter below; flowers violet/purple/blue. One cultivar has white flowers, another blue and white. *Fragrance:* Don't get near enough to smell it. *Bloom Time*: May-July for A. napellus; September–October for A. carmichaelii. *Origin:* Worldwide.

Habitat: Shady stream banks, open deciduous woods. **Earth** (soil type): Prefers deep, rich soil, but can easily handle rocky, hard soil. **Water** (moisture needs): Moderate. **Fire** (sun/shade requirements): Prefers partial shade, but can handle full sun if given enough water. **Air** (climate): US Zones 2–7.

Tips and Warnings: Because of its extreme danger, I really cannot recommend including this plant in the garden. If you must have it, put it in the back border away from children, and label it clearly. Monkshood has been called the "queen mother of poisons." All varieties of this plant and all parts are deadly poisonous; even the smell of the thing is baneful. It contains one of the most powerful of neurotoxins; ten grams of the root (the most poisonous part) can kill you. Even rubbing aconite on the body affects the heartbeat, and makes people dizzy. Although monkshood is sometimes used as a power-wash for magical implements, the stuff is dangerous. Wash your hands with great care after handling it.

Magic: Monkshood is a traditional remedy against werewolves and vampires; however, it is effective against the former only when the plant is in bloom. A famous poison, monkshood was the chief ingredient (boiled up with belladonna, poplar leaves, cinquefoil, and human fat) in the infamous "flying ointment" concocted by witches. This stuff produces a tingling feeling. Aconite seeds are supposed to produce invisibility. The few who dare use it today use it for astral projection. Monkshood may be carried as an amulet. *Those born under the sign of Cancer have the best luck with monkshood. Invoke Hecate when doing magic with monkshood. It can with care be burned during death rites.*

Moonwort *(Botrycium lunaria)* This is the herb of **Unlocking.**

Horticulture

Description: Rare succulent fern bearing a single rather fan-shaped leaf. Height under 6 inches. Name Lore: The name Moonwort comes from the crescent-shaped segments of the frond. Fragrance: Ferny. Bloom Time: This plant does not bloom, but the leaf appears in the spring. Origin: Europe and United States.

Habitat: Woods. **Earth** (soil type): Rich, cool acidic. **Water** (moisture needs): High. **Fire** (sun/shade requirements): Shade. Cannot handle sun. **Air** (climate) US Climate Zones 3–6.

Tips and Warnings: Moonwort should be planted on Monday. This fern should be gathered by moonlight to be completely efficacious.

Magic: It is traditionally believed to have the power to break locks, open doors, break hexes, loosen nails, and even un-shoe any horse who steps on it. It also attracts money and is used in love spells. It is associated with honesty. And if a woodpecker rubs his beak on it, he'll acquire the power to pierce iron. (Whether or not this would be beneficial to the woodpecker is a matter of debate. Iron objects seldom conceal grubs, the primary object of interest to woodpeckers.) It is used in divination rites. Rites involving moonwort are most effective when performed on Monday.

Mugwort *(Artemisia vulgaris)* This is the herb of **Clairvoyance.**

Horticulture

Description: Perennial herb with angled stems, alternate leaves, and small flowers. Height 1–5 feet. *Other Names:* St. John's plant (Germany and Netherlands), artemisia, felon herb, moxa, witch herb, sailor's tobacco. *Similar and Related Species:* Both wormwood and mugwort are members of the same genus, *Artemisia.* All artemisias share characteristics, including silvery foliage. However, I am listing the mugwort separately because it is frequently referred to by that name in magical texts. Another artemisia, *A. annua,* is called sweet Annie or sweet wormwood. *Colors:* Flowers yellowish. One garden species, the "white mugwort," has a creamy white blossom. *Fragrance:* Bitter. *Bloom Time*: August–September. *Origin:* Grows wild in the United States, Britain, Europe, and Asia.

Habitat: Waste places. **Earth** (soil type): Prefers dry, average to poor soil. Cannot tolerate a wet soil. **Water** (moisture needs): Moderate **Fire** (sun/shade requirements): Full sun. **Air** (climate): US Climate Zones 4–8.

Tips and Warnings: Mugwort should be planted on Friday, ideally during the full moon, for the best magical results. Easy to grow and fast growing. The white mugwort looks very well when planted alongside colorful flowers. It is an excellent choice for a moon garden. Mugwort should be picked at midnight, on the Eve of the Summer Solstice. Since it is rumored evil sprits might live in it, Christians are advised to make the sign of the cross before picking. Adherence to other traditions should also use appropriate precautions, according to their faith. Sometimes, a "coal," or remnant of old roots, will be found beneath the live roots. This "coal" is purported to have many magical powers, including the banishment of evil spirits, and the awakening of sexual passion and fertility. It is an excellent companion plant to use in gardens as it presence discourages insect pests. As silver leafed plant it is also is useful for dividing plant colors. Some sorts of artemisia need to be divided every year or so. Mugwort was often brewed as a tea with lemon balm to aid psychic powers. However, it contains the neurotoxic substance thujone and should be taken with care. Hung in closets it will help protect wool clothing against moths.

Magic: Mugwort increases psychic powers, divinations, and aids astral projection if placed at the bedside or under the pillow or drunk as a tea prior to sleep. (You may dream of your future spouse.) This will also help you remember your dreams. Having prophetic dreams is ineffective if one can't remember them afterwards. You can also simply rub your nose with it. For the same reasons, it is popular when crystal ball gazing. Use an incense of mugwort and sandalwood before reading the crystal; it also helps to drink a little honey-flavored mugwort tea. (In fact, some practitioners use a wash of artemisia to clean the crystal ball.) It is also renowned as a protector, especially of travelers, guarding people from the attacks of wild animals, and from exhaustion, sunstroke, illness, and evil spirits. (Just put some in your shoe.) An old legend says John the Baptist wore mugwort in his belt to protect him from evil influences. *Use in divination rites. When working with mugwort invoke Artemis, or Diana. It is traditional to wear a crown of mugwort or to burn it as incense at Litha (Midsummer). Mugwort may be carried as an amulet. Clothe yourself in blue.*

Mullein *(Verbascum thapsus)* This is the herb of **Light in Darkness**.

Horticulture

Description: Biennial, with furry, flannel-like leaves, and terminal spiky flowers. Only in its second year does the plant attain its characteristic height of 3–6 feet. ***Other Names:*** Candle or candlewick plant, beggar's blanket, Quaker rouge, flannel plant, velvet plant, witch's taper, hag's taper, Aaron's rod, velvet plant, flannel flower, feltwort, shepherd's club. Also sometimes called lungwort or foxglove, although these names are more commonly given to *Pulmonia* and *Digitalis* respectively. ***Colors:*** Flowers bright yellow; leaves silvery gray. ***Fragrance:*** Honey-scented. ***Bloom Time***: June–September. ***Origin:*** Europe and North America.

Habitat: Banks, roadsides, waste places. **Earth** (soil type): Roadsides. **Water** (moisture needs): Tolerant of drought and poor soil. **Fire** (sun/shade requirements): Sunny. **Air** (climate) US Climate Zone 3–9.

Tips and Warnings: For most magical results, plant on Saturday. The Romans used the plant to make a yellow hair dye. A green dye can also be made with the plant by the addition of sulfuric acid. In old

Europe, peasants would line their shoes with it for warmth. All parts of the plant are poisonous except the flowers.

Magic: The mullein's ancient use reminds us that herbal lore is one way to find light in darkness. In the old days, mullein was soaked with wax and used as a candle. For me, the mullein represents the folk-wisdom that exists in all nature. It is also used for protection and healing. When worn, it will keep wild beasts at bay. (Take some in grizzly country....) Mullein under the pillow prevents nightmares, and provides spiritual protection. A bit of mullein carried on the person attracts the opposite sex. (The down can be used for love philters.) Carried with yarrow, it brings courage. As incense, it imparts a sense of equilibrium.

Mullein is burned at Samhain and at purification rituals. *Rites involving mullein are most efficacious when performed on Saturday. Invoke Jupiter. Clothe yourself in silver. Geminis have a particular affinity to mullein.*

Myrrh (*Commiphora myrrha*) This is an herb of **Sacrifice**.

Horticulture

Description: The myrrh plant is a spiny shrub or small tree; the leaves are small and sparse. Height up to 9 feet. There are over 135 different species. Myrrh itself is the resin of the plant. *Other Names:* Karan, antew, bowl, didin, mor, stacte. *Colors:* The resin is reddish-brown after it hardens. (It emerges yellow from the plant.) *Fragrance:* Bitterly aromatic. Unusual. *Bloom Time*: Variable. *Origin:* Eastern Africa, India, and Arabia.

Habitat: Rocky areas. **Earth** (soil type): Rocky, poor. **Water** (moisture needs): Low. **Fire** (sun/shade requirements): Sun. **Air** (climate): Subtropical.

Tips and Warnings: This plant is not generally grown in the United States or Britain. The ancient Egyptians used it in embalming and fumigation; other cultures used it as perfume and slow-burning ceremonial incense.

Magic: Many people are familiar with myrrh as one of the three gifts of the Wise Men to the Christ Child, but its use is thousands of years older. The magical powers of myrrh lie in the aromatic gum resin. It is an herb of sacrifice. Why do you suppose that myrrh was selected as a gift? Myrrh was used for embalming bodies, and its presentation signifies the ultimate sacrifice that Jesus would one day be called upon to make. Burning this herb brings peace, healing, and blessing; it is also used for consecrations and exorcisms, usually combined with frankincense. It is protective of the house and can be used to bless objects and anoint candles. It can be used to banish evil spirits and break hexes. Burning myrrh also aids meditation. The oil is used to anoint magical implements. Magical necklaces may be made from myrrh wood and seeds. Magic rites with myrrh are most effective if the myrrh is placed at south end of the magical space. *Invoke Isis, Ra, and Adonis. Important festivals include Imbolc and Mabon. The most common use for myrrh is incense. Arians have a special affinity to myrrh.*

Myrtle (*Mertus communis*) This is the herb of **Creativity**.

Horticulture

Description: Evergreen shrub or small tree with glossy, fine textured, waxy, persistent oval leaves. Height 10 feet, but takes well to pruning. *Name Lore:* "Myrtle" comes from the Greek world meaning "perfume." *Other Names:* Candleberry, bayberry, tallow shrub, waxberry. *Colors:* White flowers, blue-black fruit. *Fragrance:* Leaves have a characteristic resinous smell when brushed. Flowers have a semi-sweet, distinctive scent. Fruit is also aromatic. One legend tells us that when Adam and Eve were ejected from the Garden of Eden, myrtle was one of three plants they were allowed take with them, the other two being the very practical wheat and date. But the myrtle was chosen for its fragrance. *Bloom Time*: Flowers May–August; fruits October–November. *Origin:* Western Asia and Mediterranean region.

Habitat: Open areas. **Earth** (soil type): Tolerant of most, but requires good drainage. **Water** (moisture needs): Low. **Fire** (sun/shade requirements): Full sun. **Air** (climate): US Climate Zones 8–10.

Tips and Warnings: This plant is a slow, easy grower, and lives a long time. In warmer areas, it can be made into an evergreen hedge. In colder areas, it is a good container plant. The berry has been used to make drinks, sweeten the breath, and flavor foods. The hard wood has been used to make furniture and walking sticks. The leaves can be used in a massage to tone the skin. The Russians used it to tan leather, giving the leather a distinctive fragrance. Perfumes incorporating myrtle should be worn on Monday.

Magic: Myrtle is a helpful herb in all rites involving creativity. Myrtle is supposed to preserve youth and enhance sensual love. The most potent is the sprig with three leaves in a whirl, which is hard to find, rather like a four-leaf clover. The Romans wove myrtle into garlands for their heroes. The so-called myrtle nymphs taught the Greeks the art of cheese-making, olive cultivation, and the art of building beehives. It was said that a woman desiring marriage should take a sprig of myrtle on the eve of the Solstice, and place it in her prayer book (you need to be Anglican for this to work) at the words of the wedding service where it says "Wilt thou take so and so to be thy husband?" In the morning, if the myrtle has mysteriously disappeared, the woman will soon be married. Myrtle is mixed up in the story of Hippolytus and Phaedra. The love-struck stepmother hanged herself from a myrtle while Hippolytus died when his hair got tangled up in the stuff. It can be used at handfastings and is symbolic of immortality, peace, love, passion, justice, and divine blessing. *Rites involving myrtle are most efficacious when performed on Friday. Invoke Ahura Mazda, Hathor, Astarte, Aphrodite, Brahma, or Prajapati. Rites with myrtle are most effective when Venus is visible. Myrtle may be carried as an amulet.*

Nettle (*Urtica gracilis and U. dioica*) This is the herb of **Banishment.**

Horticulture

Description: Large perennial covered with coarse stinging bristles; long, heart-shaped leaves; and tiny, petal-less flowers developing in the leaf axils. Height 2-4 feet. The sting is caused by ammonia and formic acid in the cells. *Name Lore:* The Latin name for the genus comprising the nettle is *Urtica*, which means, "burning." *Other Names:* Devil's apron (Ireland), wergulu, common or stinging nettle.

Colors: Flowers green. *Fragrance:* Bitter. ***Bloom Time***: May–September. ***Origin:*** Eurasia; they now grow all over the Northern hemisphere.

Habitat: Waste ground, roadsides, and woods. **Earth** (soil type): Ordinary. **Water** (moisture needs): Moderate. **Fire** (sun/shade requirements): Full sun. **Air** (climate) US Climate Zones 4–9.

Tips and Warnings: Nettles added to the compost pile will speed up the decaying process. And while you probably don't want a garden full of nettles, they have their uses, such as stimulating the growth of all plants in their neighborhood. They have an especially good effect on current bushes and other soft fruit. The nettle is attractive to butterflies. The substance that causes the burning sensation is chemically similar to that of bee stings. The burn from the stinging nettle is quite painful but can be relieved by rubbing leaves of dock, rosemary, mint, or sage over the skin.

Magic: Nettle is used to banish evil spirits and remove curses. To remove a hex or curse, stuff a cloth doll with nettles, write the name of the curser on it, and bury it. The curse will return to the sender. Carried with yarrow, nettle can dispel fear. *Nettle may be carried as an amulet. Arians have a particular affinity to nettle. Invoke Blodeuwedd.*

Oak *(Quercus* species) This is the herb of the **Masculine Spirit**.

Horticulture

Description: Deciduous slow growing tree with wide-spreading branches and a rounded crown. The bark is distinctly gnarled and furrowed. It was believed that the oak was the first tree created and the acorn, the first food of humankind. The slowness of its growing probably contributes to its nearly indestructible wood. Height 100 feet. Rather oddly, oaks are members of the beech family. *Name Lore:* The word Druid may mean "oak man." The root of the word Quercus means "query," referring to the power of the tree to answer questions of psychical import. Other Names: Tanner's bark. ***Similar and related species:*** Over 400 species. *Colors:* Leaves bright green above, whitish/gray beneath, turning red, purple, yellow or brown in autumn, many persist through the winter. Bark is light gray or gray-brown. *Fragrance:* Not noticeable unless the leaves are burning. ***Bloom Time***: The catkins bloom in April, but the acorns don't fully develop until fall. ***Origin:*** Northern hemisphere. Now found world-wide.

Habitat: Forests. **Earth** (soil type): Ordinary. **Water** (moisture needs): Low to Moderate. **Fire** (sun/shade requirements): Full or filtered sun. **Air** (climate): US Climate Zones 3–8.

Tips and Warnings: For most magical results, plant on Thursday or Sunday. If you have a choice, plant in the west. If an oak tree must be cut down, it should be done during the waning of the moon. Oak leaves can be made into a tonic wine. The galls of the oak are also important for many magical and medicinal purposes. (In case you're wondering, those galls are caused by wasps, and are not good for the trees.) Where oak, ash, and thorn grow together, you're sure to find fairies if you look hard enough. All oaks attract squirrels.

Magic: This is the herb of all the traditionally masculine virtues, including strength, endurance, and courage. It also represents balance, fidelity, and success. All parts of the tree are lucky or protective when carried. (Carrying an acorn also preserves youth.) To dream about an oak tree or to catch an oak leaf indicates a prosperous future. Supposedly oak leaves have the power to transfix lions, always a handy trick. And oak arrows will keep snakes away from your dung heap, in case that is important to you.

The wood is said to withstand lightning blasts, a tale stemming form the time when Thor himself hid in an oak for protection against the rages of a lightning storm. Consequently the oak became associated with the gods of thunder. Because of, or maybe despite, this, the oak is struck by lightning more than any other tree. One reason is its enormous size and low electrical resistance. When the tree is struck, it has been known literally to explode; this happens when the heartwood has rotted away and the cavity is filled with water. The lightning-struck water expands at a ferocious rate and just pops the tree open. Despite lightning's penchant for whacking oaks, folk belief insists that placing an acorn on your window will protect you and your house from lightning.

Situated at the foot of Mt. Tomarus, the sacred oak grove at Dodona was the oldest and most hallowed sanctuary in Greece. The oak is associated with Zeus and his Roman counterpart Jupiter as well as with Thor (who rode in a chariot of oak). Mjolnir, Thor's magic hammer, was created by dwarves from the wood of a sacred oak; the hammer represented the destructive power of the storms, but also fertility, death, and rebirth. Herne, an ancient British hunter-god, inhabits the oaks of Windsor Forest, and Merlin chose to work his magic in an oak grove, and used an oak branch as his wand. Oaks are also the home of dryads (whose name means "oak" in Greek).

The Druids too revered the oak above all other trees, and conducted their solemn rites only in its presence, believing it hosted the energy, power, and strength of their gods. They venerated oaks so deeply that they flayed the skin from anyone who injured one, and used the skin to heal the oak. The oak is also a good fortuneteller; the Druids used to gather beneath it to "query" the tree and to listen to the rustling of the leaves. They supposedly ate acorns before doing this; one hopes they bleached the tannin out of them first. In like manner, classical legend tells that Zeus (or Jupiter) often made his will known through the rustling of oak leaves in the grove of Dodona. Querying oak trees should be done only during the full or waxing moon. When Britain was Christianized, the custom transmogrified into giving sermons beneath oaks. These oaks were called "gospel oaks," but they were just the old querying oaks in another guise.

When mistletoe chooses to make its home there, the oak became especially sacred, for the white berries of the mistletoe were thought to represent the sperm of the gods, and so the oak became associated with the male's procreative qualities and fertility.

Burning oak leaves is said purify the atmosphere, although you may get an argument from local fire and environmental officials. Burning leaves should be for ceremonial purposes only.

In one old method of marriage divination, lovers each mark an acorn with his or her initials. They then place the acorns a few inches apart in a cauldron and watch the movements of the acorns. If they approach each other, the lovers will be married. If the acorns drift apart, there will be a separation.

The acorn is a traditional symbol of immortality, fertility, and abundance. One reason may be that acorn (*glans* in Latin) represents the glans of the penis, and is consequently a fertility symbol. Classical rulers wore oak leaves as wreaths; today, oak leaves signify military rank in the US Army. Jason's ship, the Argo, was built of oak, as was King Arthur's Round Table. King Charles II hid in an oak after being defeated in battle.

Acorns and leaves are used in many kinds of potions; especially love philters. Oak may be used at consecrations, weddings, and protection rituals as well as handfasting and fertility rites. (In ancient times, magic wands, topped with acorns, were used in fertility rites.) An acorn necklace or amulet empowers magical workings. Oak can be used as decoration at Yule, and acorns are used at Samhain. *Rites involving the oak are most efficacious when performed during Imbolc, during the month of May (especially on May 29 and June 1) with Thursday as the most propitious day. Sagittarians and Gemini seem to be able to work oak magic most successfully. Brighid, Blodeuwedd, Hercules, Jupiter, Zeus, Cybele, Bridhe, and Dagda are all associated with oaks as well, and any of them may be invoked in rites with oak. Wear black.*

Olive *(Olea europea)* This is the herb of **Peace**.

Horticulture

Description: Evergreen tree with small flowers and opposite lanceolate leaves. The olive tree has been known to live as long as 1000 years. Height 40 feet. ***Colors:*** Flowers creamy white; leaves silver-green. ***Fragrance:*** Wood slightly aromatic. ***Bloom Time***: Spring. ***Origin:*** Mediterranean.

Habitat: Dry hilly places. **Earth** (soil type): Average. **Water** (moisture needs): Low–moderate. **Fire** (sun/shade requirements): Full sun. **Air** (climate): US Climate Zones 9–10. Needs some winter chill to set fruit, but a hard freeze will kill or severely damage the trees.

Tips and Warnings: In an ornamental garden, some new fruitless cultivars are more convenient to grow than the fruited variety, and so are generally preferred. They carry the same symbolic value, but, of course, you won't have any olives. A fruiting olive tree can actually cause some problems in an ornamental garden, however. Unless you're planning to eat all those olives, they can be pretty messy. The olive is a long-lived plant that will outlast its planter by generations. The Greeks frequently used olive wood to carve statues of their gods; it is a beautiful decay-resistant wood.

Magic: The olive tree and branch has an honored place in western tradition; it plays a prominent part in biblical lore, from Genesis to Revelation. The dove returned to Noah with freshly plucked olive leaf, to let him know the deluge has passed, and Revelation records that two olive tree stand before the Lord of the Earth. The Psalmist compares himself to an olive tree, flourishing in the house of God, and Exodus records its more mundane use: "The clear oil of pressed olives for the light so that the lamps may be kept burning." The olive is a symbol of light (for its fuel), beneficence, happiness, victory, and peace. In fact, one Middle Eastern legend says that only a peaceful man may plant an olive garden.

In a contest over which god would be allowed to name the future capital of Greece, Athena struck the earth and produced an olive tree. The council of gods decided that this gift surpassed that of Poseidon's horse, so Athena was allowed to name the new city. Ever since, the olive has been associated with her, and with her Roman counterpart Minerva. So while the olive is a sign of peace for many cultures, in Greece it was a war symbol also, as Athena was quite combative. At Olympia, the chief seat of Pan-Hellenic Zeus, the sacred tree of that god was also the wild olive.

In Italian witchcraft, a drop of olive oil is placed in a basin of consecrated water in divination. Hanging an olive branch over the door keeps out evil spirits. Olive oil is used in all kinds of anointing ceremonies. *Clothe yourself in blue or lavender. Olive may be worn as amulet. Invoke Apollo, Athena, Minerva, Irene, Jupiter, and Ra. Those born under the sign of cancer have a special affinity with olive.*

Oregano (*Origanum vulgace*) This is herb is **Proof Against Satanic Influences**.

Horticulture

Description: Perennial, bushy herb with a square stem, oval hairy leaves, and tubular blossoms in broad terminal clusters. ***Other Names:*** Origanum, wild marjoram. ***Similar and related species:*** See Marjoram. *Colors:* Flowers white to rose. ***Fragrance:*** Sweet. ***Bloom Time:*** July–September. ***Origin:*** Mediterranean region, naturalized all over Europe and America.

Habitat: Dry slopes. **Earth** (soil type): Well-drained, rocky, dry. **Water** (moisture needs): Oregano is drought resistant. **Fire** (sun/shade requirements): Sunny. **Air** (climate) US Climate Zones 6–9.

Tips and Warnings: Prune regularly for best shape. An excellent choice for **Air** Gardens. Oregano is frequently included in tomato-based dishes and soups. A reddish brown dye can be made from oregano.

Magic: This plant is reportedly highly effective against witches and satanic influences. In a dark historical footnote, it is said that officers of the Inquisition burned oregano while torturing reputed witches to avoid being harmed by them. Oregano is associated with intellectual development. *Geminis and Scorpios have a particular affinity for it. Oregano is used primarily in rites of protection.*

Orris See Iris

Pansy See Violet.

Parsley (*Petroselinum crispum, or P. sativum*) This is the herb of **Dark Forces**.

Horticulture

Description: Biennial herb usually gown as an annual with an erect stem, alternate leaves, and small flowers. Height 8–12 inches. ***Name Lore:*** *Carum Petroselinum* comes from *petros*, which means "rock," and *selinon*, a word indicating the celery family. ***Other Names:*** Devil's oatmeal, death plant. *Colors:* Leaves bright green and crinkled; flowers greenish, white, or yellow. *Fragrance*: All parts of the plant have a strong, tart smell. ***Bloom Time***: June–August. ***Origin:*** Mediterranean and Europe, grown throughout the world.

Habitat: Waste places, old walls. **Earth** (soil type): Moist, composted, humus-rich, and well-drained. **Water** (moisture needs): Prefers to be well watered. **Fire** (sun/shade requirements): Partial shade to full sun. **Air** (climate) US Climate Zones 5–9.

Tips and Warnings: Only the wicked grow parsley. This is not necessarily my opinion, but it's a very old saying. Parsley is so slow to germinate that one old tradition says it has go nine times to the devil before coming up; the same story claims if the seed fails to germinate, the planter will die within the year. It was also said that if parsley is transplanted it will bring about the downfall of the house. Sow or plant (if you dare) during the first quarter of the moon on Wednesday or Sunday for best magical results. Good Friday, which never falls during the first quarter of the moon, is also a good day. Pregnant women are said to have the most luck with it. Harvest on Friday beneath a waxing Moon. The Greeks thought it was sacred to oblivion and to the dead and so did not use it at meals. The Romans, however, felt differently about it. They called it the "herb of festivity" and used it to cleanse the breath during their interminable orgies. It was also supposed to prevent drunkenness. They thought it was antidote to all poisons, and placed it on the plate to serve guests (I suppose just in case anything should happen to go wrong with the serving). Parsley provides a good larval food for desirable butterflies like swallowtails. You may lose some parsley, but you'll have the butterflies. It's a fair trade. Parsley draws bees too, as well as beneficial wasps. It is said to increase the scent of roses. Parsley has been used as a flavoring for soups, meats, salads, and also as a garnish. The ancients used to feed their warhorses upon parsley, but for what purpose I cannot ascertain.

Magic: There is something not quite right about this herb. In the Middle Ages, parsley reverted to its older, sinister meanings. In fact, the plant has a long association with the devil. Parsley has been a traditional ingredient in the initiation of werewolves. It is traditionally unlucky if given or received as a gift; many people say that parsley ought never to be brought into the home. However, Native Americans made a love-potion that included wild parsley. The Greeks said that parsley sprang from the blood of Archemorus, who was gobbled up by snakes after having been carelessly left on parsley leaves.

The winners of the Greek Isthmian Games, a sort of poor cousin of the Olympics, were crowned with parsley. If you powder your hair overnight three times a year with parsley you will never go bald. *In its more cheerful aspect, parsley, combined with vervain and potentilla (cinquefoil), makes a superior anointing oil. It can also be an aid to meditation. Invoke Aphrodite, Persephone, or Venus. If you are a Christian you might invoke St. Peter, also a guardian to the Otherworld. Parsley is used primarily for rites of the dead and purifications. Rites with parsley are most effective when Mercury is visible. Parsley may be worn as an amulet or used as a bathing herb where it brings one into affinity with the Yin (feminine) side of the cosmos. Librans have a special affinity to parsley.*

Pasqueflower See Anemone.

Pennyroyal (*Mentha pulegium, Hedeoma pulegioides*) This is an herb of **Calming**.

Horticulture

Description: The smallest of the mints, pennyroyal looks rather different from the others. It comes in two common forms: the variety *decumbens*, with weak, prostrate stems, and opposite, short-stalked, somewhat hairy leaves and whorled clusters of flowers. The other variety, *erecta*, has thicker, stronger stems. This type is more suitable for cultivation, as it can be reaped and tied up in bundles. American pennyroyal (*H. pulegioides*) is an annual and is similar to *M. pulegium* in its uses. ***Name Lore:*** *Pulegium* came from Latin, from *Pulex,* or "flea," for its reputed ability to banish fleas. "Pennyroyal" is a corruption of "Pulioll-royall," or sovereign remedy against fleas. ***Other Names:*** English pennyroyal, lurkin-the ditch, tickweed, mosquito plant, piliolerial, pudding grass, squaw mint, run-by-the-ground. *Colors:* Flowers reddish purple to lilac blue. *Fragrance:* Pronounced. ***Bloom Time***: July–August. *Origin:* Europe. *M. pulegium* has been introduced to North America.

Habitat: Borders of ponds and streams. **Earth** (soil type): Moist. **Water** (moisture needs): Pennyroyal can withstand drought. **Fire** (sun/shade requirements): Shade. **Air** (climate): US Climate Zones 4–8.

Tips and Warnings: For most magical results, pennyroyal should be planted on Friday. It can be planted in pathways or under the gate where people can step on it to release the fragrance. Pennyroyal is perfect for the **Air** Garden. Pennyroyal is dangerous to pregnant women. In large doses, pennyroyal taken internally can produce convulsions and coma. In addition, the plant and the oil can cause dermatitis. It can be used in cupboards to get rid of ants, fleas, flies, and mosquitoes.

Magic: Pennyroyal protects against the evil eye, and is an herb of peace and calming when placed in the house. It was said that carrying pennyroyal flowers at sea will prevent seasickness, and scattering pennyroyal on the seas will calm them. When attached to the bedpost it is said to sharpen the intellect. Placed in the shoe, it prevents weariness. Pennyroyal was used during rites of love and rebirth and of death and immortality (when it was used to bathe the corpse). It is said that the Greeks used pennyroyal in the initiations of novices in the Eleusinian mysteries. Rites involving pennyroyal are most efficacious in summer. *Pennyroyal may be worm as amulet. Scorpios have a special affinity to pennyroyal. Invoke Demeter.*

Peony *(Paeonia* species) This is the herb of **Honor.**

Horticulture

Description: Perennial shrub that can attain a height of 4 feet. Showy, ruffled, globelike flowers, some attaining a width of 8 inches. *Name Lore:* The name apparently refers to Paeon, a very ancient physician to the gods. It is not clear why gods need physicians, but there you are. Some stories claim that he was changed into this plant by Zeus to save him from the jealous rages of Asclepius. *Colors:* Flowers white, pink, red, yellow, and purple; foliage deep green. *Fragrance:* Variable, usually sweet and rich. Certain pink and white varieties are the most fragrant. ***Bloom Time***: May–June. *Origin:* China and southeastern Europe, widely introduced.

Habitat: Meadows. **Earth** (soil type): Rich, well-drained, humous. Tolerant, but does not like light or alkaline soils. **Water** (moisture needs): Prefers to be well watered. **Fire** (sun/shade requirements): Full sun to light shade. **Air** (climate): US Climate Zones 3–8. Strong winds are damaging to peonies.

Tip and Warnings: Easy to grow, peonies are very resistant to insects and disease. Peonies usually flower the second year after planting. Some of the most fragrant varieties may topple after a rain and should be staked. A peony can easily live a century or more, especially if left undisturbed. The peony looks wonderful with the bearded iris (at least in my garden). The foliage disappears in the summer. Seeds should be harvested and dried under a full moon. One charming story, to whose veracity I cannot attest, says that if a woodpecker sees you harvesting peony roots, it will peck out your eyes. All parts of the pant are poisonous, especially the flowers.

Magic: While the peony has only a thin magical tradition in the west, it is considerably more important in its home, China, where it is known as "Queen of Flowers" and where is associated with honor, dignity, and wealth. This is an excellent plant in business to attract customers. In Europe, it is considered "a rose without thorns." It is good luck when carried, and sailors also carried the roots as a protection against storms. In fact, peony roots are generally considered protective in general. At one time, peony seeds, where much of the magic is stored, were thought to glow in the dark; the seeds are frequently burned to banish evil spirits. Peony is linked to Pan, but fairies can't stand the stuff, and won't come near a garden where it's planted. That's another advantage, from my point of view. My garden is loaded with it. *It may also be used in exorcisms, one of the pleasanter herbs for that purpose. Clothe yourself in pink. Peony may be worn as an amulet.*

Peppermint *(Mentha piperita)* This is the herb of **Change.**

Horticulture.

Description: Perennial with spear-shaped leaves and a neat, beautiful habit. The plant is a cultivated cross of water mint and spearmint. Height 24–30 inches. **Other Names:** Balm mint, brandy mint, lamb's mint. **Colors:** Leaves dark green. Stems reddish. Flowers reddish-violet. **Fragrance:** Cool. **Bloom Time**: July–September. **Origin:** Eurasia.

Habitat: Damp waste places. **Earth** (soil type): Rich, moist. **Water** (moisture needs): High. **Fire** (sun/shade requirements): Full sun or partial shade. **Air** (climate): US Climate Zones 3–10.

Tips and Warnings: Peppermint should be planted on Friday. Peppermint is a good choice for the **Air** Garden. Easy to grow, but peppermint can be invasive, and needs to be isolated or contained in a pot. Pick in early to midsummer. Peppermint leaves, dried or fresh, can be used as a tea. It is also used as garnish and ingredient in jellies, punches, and candy.

Magic: Use peppermint, especially peppermint oil, when you want to make a change in your life. Peppermint is an herb of purification, happiness, and healing. It can be relaxing as well. In the Victorian language of flowers, peppermint represents a false heart, possibly because it signals change. In an herbal bath, peppermint produces a feeling of peace. *Clothe yourself in red. Peppermint may be worn as an amulet.*

Periwinkle *(Vinca minor* and *V. major)* This is the herb of **Wizards and Sorcerers**

Horticulture

Description: A perennial low, trailing evergreen with opposite, short-stalked leathery leaves. It is a member of the dogbane family. **Name Lore:** *Vinca* comes from the Latin Vincio, meaning, "I bind," referring to the long stems that suppress other plants. **Other Names:** Devil's eye, sorcerer's violet, joy-on-the-ground, violet of the sorcerers, and myrtle – not to be confused with the Mediterranean myrtle (*Mertus communis*), although the leaves are similar (tough and shiny). **Colors:** Flowers are blue, bluish-purple, or white. **Fragrance:** Subtle. **Bloom Time**: April–May. **Origin:** Mediterranean.

Habitat: Woods, copses, hedge banks. **Earth** (soil type): Wee-drained moist (but not wet) humus rich. **Water** (moisture needs): Moderate. **Fire** (sun/shade requirements): Partial shade to full sun. **Air** (climate): US Climate Zone 4–8 for most cultivars.

Tips and Warnings: The greater periwinkle (*V. major*) can be invasive, but the lesser periwinkle (*V. minor*) is usually safe. It can survive well even very close to trees, and is attractive there.

   Periwinkle is mildly poisonous. In olden times, it was said that eating a few leaves of periwinkle would stop quarreling between a husband and wife; since the plant is toxic, it might stop the quarreling in an unexpected way.

Magic: Much magic, both good and evil, can be wrought from the humble periwinkle, so not for nothing is it known as the violet of sorcerers. German wizards called it an herb of immortality, and the Welsh sorcerers (they say) used it to make body materialize in graveyards. For this reason, perhaps, it has also been called the flower of death. The greater periwinkle (*Vinca major*) was placed as a crown on the heads of dead children and was frequently planted in graveyards, especially on the graves of children. A wreath of the stuff was supposedly hung around the necks of those condemned to hang. It is unlucky to bring fewer than seven blooms into the house, but hanging periwinkle on the door is supposed to be protective against negative influences. Periwinkle is considered efficacious against the evil eye and in exorcisms. On a lighter note, some say that staring at periwinkle will bring back lost and pleasant memories. *Periwinkle may be worn as an amulet.*

Pine *(Pinus* species) This is the herb of **Dispelling Negativity**.

Horticulture

Description: Tall, straight coniferous evergreen. Height up to 100 feet. ***Similar and Related Species:*** Many species exist, most with the same magical powers. Many magical powers are attributed to the Scots Pine (*Pinus sylvestris*), the only pine native to Britain, and one of only three native needle-leaved trees occurring naturally in the UK, the other two being yew and juniper The white pine (*P. strobes*) is common in the United States. *Colors:* Scots pine has a coppery red bark. Both Scots and white pine have bluish-green needles. Pollen yellow, the actual "flower" is a budlike object. ***Fragrance:*** Characteristic mild, resinous fragrance most noticeable on warm days. ***Bloom Time***: Flowers insignificant. Early spring for the pollen. ***Origins:*** Worldwide.

Habitat: Woods, open places. **Earth** (soil type): Not fussy, does well in sandy soil where other kinds of trees don't grow. **Water** (moisture needs): Moderate. **Fire** (sun/shade requirements): Full sun. **Air** (climate): US Climate Zones 2–10 (dependent on species).

Tips and Warnings: For strongest magical effect, gather the needles on Midsummer's Day. If possible, plant pines to the east, from which direction they gain the strongest magic. The white pine is a very rapid grower; it is also easy to transplant. For best magical results, plant on Sunday during the second quarter of the moon.

Magic: Tipping a magic wand with a pinecone increases the power of magical rites, or the wand itself may be made of pine. There is also a connection between the pine and the birth of children, possibly because storks nest in pines. Burning pine in the home is purifying. Pine needles ward off evil spirits;

if you burn the needles, you will send evil spells back to their originator. Burning pines needles also brings comfort to bereaved folks. In Egypt the pine tree was connected with Osiris, images of whom were made from the heart of a hollowed-out pine tree and then placed within the tree. The Greek goddess Cybele turned her faithless lover Attis into a pine. (Some say he castrated himself first.) There is also an association with Pithys, a nymph, who while fleeing from the unwanted attentions of Boreas, fell against a rock and changed into a pine.

Pines are considered symbolic of winter, but fairies, who so love summer, will dance around pine trees. Decorating a home with pine symbolizes healing, life, good health, and joy. Even pressing your fingers against the pinecone when you are tired brings freshness and revitalization to a tired body. The characteristic pyramidal shape of the pine suggests immortality. In China, the Scots Pine (*P. silvestris*) is the tree of life and a sign of a happy marriage. (What a Scots pine was doing in China is a whole other tale.) It is featured in Chinese art, representing longevity, self-discipline, and steadfastness. For many people, including the Iroquois nations, pines are trees of peace. Use pinecones for decoration at Litha and Yule, and for rites of prosperity, protection and consecration. In ancient Siberia, a pine fire was often used for initiation ceremonies. Pine branches are sometimes used to sweep and area ritually clean in outdoor magical rites. *Rites involving pine are most efficacious when performed in the winter and spring; Thursday is the best day. Clothe yourself in brown. Invoke Jupiter, Dionysus, Attis, Cybele, Venus, Osiris, or Bacchus. Pine may be used as incense, and as a bathing herb to dispel negativity, and as an amulet.*

Pomegranate *(Punica granatum)* This is the herb of **Sexuality.**

Horticulture

Description: Deciduous, twiggy shrub or small tree with oblong shiny leaves. ***Name Lore:*** The old French word means "apple with many seeds." ***Other Names:*** Chinese apple, grenadier, malicorio. ***Colors:*** Orange flowers, red fruit. ***Fragrance:*** Mild. ***Bloom Time***: June–September. ***Origin:*** Eastern Mediterranean and Near East.

Habitat **Earth** (soil type): Prefers dry soil. **Water** (moisture needs): Drought tolerant. **Fire** (sun/shade requirements): Full sun. **Air** (climate): Tropical and subtropical.

Tips and Warnings: For the best magic, plant on Thursday. The pomegranate is easy to grow, especially the dwarf varieties with their ornamental fruit. The blossoms are attractive to hummingbirds. Pomegranate was once used to create a red dye. Grenadine syrup comes from the seeds.

Magic: The pomegranate is a plant of general good luck and is useful when working with a spell involving material objects. It has strong sexual connotation, especially when split open. On a less erotic level, the split pomegranate is said to represent generosity, or God's love. Today a bride may cast a pomegranate upon the ground; the number of seeds spilled indicates the number of children she will bear. In ancient times pomegranates were planted on the graves of heroes, probably in the hope that the heroes would produce many others like themselves. In Greece, the most famous myth associated with the pomegranate is that of Persephone; because she ate the fruit, she had to spend a portion of the year in the Underworld. Another story says that pomegranates come from the blood of Dionysus.

The pomegranate was a favorite plant of the biblical King Solomon, at least to judge by the amount of pomegranate design he ordered for the Temple at Jerusalem. The connection may be that the fruit has a definite crown-like appearance. *The pomegranate also symbolizes love, marriage, childbirth, abundance, and the oneness of the universe. Clothe yourself in red. Invoke Dionysus, Pluto, and Ramman. Pomegranate may be worn as an amulet.*

Poplar *(Populus* species) This is the herb of **Sympathy**.

Horticulture:

Description: Deciduous, fast-growing broadleaf. Height 75 feet. About 35 species. *Other Names:* Cottonwood, aspen. Several are common in the United States as landscape plants, including white poplar (*P. alba*); Balm of Gilead poplar (*P. candicans*), sometimes used instead of the true balm of Gilead (*Comminphora meccanensis*, a native of Asia and Africa with aromatic leaves); Fremont cottonwood (*P. fremonti*); Lombardy, or black poplar (*P. nigra*); and quaking aspen (*P. tremuloides*). The latter species is the most widespread tree in America. Poplars common in Britain include P. *alba*, several hybrid black poplars (*Populus x Canadensis*), Grey poplar (*P. canescens*), and European Aspen (*P. tremula*). *Similar and related species:* The yellow poplar or tulip tree is actually of a different genus (*Liriodendron tulipifera*). *Colors:* Brilliant autumn color. *Fragrance:* In spring, the unfurling leaves are covered with a sticky substance that gives off a woodsy, bittersweet, resinous scent. *Bloom Time*: April for most species. Aspen can bloom as early as February. *Origin:* Northern hemisphere.

Habitat: Variable depending on species; wet woods and stream banks. **Earth** (soil type): Ordinary garden soil. **Water** (moisture needs): Moderate. **Fire** (sun/shade requirements): Sun to part shade. **Air** (climate): US Climate Zones 1–9.

Tips and Warnings: Plant late fall to early spring. Poplar is most magical if planted to the south of the garden. The roots of the poplar can be destructive to sidewalks and underground utilities; care is needed in planting. Most useful around stream banks and ponds. Tolerant of pollution, and often grown on city streets and in parks.

Magic: The poplar is a tree of success, inspiration, and knowledge. However, the white and black poplars have somewhat different magical uses. (It doesn't help that the white poplar is sometimes called the quaking aspen, whereas in reality they are quite different trees.) In sacrifices to Zeus and also to Pelops the wood of the white poplar was used and no other. In Greek myth, poplars were also sacred to Hercules. In another tale, Hades fell in love with the nymph Leuce. When she died, he transformed her into a poplar. One variety of poplar, the quaking aspen, has its own collection of myth. In French folklore, the cross of the Jesus was made from quaking aspen, and it was this circumstance that caused the tree to quake in the first place. A German legend claims that it quakes because Jesus cursed it. Because the quaking aspen trembles with every breeze, it was believed to have strong sympathetic magic. Because the two sides of the leaf are different, the quaking aspen represents the Tree of Life, the white underside representing the moon and water, the rich green of the top representing fire and sun. The ancient Greeks used the black poplar as a funeral tree, sacred to the earth mother. Later on, the buds and leaves were an ingredient in witches' "flying ointments" for astral projection and to summon spirits. *Poplar can be burned as incense. In divination, the black poplar means the loss of hope.*

Use the white or quaking poplar to achieve hope, protection, and powers of speech. Magic with poplar is most effective when Jupiter is visible. Mabon (Fall Equinox) is a time of special power to perform rites with poplar. Wear red.

Poppy *(Papaver species)* This is the herb of **Dreams**.

Horticulture

Description: One hundred species of annual, biennial, and perennial herbs. Poppy flowers are generally large and cup-shaped. The blooms have a crepe-paper-like quality. The poppy most generally used in magic is the annual field poppy (*P. rhoeas*). ***Other Names:*** Corn poppy, common poppy, corn rose, headache, manseed, head waak, blind bluff. ***Similar and Related Species:*** The California poppy is of a different species (*Eschscholzia californica*); the Iceland poppy (*P. nudicale*) is a nice variety, as is the Iranian poppy (*P. bracteatum*), native to southeast Asia. ***Name Lore:*** The Latin name of *P. somniferum*, or opium poppy, comes from the Roman god of sleep, Somnus. (The Iranian poppy actually produces more codeine per acre than the famous opium poppy.) ***Colors:*** Blooms all shades of pink, lilac and orange, also a white variety. Foliage dark green. ***Fragrance:*** Subtle. ***Bloom Time***: May–June. ***Origin:*** Asia, Europe.

Habitat: The field poppy thrives in areas that have been newly turned; the new seeds need light to germinate. This is why they grew so well on battlefields. **Earth** (soil type): Moist, loamy, well-drained soil but can handle poor, dryish, sandy soil. **Water** (moisture needs): Moderate. **Fire** (sun/shade requirements): Full sun or light shade. **Air** (climate): US Climate Zones 3–8.

Tips and Warnings: John Ruskin said the poppy was "All silk and flame," and that is an apt description of the beautiful flower. The poppy is best in informal gardens and the **Water** Garden. For best results, plant on Thursday during the first quarter of the moon. Once planted, they are hard to get rid of, although they don't like to be crowded. Since the petals are translucent, it's lovely to have the light behind them at least some of the time. Poppies cannot be transplanted; throw the seeds where you want the plants to grow. Even then the poppy is pretty quirky, but as a rule it is easy to grow. The spent foliage of the perennial poppy is nasty looking, though it fades away quickly, and is replaced by new, attractive growth in September. Taller poppies need to be staked. And no poppy can stand to be picked. Poppy is the source of opium, and the main source of morphine and codeine. The seeds of the opium poppy are widely used in cooking and baking. (They are not narcotic.) The common poppy (*P. rhoeas*) is slightly poisonous. All parts of the opium poppy except the seeds are highly poisonous. It is illegal to grow the opium poppy in the United States and many other countries. The opium poppy is a very popular garden plant in Britain, where the climate makes opium production unlikely. Poppies attract wildlife.

Magic: Paracelsus said that the poppy granted immortality, and one tradition claims that poppies insure fertility and eating its seeds insures pregnancy. Poppy seeds may also be added to money charms.

In Greek depictions, the gods of night (Nix, Thanatos, Hypnos, and Morpheus) were crowned with poppy wreaths. (Somnos is also associated with poppies.) It is also said that the Greek goddess

Demeter used poppy to help her forget the sorrow of losing her daughter Persephone to Hades. In addition, it is said that Aphrodite cried when she mourned for her beloved Adonis, and that from her tears poppies sprang. The Romans often laid poppies on the graves of their departed, and the European field or corn poppy (*P. rhoeas*) is considered the emblem of sleep and forgetfulness. This is the flower that blooms on the blood-drenched fields of Flanders. Thus, symbolically, it memorializes those who died in war. *Poppy may be worn as an amulet. Invoke Ceres or Demeter.*

Potentilla   *(Potentilla* species) This is the herb of **Power.**

Horticulture

Description: Five hundred species of annuals and perennials ranging from small creeping plants to 4 feet high shrubs. All have five deeply toothed leaflets and buttercup like flowers. Shrubs have peeling winter bark, and fruit borne in clusters. *Name Lore:* The very name "potentilla" suggests its power, although it is known more commonly as cinquefoil. *Other Names:* Cinquefoil, silverweed, pentaphyllon, five-finger grass, synkefoyle, witches weed, five leaf, tormentilla, sunkfield, and bloodroot. *Colors:* Traditionally yellow, but there are some red, cream, white, apricot, and pink cultivars. Spring foliage silvery-green. In summer leaves dark green above and light below. *Fragrance:* Bittersweet. *Bloom Time*: April–September. This is one of the few perennials that bloom all summer. *Origin:* Europe but naturalized in the United States.

Habitat: Roadsides, fields, prairies, dry open spaces. **Earth** (soil type): Prefers average, well-drained, but is tolerant of poor, dry soil and drought. **Water** (moisture needs): Varies according to species. **Fire** (sun/shade requirements): Full sun to partial shade. **Air** (climate): US Climate Zones 3–8.

Tips and Warnings: Some potentillas need a prop – you can use a steadier, wirier-stemmed plant for this purpose. Most mix very well with perennials. Usually best for magical purposes when gathered at midnight under a waxing moon; however it is most powerful when picked on the morn of the Summer Solstice.

Magic: As its name suggests, potentilla is a potentiator of any magic spell. It is an herb of justice, clairvoyance, abundance, and protection (especially against evil sprits while you sleep – and witches all the time). Carrying the root supposedly endows its wearer with eloquence, persuasion, and visionary powers. It is also said to strengthen the five senses and can help one attain divinatory dreams, especially ones offering guidance in love.

Filling a drained eggshell with potentilla is supposed to protect property. (More simply, you can hang potentilla over the door.) Possibly because of its five "fingerlike" leaves, the plant is often used as a love charm. Potentilla, especially combined with parsley and vervain, makes a superior anointing oil. Each of its five petals represents a different treasure: riches, health, love, wisdom, and power. It also represents a beloved daughter.

Witches used potentilla as part of their famous flying ointments, mixing it with water hemlock, thorn apples, deadly nightshade, and spiders legs. (The spider legs are not necessary; no true magic depends on the death of a living creature. It is extremely awful karma to kill one.) Drinking tea from white potentilla encourages a pregnant woman to give birth to a girl; if the blossoms are yellow, it will be a boy.

Rites involving cinquefoil are most efficacious when performed on Thursday. It may be used as a purifying bathing herb. Traditionally burned at Ostara, Beltaine, and Litha. Clothe yourself in purple. Taurians have the most luck with it.

Primrose *(Primula vulgaris* syn *P. officinalis)* This is the herb of **Inner Beauty**.

Horticulture

Description: Perennial with leathery, crinkly leaves; evergreen in some cases. There are over 400 varieties of primula. ***Name Lore:*** *Primrose* means, "first rose," and so it is. ***Other Names:*** English Primrose, Cowslip (*P. veris*), fairy cup, butter rose, drelip, English cowslip, herb Peter, password, and Our Lady's keys. ***Similar and related species:*** The cowslip (*P. veris*) can cross with the primrose to produce the Oxslip (*P. elatior*). ***Colors:*** All colors. The cowslip, is deep yellow, yellow or cream. The English primrose *P. vulgaris* is also usually yellow. Other pastel shades available. ***Fragrance:*** Delicate, bittersweet or sweet, spring like. ***Bloom Time***: April–June, depending on variety. ***Origin:*** Northern Hemisphere.

Habitat: Woodland near brooks. **Earth** (soil type): Moist, rich, moisture retentive, humus rich. **Water** (moisture needs) High. **Fire** (sun/shade requirements): Partial or half shade. **Air** (climate): US Climate Zone 3–8, depending on species.

Tips and Warnings: This is a short-lived plant in most areas, and is difficult to maintain. Primrose needs to be divided every year or so. They are beautiful planted in a rock garden, the **Air** Garden, or along a stream. They are also beautiful as an under-plant for tulips. Some primulas cause dermatitis in sensitive people. Bathe in primrose water to enhance your inner beauty.

Magic: This is an herb of love, peace, and immortality. Even with all these nice attributes, however, it is unlucky to bring primroses into a home, unless the bunch totals more than thirteen, in which case it is a good house-guardian. You can also hide primrose in front of the home to keep unwelcome visitors away and protect the house. You hide it by growing it in a pot and hiding the pot. It is lucky to sew a primrose into a child's pillow; doing so will make the child behave. (This is a circumstance in which it is safe to bring one primrose into the house.)

Some believe that primrose wards off illness. Primrose is also good for locating treasure and for making one more attractive. Eating primrose may let you see the fairy folk. Just planting them may do the trick. Blue and red primroses are especially good in this regard; it is said fairies like to hide in them during the rain. *Used in healing rites, and rites of love. Use at Beltaine. Librans have the best chance of succeeding with primrose. Clothe yourself in green. Invoke Aphrodite, Venus, Freya, Blodeweudd, or Lakshmi. Primrose may be carried as an amulet.*

Purslane *(Portulaca oleracea)* This is the herb of **Night Protection**.

Horticulture

Description: Annual with prostrate, succulent stems and 4–6 petals. 2 feet in length. ***Colors:*** Blooms pale yellow. ***Fragrance:*** Subtle. ***Bloom Time***: May–October. ***Origin:*** Europe but widely adapted to the US.

Habitat: Waste place and fields. **Earth** (soil type): Humousy, well–drained, sandy. **Water** (moisture needs): Moderate. **Fire** (sun/shade requirements): Purslane can handle some shade, but prefers full sun. **Air** (climate) US Climate Zones 4–8.

Tips and Warnings: For the best results, plant on Thursday. Purslane can be grown between stones on a garden path, or between herbs in the herb garden. The Puritans used it to treat scurvy. My garden is full of the stuff, even though I never attempted to plant it. Young plants can be cooked or eaten raw in salads.

Magic: This is an herb of good luck, purification, and counter-magic. It will also help one forget a lover. Placed beneath a pillow or strewn around the bed, it provides spiritual protection during the night from evil spirits. *Most effective rites are performed under the full moon.*

Rose *(Rosa species)* This is the **Herb of Romance**.

Horticulture

Description: This perennial shrub is one of the oldest flowering plants known. It is too familiar to need a description. "There is simply the rose; it is perfect in every moment of its existence," said Emerson. All roses are thorny, although the roses in the Garden of Eden remained thorn-less until the Fall! *Name Lore:* Today the name of the rose is inextricably embedded in "rosary," a litany of prayers dedicated to the Virgin Mary, who was considered the rose without thorns. The so-called dog rose (*Rosa canina*) was given that name in the belief that it has powers over the bite of a rabid dog, at least according to Pliny. *Other Names:* Love flower. *Colors:* One of the few plants with true clear red. Roses come in all colors except blue, but the true old roses are mostly red and pink. The red rose is supposed to come from the blood of Adonis. *Fragrance:* A substance called geraniol dictates the characteristic rose fragrance. The scent may be spicy (tea roses), fruity (old roses), lemony, or cinnamon-like. Some are bittersweet. As a rule, the deeper the red, the stronger the fragrance. Yellow roses are less likely to have scent, although some certainly do. *Bloom Time*: May–September. *Origin:* Asia, now worldwide in temperate zones.

Habitat: Fields. **Earth** (soil type): Average. **Water** (moisture needs): **Water** deeply, but infrequently.
Fire (sun/shade requirements): Full sun. **Air** (climate): US Climate Zones 3–9.

Tips and Warnings: Plant during the first or second quarter of the waxing moon (Thursday is the best day). For utmost magical power, include both red and white roses in the garden; this is an old alchemical secret. The old-fashioned roses are more suited to magical purposes, although any rose will do in a pinch. Old-fashioned and species roses do very well in a mixed garden, combining perfectly with salvia, geraniums, lupines, mugwort, irises, carnations, lavender, and sage. It's a sort of garden maxim that hybrid tea roses look best with other roses and don't mix well, but with care, you can

blend them. I've done it. Rose hips can be made into jellies, tea, and wine. A rosebud chain around the ankle is said to heal sprains. You can make a surprisingly durable (and sweet-smelling) rosary out of rose petals. Rose-smelling perfumes should be worn on Friday.

Magic: The rose is truly the master herb of love. Even bathing in rose water, or wearing a necklace of rosebuds, will draw a lover. The rose also brings peace to a household, either by itself or in an herbal bath. Rose hips or buds carried on the body in a red cloth bag, beneath the clothes, are said to attract love. Add a bit of rose oil to any spell where you need courage.

In ancient Greece, diviners used rose petals to tell the future. A concave-shaped petal was selected, and the diviner, having entered into a trance, would hold the petal in her right hand, clap her hands hard together and then examine the petal. If the petal remained whole, the answer to the question is Yes. If it broke, the answer to the question is No.

The Roman nobility liked to sleep on rose petals; they also wore rose garlands about their heads in the belief that this would temper the effects of wine. Petals and buds thrown into a fire bring good luck, and supposedly, merely swallowing one petal of the apothecary rose (*R. gallica*) will cure infertility. The whole plant is generally lucky, although the dog rose should not be brought into a home. Fairies are fond of roses. The red rose symbolized the blood of martyrs and Jesus for the early Christian church, while the white rose symbolized the celibacy of the clergy. It may also symbolize compassion or even death; in Roman times a white rose was planted over the grave of a virgin, and red rose over the graves of other virtuous folk. The rose, especially the pink rose, is a symbol of a powerful love that surpasses even death. The red rose symbolizes passion. *Modern practitioners use roses in divination and love spells. Invoke Brahma, Vishnu, Blodeweudd, Adonis, Demeter. Buddha, or any love deity. Clothe yourself in pink. Librans and Taurians can make particularly effective magic with the rose. A rose may also be carried as an amulet. May 23 is an extremely auspicious day, as is Beltaine, for rose magic.*

Rosemary (*Rosmarinus officinalis*) This is the herb of **Self-Confidence**.

Description: Perennial, evergreen shrub. Some varieties are upright, some sprawling.
Other Names: Compass weed, incensier, polar plant, rosmaris, rosmarine, seadew, rosemarie, guardrobe. *Colors:* Flowers white or bluish; branches pale green; leaves dark above and pale below.
Fragrance: Leaves are sweetly fragrant, often redolent of pine. The scent of the plant is supposed to stem from the time Mary hung the baby Jesus' swaddling clothes over a rosemary bush to dry. (This connection may be clearer to the reader than to me.) *Bloom Time*: Spring. *Origin:* Mediterranean, now widely cultivated.

Habitat: Open places. **Earth** (soil type): Prefers a well-drained more alkaline soil than many plants. **Water** (moisture needs): Likes dry soil, but can also handle moisture. **Fire** (sun/shade requirements): Sunny. **Air** (climate): Needs shelter from wind.

Tips and Warnings: Rosemary is best in an informal garden, although upright rosemary can be made into a hedge. For best magical effects, rosemary should be planted on Sunday. Where rosemary flourishes – the woman rules. It is also a good choice for a moon garden. Sprawling varieties can be substituted for juniper. Clipping rosemary frequently not only makes it look neater, but also releases its characteristic and magical scent. But don't clip too much – the scent is also released when you brush against the plant. It looks lovely against a brick wall. Wait until the tip of the top branch starts to droop before you water; if the tips of the leaves are brown, the plant is getting too much. Rosemary is beneficial to cabbage. It is excellent in the **Fire** Garden. It used to be placed in wedding cakes and Christmas puddings. Now it is generally added to meats, soups, and vegetables. It is good in poultry stuffing. It can also be used in incense, as well as in bathing and shampooing products.

Magic: Rosemary brings good luck; it is one of the totally energizing plants. It brings success to any undertaking. It fosters courage, happiness, love and friendship. It can also be used to banish evil spirits and illness. When carried or worn in a chaplet it improves the mind (especially memory) by promoting commonsense and self-assurance. It was believed to be a guardian of churches. When placed beneath a pillow at night it provides spiritual protection, and will help you remember your dreams. There is a magical rite for seeing one's future mate involving rosemary and thyme, but since the rite involves urinating on the sprig and then putting it in your shoe, we will omit it. There are pleasanter and equally efficacious ways to dream of one's future husband. Just smelling a box made of rosemary wood was supposed to preserve youth.

Rosemary has ancient connections with Christmas and the Virgin Mary, although that association is weak now. (It was once said the flowers turned from white to blue when she lay her mantle over them.) Rosemary may attract fairies and elves. It has the power to rekindle lost energy, remembrance, friendship, fidelity, and love. It can be burned at Yule and is considered to be an auspicious New Year gift. Rosemary sprinkled on the head is also supposed to cure headaches, and it is useful in all healing rituals). As the plant of remembrance, it is traditionally given when friends and lovers must be parted from each other. Rosemary is used at blessings, cleansing rituals, rites of protection, and death rites (placed on the coffin). *It was equally important for handfastings, where wedding crowns were made of it, and sprigs were given to the groom to assure his faithfulness. Arians work well with rosemary.*

Rowan *(Sorbus aucuparia)* This is the herb of **Empowerment**.

Description: Deciduous shrub or small tree with slender, alternate, pinnately compound, upward pointing branches, glossy bark, five-petalled flowers, and sour fruit. Height up to 30 feet. It can live for over 200 years. **Other Names:** Witchwood, quickbane, wicken tree, mountain ash, roan, roddan, rantry, Thor's helper, quickbeam, wild sorb, ran-tree, witchbane, witchwood, and witchen. **Related and Similar Species:** When the rowan is called the European or American mountain ash, it is sometimes confused with the true ash. The true ash *(Fraxinus* species) has alternate leaves; the rowan has opposite leaves. **Colors:** Flowers creamy-white. The red berries are said to derive their color from the blood of the ancestors who live in the tree. Bark can be any color from gray to purplish. Leaves turn gold, pink, and scarlet in the fall. **Fragrance:** Subtle. **Bloom Time**: May–June; berries autumn. **Origin:** Europe.

Habitat: Edges of woods, open areas. **Earth** (soil type): Light, peaty soil with good drainage. **Water** (moisture needs): High. **Fire** (sun/shade requirements): Prefers full sun, but can tolerate light shade. **Air** (climate): US Climate Zones 2–9. Tolerates pollution.

Tips and Warnings: For best magical results, plant a rowan tree during the second quarter of the moon. Rowanberries attract birds. Unripe seeds can be poisonous.

Magic: This is a tree of general protection, purification, divination, knowledge, counter-magic, and healing; it enhances all magical rites. Branches and leaves of this tree are lucky when brought into the home, especially if the branches are formed in the shape of cross. The wood was frequently used for ship masts to ward off evil. (If you touch a witch with even a single leaf, she goes straight to the devil.) Ancient Irish lore says that dragons and serpents guard rowan groves. Putting a rowan branch over stable doors will keep out witches. Because pagan people held this tree in such high repute, the church condemned it.

The berries, if eaten, are supposed to endow the eater with supernormal powers and protection from Satan. (This is one reason why the rowan was planted in churchyards.) Magic wands or staffs made from the wood of the rowan are considered especially powerful for protection, and small crosses made of rowan hidden in the clothes are also protective. However, when you go out to collect the wood for the crosses, be sure to take a different route going and coming, and do not use a knife to cut the twigs.

Some say that rowan trees come from fairyland. Deck your barn on May 2 with rowan to keep your cows free of evil influences and keep the milk from going sour. You can make rowan hoops for your sheep to jump through as well; that will protect them. Rites involving rowan are most effective when performed on Wednesday. *Rowan may be used as incense. This tree is especially useful during times of major strife or conflict. Rites with rowan are most propitious on January 21, May 2 or 3, and July 15, or in December. Choose a time when Mars is visible if possible. Invoke Thor, Brighid, Dagda, Lugh, or Brigantia. Sagittarians have strong connections with rowan.*

Rue *(Ruta graveolens)* This is the herb of **Witches**.

Horticulture

Description: Perennial evergreen herb with erect stems. Height up to 6 feet. *Name Lore:* The Latin name graveolens means "strong-smelling." Our modern word "ruefulness" comes from the name of this plant. *Other Names:* Herb of Grace, herbygrass, ruta, garden rue, herb of repentance. *Colors:* Flowers bright yellow; foliage blue-green or gray-green. *Fragrance:* All parts of the plant are bitterly aromatic. *Bloom Time:* All summer. *Origin:* Southern Europe.

Habitat: Open places. **Earth** (soil type): Prefers a well-drained more alkaline soil than many plants. **Water** (moisture needs): Rue is drought tolerant. **Fire** (sun/shade requirements): Sunny. **Air** (climate): US Climate Zones 5–8.

Tips and Warnings: It has been said from time immemorial that the best and most magical rue must be stolen from somebody else's garden. I am not advocating theft, I'm just telling you what they say. Rue should be planted on Sunday. Rue looks good next to plants with silver foliage. Because its volatile oil can cause blistering on sensitive skin, it should not be planted in the front of the garden. Rue is bad for cabbages, and bad near most other herbs, especially basil. Use gloves when picking. It is a good choice for the **Earth** Garden. All parts of the plant are slightly poisonous, especially the essential oil. Use sparingly in cooking to flavor cheese and stews; when dried it loses its aroma but not its taste. Rue can be put in a cupboard to get rid of ants.

Magic: In the Middle Ages, a sprig of rue was a sign for a witch and at one time any woman who even had rue in her possession was so classified, at least by some people. But this was a grievous error, and a misunderstanding of its power. The Eastern Orthodox Church understood its powers more clearly and used it to invite the divine grace into a sacred space. Shakespeare, too, knew rue as the herb of grace (Hamlet). The Romans nibbled on rue to protect themselves from the evil eye, and the Catholic Church used it to repel demons and negative influences. You can too. Here's how: Just tie some rue with a red ribbon and place it in your doorway. Sniffing fresh rue will take your mind away from any problems concerned with love and will restore you to level-headedness. It will also clear your head of envy, and revitalize you in general. It may give you second sight.

Rue is good for all consecration, protection, and purification rites; it is generally sprinkled around a ceremonial site for the purpose. When purifying a site with rue, clothe yourself in blue. *Invoke Diana or Faunus. Leos have a particular affinity to rue.*

SAFFRON *(Crocus sativa)* This is the herb of **Luxury.**

Horticulture

Description: Perennial. Has an underground corm, a large six–lobed flower, and linear leaves with a pale midrib. This plant is the origin of saffron, and has been cultivated for more than 4000 years. The name saffron comes from the Arabic *za'faran*, referring to the orange-gold stigmas. Height 6 inches. *Other Names:* Autumn crocus, Spanish saffron. *Similar and Related Species:* The true autumn crocus is *Colchicum autumnale,* also sometimes called meadow saffron. Meadow saffron is *poisonous*, so a careful distinction must be made. *Colors:* Pale purple flower. *Fragrance:* Subtle. *Bloom Time*: Fall. (Most other crocus species bloom in early spring.) *Origin:* Middle East.

Habitat **Earth** (soil type): Light, fertile, well-drained. **Water** (moisture needs): Moderate. **Fire** (sun/shade requirements): Part shade. **Air** (climate): US Climate Zones 6–9.

Tips and Warnings: If possible, plant in the west of the garden. Very large doses of saffron can be poisonous; ten grams is a lethal dose. It is the main seasoning in Spanish paella. Perfumes incorporating saffron should be worn on Friday.

Magic: Saffron is an herb of luxurious happiness and clairvoyance (at least the Egyptians considered it so), and it has been used to raise the winds. *Rites with saffron are most efficacious if done during the day or at night when Venus is visible. Saffron may be carried as an amulet. Leos have a special affinity to saffron.*

SAGE (*Salvia officinalis*) This is the herb of **Wisdom.**

Horticulture

Description: Hardy, perennial, evergreen sub-shrub. It has square, hairy stems. Leaves are grey-green and pointed at the end. Height 1–3 feet. *Name Lore: Salvia* is derived from the Latin "to be in good health. *Other Names:* Purple sage, sawge. *Similar and Related Species:* The tender annual ornamental salvia is also called scarlet sage. *Colors:* Shades of white through blue, blue-violet, and purple. Leaves whitish green, green-gray with purple. *Fragrance:* All parts of the plants sweetly aromatic and somewhat fruity. *Bloom Time*: June–September. *Origin: S. officinalis* is native to the Mediterranean and Asia Minor.

Habitat: Dry meadows. **Earth** (soil type): Average to poor sandy, light, or rocky soil. Prefers a more alkaline soil than many plants. **Water** (moisture needs): Low; very drought tolerant. Can stand some moisture, but over watering causes root rot. **Fire** (sun/shade requirements): Full sun to light shade. **Air** (climate): US Climate Zone 4–9 for most varieties.

Tips and Warnings: Sage is best in the informal garden. For best results, plant sage on Thursday. Sage is low maintenance, easy to grow, and beneficial for cabbages. Sage is attractive to hummingbirds, bees, and several species of birds such as goldfinch, sparrows, and quail. Deer, on the other hands don't like the plants. Perhaps it's the smell. Sage can be made into a tea and can be used to flavor soups and fish. Sage has a strong flavor and tends to dominate other spices in cooking, so be careful with it. An old Arab saying credits sage with the ability to prolong life forever: "How can a man die with sage in his garden?" At the very least it prevented gray hair.

Magic: Sage is the herb of virtue, consecration, purification, inspiration, protection, immortality, and salvation, and is used to combat death, especially if eaten in May (the early part of the month is best). It can also help develop wisdom (hence the name "sage"), calm passions (part of wisdom), make wishes come true, banish evil spirits, and attract money. In fact, merely growing sage in the garden was at one time considered a sign of prosperity. It absorbs and destroys negative influences.

Here is an old marriage-divination using sage: Go silently into the garden at the witching hour on Halloween. Pluck twelve sage leaves (if there are any left), one at each stroke of the clock. At the twelfth stroke (and leaf), the face of one's future husband will appear and you'll be married within a year. If no face appears, there's no wedding in the next twelve months. This rite can be performed only once or it will bring bad luck. *Sage can be burned at Mabon (Fall Equinox), Samhain, and Yule as well as at divination, healing, and prosperity rites. Taurians have especially good luck using sage. Sage may be carried as an amulet, used as incense, or included in a ritual bath.*

ST. JOHN'S WORT *(Hypericum perforatum)* This is the herb of **Litha Midsummer**.

Horticulture

Description: Hairless, branched perennial with five-petalled flowers and opposite, stalkless, oval leaves. Height 1–2 feet. *Other Names:* Leaf of the blessed, hypericum, Klamath weed, herba jon, John's wort, goat weed. *Colors:* Blooms bright yellow with bright yellow stamens at the centre; leaves spotted with red or black. The spots appear around August. *Fragrance:* Bittersweet; the scent alone is supposed to dispel evil spirits. *Bloom Time*: Mid summer to early fall. *Origin:* Europe, North Africa, and western Asia. Naturalized in the US.

Habitat: Roadsides, fields, waste places. **Earth** (soil type): Ordinary. **Water** (moisture needs): Moderate. **Fire** (sun/shade requirements): Can tolerate some shade. **Air** (climate): US Climate Zones 4–9.

Tips and Warnings: St. John's wort should be planted on Sunday. St. John's wort is always supposed to be picked with the left hand at Midsummer, and the gardener should pray and ask permission of the summer gods beforehand. Robert Burton, in his famous *Anatomy of Melancholy*, opined that St. John's wort worked best if gathered on Friday and hung around the neck. Some recent studies show that St. John's wort doesn't work as well against depression as formerly believed. Perhaps the scientists picked it on the wrong day. It was also supposed to ward off fever, and is said to make one invincible in war. It is best dried over the Midsummer fire. For magical usage, the earth must be loosened and the entire plant plucked out, roots intact.

Magic: This is an herb of healing, love, protection, and fertility. It also strengthens the will. The ancient Greeks placed this energizing plant above the statues of their gods and in their homes for protection against evil spirits. St. John's wort is reported to be a perfect blend of water and fire, which enhances its healing properties. St. John's wort may attract fairies. It is supposed to be one of the most powerful of all herbs against satanic powers; its yellow blooms represent the sun (St. John's Day is close to the Summer Solstice), and the red on the leaves represents the blood of the martyred saint. This is a good luck plant for a home. For extra protection, gather the plant on St. John's Eve (June 23) and hang the sprigs over your windows and doors. The leaves can also be soaked in olive oil for the same purpose. If St. John's wort oil is dropped on the belt of the beloved, your love is assured. Young women would gather the herb at midnight on St. John's Eve. If the blooms were still fresh in the morning, a healthy child would soon be born. If the blooms were withered, it was said to indicate sterility. *Those born under the sign of Leo have very good luck with St. John's wort. In rites of protection the plant can be burned at Litha. Rites involving St. John's wort are most effective if performed on Sunday. Invoke Balder.*

SANDALWOOD *(Santalum album)* This is the herb of **Spirituality**.

Horticulture

Description: Tropical semi–parasitic evergreen tree with lanceolate leaves. Grows on the roots of other trees. Height 40 feet. *Other Names:* Santal, white saunders, white sandalwood, yellow sandalwood. *Colors:* Flower pale yellow to purple; fruit nearly black. *Fragrance:* Sweet, woody. *Bloom Time*: Variable. *Origin:* South Asia, especially eastern India.

Habitat: Semi parasitic. Lives on roots of host plants. **Earth** (soil type): Roots. **Water** (moisture needs): Moderate. **Fire** (sun/shade requirements): Sunny. **Air** (climate): Tropical.

Tips and Warnings: Perfume incorporating sandalwood should be worn on Tuesday.

Magic: Burning sandalwood makes a wish come true if accompanied by the ancient Hebrew words invoking Lord God, "Adonai, Elohim; Adonai, Elohim; Adonai, Elohim." Sandalwood has been used both to call up and banish spirits. Placing sandalwood on the forehead is supposed to focus the mind. Its very scent is supposed to open the spiritual faculties, especially when combined with frankincense. Combined with lavender, it is supposed to open a path into the Otherworld of the spirit. Oil of sandalwood can also help the seeker achieve knowledge of previous lives. Use sandalwood in rites of clairvoyance, protection, consecration, love magic, and healing. *Rites incorporating sandalwood are most effective when Mercury is visible and the moon is as close to full as possible. Invoke Isis. Clothe yourself in white. Sandalwood is used primarily as incense, but it can also be carried as an amulet. Those born under the sign of Virgo have great luck with sandalwood magic.*

SELF-HEAL

See Heal-all.

SHAMROCK

See Clover.

SOMA

Alas, this is a true magical herb, and can no longer be grown. In the Hindu tradition the most powerful of magic herbs is soma. Soma (*haoma* in the Zoroastrian tradition) may or may not have once been an extant plant. If it ever was, the consensus is that the plant no longer exists. There is no agreement even about what kind of plant it was. The ancient Rig Veda sometimes describes it as clear, sometimes as amber or ruddy. Sometimes it refers to it as grass, at other times as a liquid pressed between stones. Today, the effects of soma may be approximated by various secret formulas. Whatever its composition, soma was clearly a mind-altering substance. It is not for nothing that the ancient *rishis,* immemorial singers of the Rig Veda, called it the God of Delight. Today, practitioners of the art of Tantra have developed their own formulas evoking the legendary power of soma. Most of these formulas contain alcohol, marijuana, psychedelic mushrooms, and other visionary drugs. The western version of the drink is ambrosia, which shares many of its qualities.

SOUTHERNWOOD *(Artemisia abrotanum)* This is an herb of **Seduction.**

Horticulture

Description: Perennial, compact, woody sub-shrub. Tiny flowers, and feathery pinnate leaves. *Other Names:* Old man, lad's love, appleringie, garde-robe, maiden's ruin. *Colors:* Blooms yellow. Leaves gray/green. *Fragrance:* Pleasantly strong and lemony. *Bloom Time*: August–September. *Origin:* Southern Europe.

Habitat: Fields. **Earth** (soil type): Average, well-drained, slightly acid. **Water** (moisture needs): Drought tolerant. **Fire** (sun/shade requirements): Prefers full sun. **Air** (climate): US Climate Zones 5–9.

Tips and Warnings: Easy to grow but may not flower in northern gardens. It makes an excellent addition to a moon garden; it is also a good choice for the **Earth** Garden.

Magic: The leaves and stems are the parts used. Young men are traditionally supposed to include a sprig of southernwood in gifts to their ladies. It is traditionally used as air freshener, in the bath, and as a hair rinse, and is used for counter-magic and spell breaking. *Geminis are particularly adept at working with southernwood.*

STAR ANISE

(*Illicium anisatum, I. verum*) See Anise. The two have identical magical properties.

SUNFLOWER (*Helianthus annus*) This is the herb of the **Sun**.

Horticulture

Description: Tall, branched annual herb with an erect hairy stem, large pointed leaves, and showy flowers. The wild sunflower has more and smaller flowers than the garden variety. Height up to 10 feet. *Name Lore:* Named after Helios, the Greek sun-god (who was later drowned by his uncles). *Other Names:* Marigold of Peru. *Similar and Related Species:* Tickseeds, coneflowers, and black-eyed Susan all belong to the same family. *Colors:* Yellow flower rays, purplish-brown disc flowerets. *Fragrance:* Subtle. *Bloom Time*: June–September. *Origin:* North and Central America.

Habitat: Prairies, waste places, roadsides, grasslands. **Earth** (soil type): Rich, well-drained. **Water** (moisture needs): Average. **Fire** (sun/shade requirements): Full sun. **Air** (climate): US Climate Zone 5–10.

Tips and Warnings: For best magical results, plant during the first, third, or fourth quarter of the moon. An excellent plant for the **Fire** Garden. A yellow dye can be extracted from sunflowers and the seeds make an important bird food. At one time it was believed that planting sunflowers around the house would ward off malaria, and the leaves and flowers were used to treat malaria.

Magic: The ancient Aztec priestesses carried sunflowers and wore them as crowns and necklaces. At one time, women believed that eating sunflower seeds during the waxing moon would help them conceive. The sunflower may attract fairies. In the Victorian language of flowers, the sunflower stands for devotion, a notion probably derived from the way it follows the sun. It also represents self-respect or even haughtiness. *Sunflowers are good for material magic. Invoke the name of Helios during the rites. Sunflower can be carried as an amulet.*

TANSY (*Tanacetum vulgare*) This is an herb of **Repulsion**.

Horticulture

Description: Hardy perennial herb with an erect, almost hairless stem, floret flat-topped and rayless. It is a member of the aster family. Height 2–3 feet. ***Name Lore:*** The Greek name for the plant, *athanatos*, means "deathless." ***Other Names:*** Bitterbuttons, scented fern, stinking Willie. ***Colors:*** Flowers bright yellow. Fruit greenish-white. Leaves dark green. Stems reddish. ***Fragrance:*** Camphor–like, strong. ***Bloom Time***: July–September. ***Origin:*** Europe and Asia. Naturalized in America.

Habitat: Roadsides, hedgerows, waste places. **Earth** (soil type): Needs lots of space. Tolerates poor soil. **Water** (moisture needs): Moderate. **Fire** (sun/shade requirements): Prefers full sun, but can handle shade. **Air** (climate): US Climate Zones 4–10.

Tips and Warnings: Tansy can be invasive, and so actually does "best" in poor, dry soil, where it can be more easily contained. Tansy is attractive to beneficial wasps. Planted close to the door, tansy will repel ants and if you hang it upside down near the door, it will keep flies out of the kitchen, even if the kids forget to shut the door. It gets rid of fleas, too. Laying the bruised leaves on the stomach of a pregnant woman is supposed to prevent miscarriage. Tansy used to be made into a healing tea, but the stuff tastes terrible. It is better to be sick. This plant is dangerous if used internally, which seems to be counterproductive for a plant of immortality, or at least longevity.

Magic: In ancient days, the purifying tansy was used to preserve corpses, and partly for that reason (or perhaps it was the other way around) it was known as the herb of immortality. Tansy is protective of all gentle spirits. In the Victorian language of flowers: "I declare against you!" (In this case the "you" must refer to mice and other pests.) Today this herb is used for healing rituals. In the past, tansy cakes were popular at Easter. *Gemini and Librans are usually the best at dealing with tansy. Tansy may be carried as an amulet.*

THISTLE (*Echinops, Cirsium* or *Sonchos* species) This is the herb of **Autumn**.

Horticulture

Description: Spiny annual, biennial, perennial plants with erect stem. Many species. The thistle is the national flower of Scotland (because the Danes, who were sneaking around barefoot trying to take over the place, cried out when they stepped on them and thus made know their presence.) Height up to 5 feet. ***Other Names:*** Lightning plant. ***Similar and Related Species:*** Bull thistle (*Cirsium vulgare*), Canada thistle, and musk thistle. See also: Blessed Thistle, treated separately. One good garden thistle is the *Echinops,* or the Globe Thistle. ***Colors:*** Flowers blue, purple, and white. ***Fragrance:*** Subtle. ***Bloom Time:*** July–September. ***Origin:*** Worldwide.

Habitat: Fields woods, roadsides, waste places. **Earth** (soil type)Average too poor, well-drained **Water** (moisture needs): Moderate. **Fire** (sun/shade requirements): Full sun. **Air** (climate): US Climate Zones 4–9.

Tips and Warnings: For best magical results, plant on Sunday. Cut down all the plants before Midsummer, or you'll have a lot of problems with them. There are ornamental thistles, however, that create a wonderful accent plant. I suggest you try them! The bull thistle (*Cirsium vulgaris*) is attractive to butterflies.

Magic: If a pregnant woman eats thistle, she will have a boy. The thistle is also a great revitalizer and energizer. It represents defiance. Magically, the thistle is sometimes used to summon as well as banish spirits. It is said that thistle grown in the garden will ward off thieves, but the thistle might give you more trouble than the thieves. *It can be burned at Mabon (Fall Equinox). People born under the sign of Aries have particular luck with thistles. Invoke Thor. Thistle can be carried as an amulet.*

THYME *(Thymus vulgaris)* This is the herb of **Resolve.**

Horticulture

Description: Minty herb with fine hairy leaves and tiny flowers. Height 6 inches. *Other Names:* Bitter mint. *Name Lore*: The name possibly derives from the Greek word *thumon* referring to an herb used in sacrifices. *Colors:* Flowers purple, mauve, white, lavender, or pink. Foliage silver-gray. *Fragrance:* Aromatic foliage; some bittersweet, some lemony (*T. x citriodorus*). Often most noticeable on a hot day. *Bloom Time*: May–June. *Origin:* Mediterranean.

Habitat: Usually found in gardens. **Earth** (soil type): Prefers a more alkaline, chalky soil than many plants. Well drained, dry soil. Tolerates poor soil. **Water** (moisture needs): Prefers dry conditions, but can handle humidity. **Fire** (sun/shade requirements): Full sun. **Air** (climate): US Climate Zones 6–10. Heat tolerant.

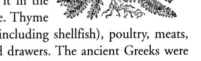

Tips and Warnings: For best results plant thyme during the first quarter of the moon. Thyme is excellent in the knot garden, if you use the old, tough upright variety. It's also a fine choice for a moon garden. The modern cultivars are best in an informal setting, including rock gardens. Creeping thyme (*Thymus praecox*) has a wonderful scent. Plant it in the garden pathways so people can step on it to release the fragrance. Thyme is beneficial to cabbage. It is used to flavor soups, bread, fish (including shellfish), poultry, meats, vegetables, eggs, cheeses, and desserts, and to freshen closets and drawers. The ancient Greeks were especially fond of it, rubbing themselves with it after baths.

Magic: Thyme is an herb of courage and love. Burning this herb brings health to the entire household. It banishes venomous creatures and helps communion with the dead and the Otherworld. Putting thyme in a pillow will ensure good dreams and provide spiritual protection. Thyme is home to certain varieties of fairies. It fact, it enables one to see them. *Thyme may be burned at Litha (Midsummer) and used in purification, healing, and divination rites. It can be worn as an amulet, and used as incense or as a fumigator. Rites involving thyme are most efficacious when performed on Friday. Arians have strong connections with thyme.*

VALERIAN *(Valeriana officinalis)* This is the herb of **Transformation.**

Horticulture

Description: Perennial herb with a large root system with finely cut, ferny leaves and clustered flowers. Height 3–5 feet. *Other Names:* Garden heliotrope, amantilla, blessed herb, setwell, phu, capon's tail, amatilla, all heal, cat valerian. This plant may also be the biblical spikenard. The name "phu" stems from its nasty smell. ***Colors:*** Flowers pale pink or white. ***Fragrance:*** Foul and sour. "Valerian! The most infernal, diabolical smell that was ever emitted from any known or unknown substance." Alice Jones and Ella Merchant, *Unveiling a Parallel: Romance*.) ***Bloom Time:*** June–August. ***Origin:*** Europe; now found in all temperate regions.

Habitat: Marshy places. **Earth** (soil type): Rich. **Water** (moisture needs): High. **Fire** (sun/shade requirements): Sun to shade. **Air** (climate) US Climate Zones 4–8.

Tips and Warnings: Valerian is most suited to the informal garden. This deeply rooted plant will help to break up a heavy, clayey soil. Valerian is best in the **Earth** Garden. Internal use over a long period can produce depression. I personally dislike this herb so much that being around it even for a second depresses me.

Magic: Valerian is consecrating and purifying (when sprinkled). It is also considered an herb of peace. Placed beneath the pillow, it brings on sleep. Burning it banishes evil (and everything else). The Pied Piper supposedly carried valerian in his pocket. (One would think it would have had the opposite effect than the one it did.) It is considered important in love charms. Cats are sometimes attracted to this plant, and a tiny bit of valerian root may be added to lavender and betony in a cachet to attract men. Valerian mends a broken heart, and overcomes opposition. It is important in all kinds of transformations of the spirit. For medieval monks, the herb was holy to the Virgin Mary. *Clothe yourself in blue or lavender. Valerian may be carried as an amulet. Scorpios have good luck with valerian.*

VERVAIN (*Verbena officinalis*) This is the herb of **Enchantment**.

Horticulture

Description: Perennial hairy herb with a square, erect, leaves and tubular flowers resembling a candelabrum borne in terminal spikes. Produces broad mats. Height 1–4 feet. ***Other Names:*** Verbena, the enchanter's plant, Juno's herb, blue vervain, herb of grace, Juno's tear, pigeon's grass, herb of grace. The name vervain comes from Celtic roots and means to "drive away stones," such as bladder or kidney stones. ***Colors:*** Purple, white, or lilac. ***Fragrance:*** Faint but bitter, although it can be made into a heavy perfume traditionally used in witches' sabbats. ***Bloom Time:*** May–October. ***Origin:*** Europe, North Africa, China, Japan. Some species are native to North America.

Habitat: Moist ground. **Earth** (soil type): Average, well-drained. **Water** (moisture needs): Can handle humid conditions. **Fire** (sun/shade requirements): Full sun. **Air** (climate): US Climate Zones 6–10.

Tips and Warnings: Vervain should be planted on Friday for the most efficacious results. It is said that burying it in your garden will assure a bountiful harvest. The plant is traditionally gathered on Midsummer's Eve or when Sirius the Dog Star rises. It can also be gathered on the first day of the new moon before sunrise. After being picked, it should be raised high in the left hand. If gathered at other times, the plant is not effectual. Vervain is also considered good for other plants, both indoors and out. It can be sprinkled on growing things.

Magic: Vervain is an herb of energy, justice, peace, good fortune, and happiness. Burning vervain will rid the practitioner of the chains of unrequited love. Ancient texts say that burning vervain and frankincense together, along with the repetition of a solemn chant, can draw down the moon, or make a snake burst open. (I don't recommend either of these practices.) One can then "bind" one's love to one's heart. The Druids also held vervain in particular regard, and sprinkled it upon worshippers as a blessing. Vervain also dispels fears and wards off illness and insects. Merely touching your intended after you have washed your hands in vervain-infused water will bring about the desired result, or for stronger magic, place some in your mouth and kiss your beloved. Hung around the neck, it will prevent dreams; placing vervain beneath the pillow guarantees a restful night. Vervain reportedly acts as an aphrodisiac, although some sources say it has the opposite effect, depending upon how it is prepared. Vervain also protects soldiers from their enemies and brings quarrels to an end.

Vervain makes a superior anointing oil, especially when combined with cinquefoil and parsley. Some believe that vervain can help recover lost items, and it is considered as helpful in obtaining material objects. If placed in a baby's crib, it will help the child's emotional and intellectual development. As incense, it stimulates creativity, especially in the arts, and is associated with intellectual prowess. It can be used as a charm to catch fish and hive bees. Wearing vervain or bathing in it places one under the influence of Diana. Vervain was also a most important herb in the mystical cauldron of Cerridwen. Vervain attracts fairies. It is used in blessings, love magic, protection, and purification rituals. It is customary in some circles to wear a crown of vervain while performing magic. The white variety is considered to be the most potent. *Rites involving vervain are most effective near the full moon. Monday night is the best time. Vervain may be carried as an amulet. Geminis have good luck with vervain. Vervain may be burned at Litha. Invoke Isis, Jupiter, Mars, or Venus*

VIOLET and PANSY (*Viola* species) This is the herb of **Immortal Love.**

Horticulture

Description: Small perennial; most species, and there are scores of them, have five sepals and five petals. Popular types include the pansy (*V. x wittrockiana*) and Johnny-jump-up (*V. tricolor*). The most common blue violet in the US is the *V. papilionacea*, which are actually more lilac colored. One color variation is the Confederate violet (white with purple veins) that tends to grow in more southerly regions of the United States. In the UK the dog violet (*V. riviniana*) is the most common wild violet. The sweet violet (*V. odorata*) is the most fragrant. ***Name Lore:*** In Greek the word *io* means "violet." ***Other Names:*** Pansy, heart's ease, Johnny-jump-up, blue violet. ***Similar and Related Species:*** Pansies and violets are closely related and are often interchangeable for magical use. ***Colors:*** Blue or white. ***Fragrance:*** Sweet, but elusive. The common wild violet is practically odorless, so if fragrance is important to you, you'll need to find a sweet-scented cultivar. ***Bloom Time***: April–June, depending on the variety. ***Origin:*** Eurasia and North America.

Habitat: Shady woods for most; some like meadows. **Earth** (soil type): Wooded area; moist, limy, rich humusy soil. **Water** (moisture needs): Moderate, does better if kept moist. **Fire** (sun/shade requirements): Shade, half shade, partial shade, or dappled sunlight. They like the high shade of deciduous trees. The Johnny-jump-up can handle full sun. **Air** (climate): US Climate Zones 4–8 for most species. Most violets and pansies can handle a light frost. If you live in the south or in most parts of the UK you can plant them in the fall for a winter garden.

Tips and Warnings: Most of the large garden-variety violets have no scent. You must head for the woods to enjoy the sweet scent of the *V. odorata*. Violets have been made into wine and conserves, as well as tea. Wearing a violet wreath was supposed to dispel the odors of wine. (Sniffing violets was rumored to cause a temporary loss of smell.) Violet perfumes should be worn on Friday. Violet is most magical if grown in the south of the garden. Roman women used to mix violets and goat's milk to help their complexions. The Romans often wore garlands of violets on their heads during banquets, believing they cooled the brow. (They could probably have achieved much the same effect by eating less.) Pliny said violets induced sleep. Violet oil is healing when added to baths. Violets should be planted on Thursday (luck charms) or Friday (love charms) for greatest efficacy. Most violets are invasive – in some places they are even considered weeds! Violets create a beautiful softening effect in every garden, and they naturalize well. If properly fertilized, many bloom again in the fall. They look well planted with daffodils and are good for the **Air** Garden.

Magic: The modest violet has a rich and mystical past. This is an herb of justice as well as love. Violets attract the blessings of beneficent spirits, and gives off healing vibrations. In *Midsummer Night's Dream* Puck uses violet juice for a love potion. Violet is in fact a standard ingredient in most love potions, often combined with roses, yarrow, lavender, and apple blossoms. The leaves are also considered protective. The Greeks claimed that violets were born from their god Attis. However, never being satisfied with just one theory, they also suggested that violets were the tears of Io whom Zeus had changed into a white heifer to protect her from his jealous wife Hera. Fairies like them, especially pansies. The Victorians regarded the violet as symbol of simplicity and steadfastness. Violets represent innocence and modesty (white violet), as well as loyalty and constancy (blue violet). White violets are emblems of St. Fina. The Bonapartists of France also chose the violet as their symbol, since Napoleon said he would return with the violets in spring. (He did, too.) Romans had a special day just for violets, the *dies violaris*, in which they remembered their dead; in some places violets were traditionally placed on the graves of children. Today they are frequently a part of wedding bouquets. *Rites involving violets are most effective if performed on Wednesday or Friday. Violet may be carried as an amulet. Invoke Jupiter.*

WALNUT *(Juglans* species) This is the tree of **Secret Treasure.**

Horticulture

Description: Large deciduous tree producing edible nuts. Height 20–100 feet. The black walnut (*J. nigra*), the English walnut (*J. regia*), and the butternut, or white, walnut (J. *cinerea*) are all large, handsome trees grown for their fruit – the walnut – their wood, and their ornamental value in parks and large gardens. ***Other Names:*** Tree of evil. ***Colors:*** Bark ash-gray (*J. regia*), brown and ridged (*J. nigra*). Flowers yellow. Leaves light or mid-green. ***Fragrance:*** The leaves of the black walnut have a pungent odor. English walnut leaves are aromatic when bruised. ***Bloom Time***: June. ***Origin:*** Southeastern Europe and western Asia (*J. regia*).

Habitat: Forest. **Earth** (soil type): Fertile, well-drained. **Water** (moisture needs): Moderate. **Fire** (sun/shade requirements): Does best in full sun. **Air** (climate): US Climate Zones 5–9 for the black walnut; Zones 3–9 for other species.

Tips and Warnings: The shade of the walnut tree is considered harmful. The tree does not transplant well. The black walnut carries in its roots a substance called juglone that destroys nearby trees, especially fruit and oak trees. The walnut is too large for most gardens. Trees do not fruit until they are least eight years old.

Magic: The nut of the tree is reported to contain great and secret treasures. Witches used to dance in their shade. There's an Italian story dating back to the seventh century about a walnut tree frequented by witches. The tree remained in leaf all year round; when missionaries cut it down, the witches replanted it from seed. Dreaming about walnuts is supposed represent your attempts to solve a difficult problem (a "hard nut to crack"). But dreaming of walnuts is not perhaps very common. At one time walnuts were believed to cure mental diseases, perhaps because of their resemblance to the brain. Walnuts may be used at handfastings. *Invoke Diane, Hecate or Artemis, who received walnut tributes from the Greeks. Walnuts may be carried as an amulet.*

WATER HEMLOCK *(Cicuta virosa)* This is the herb of the **Magical Sword.**

Horticulture

Description: This poisonous biannual has coarsely toothed leaves. *Name Lore:* This plant derives its other name, cowbane, from the fact that it is deadly to cattle. *Other Names:* Cowbane. *Similar and Related Species:* The plant is sometimes mistaken for parsley or sweet cicely. *Colors:* Leaves are purple spotted or streaked. *Fragrance:* Parsley-like and strong (leaves). *Bloom Time*: June–August. *Origin:* Northern and Central Europe and Asia.

Habitat: Marshes, wet meadows, ditches. **Earth** (soil type): **Water** hemlock has an aquatic habitat. **Water** (moisture needs): **Water** plant. **Fire** (sun/shade requirements): Sun or shade. **Air** (climate): US Climate Zones 4–8.

Tips and Warnings: Although the plant has a sweet smell and taste, all parts of water hemlock are lethal. It should never be used for medicine, magic, or food. This is related to the plant that killed Socrates (poison hemlock, Conium maculatum)

Magic: In ritual, the plant is used to purify magical instruments, especially swords and daggers. It was also used to curse men by making them impotent. *Invoke Hecate.*

WATER LILY

(Nymphaea) See Lotus. The two herbs have identical magical powers.

WILLOW *(Salix* species) This is the tree of **Sorrow.**

Horticulture

Description: Deciduous fast growing tree with tiny flowers. Common landscape varieties include the white, or European willow (*S. alba*), the weeping willow (*S. babylonia*), the goat or pussy willow (*S. caprea*), and the corkscrew willow (*S. matsudana*). Altogether there are over 400 species of willow, including the white willow, peachleaf willow, weeping willow, Bebb willow, coastal plain willow, sandbar willow, Florida willow, crack willow, black willow, white willow (*Salix alba*), balsam willow, and basket willow. ***Name Lore:*** The words "willow" and "witch" may be related, both stemming from the Old English *wigle* meaning "divination." According to a very inaccurate legend, the exiled Jews in Babylon hung their harps on the willow, making its branches droop. Hence the weeping willow (*S. babylonia.*) ***Other Names:*** Tree of Enchantment, witches' aspirin, arovous, osier, saille. ***Colors:*** Flowers yellowish or greenish. Bark is gray, red, or brown depending on species. Foliage bright green in the spring, yellow in fall. ***Fragrance:*** Slightly woody. ***Bloom Time***: Early spring. ***Origin:*** The weeping willow (*S. babylonia*) is native to China, others native to central and southern Europe.

Habitat: Stream and riverbanks. Wet woods. **Earth** (soil type): Moisture-retentive, but well-drained. **Water** (moisture needs): Heavy, unless naturally supplied, which is best. **Fire** (sun/shade requirements): Full sun or light shade, depending on cultivar. **Air** (climate): US Climate Zones 4–9.

Tips and Warnings: Easy to grow and attractive in the winter garden. Willows are attractive to bees. According to Cunningham, willow should be planted to the west of the garden. Set willows well away from house foundations and drainage systems. Their root systems can be damaging. In the Middle Ages, it was believed that if the saliva of a sick person were placed under a willow, the person would be healed. It is bad luck to tell a secret while standing beneath a willow: the wind that blows through the leaves will reveal the secret to everyone. Striking any animal or child with a willow twig (as if one would!) will stunt their growth.

Magic: Willows have been used to summon spirits, divine the future (in divination rites, a bundle of 5, 7 or 9 branches is used) and to protect against evil influences, sorcery, and the evil eye. Bearing a sprig of willow will free you from fear of death. To dream about a willow, however, indicates a coming sorrow. Because willow wood is flexible, belonging to the ever-changing moon, it reminds the practitioner that the tides of sorrow will eventually turn, and that change is part of the natural rhythm of life. Willow is used to bind witches' brooms, and witches often tie a knot in a willow whip while casting a spell. Once the magic takes effect, the knot is untied. Willow wands are wonderful for wishing magic. In China, willows were frequently used in rain charms; practitioners would wear willow wreaths upon their brows during the rites. If you come upon a willow branch that seems to have knotted naturally, leave it alone. The fairies did it. In Britain the willow typically stands for death, although an alternate tradition suggests the stubborn power of life over adverse circumstances. In other places willow bears still different meanings – Chastity (Europe); female sexuality and spring (China); joy (Egypt); fertility (Greece). At one time broken willow twigs were also given as parting gifts, suggestive of sorrow at the departure. In China one was expected to wear a willow wreath on the feast of Qingming, held 105 days after the winter solstice; those who failed to do so are to be reborn as yellow dogs. In parts of Britain it is believed it is bad luck to burn willow on Bonfire Night (Guy Fawkes Day, November 5). The Druids used willow baskets for their human sacrifices, but the Druids were not always quite so nice as one might wish.

Many potent spells are written upon willow bark. Willow wands are ideal for carrying around a Maypole at Beltaine. This is an important herb to use for those who are in mourning and who are unlucky in love or breaking off an affair. Rites involving willow include women's rites, wish-magic, death passage rites, rites of divination and healing, and rites done under the moon. *Invoke Hecate,*

Circe, Ceres, Mercury, Artemis, Hera, or Persephone. Rites involving willow are most efficacious on Monday. The most auspicious dates are April 15 and October 22 or in February. Willow may be carried as an amulet. Rites with willow are most efficacious when the moon is full. Rites with willow are most effective when performed by women.

WINDFLOWER

See Anemone.

WOODRUFF (*Galium odoratum* or *Asperula odorata*) This is the herb of **Encouragement.**

Horticulture

Description: Perennial herb with unbranched, hairless erect stems, and small, star-shaped flowers. Height 4–6 inches. *Other Names:* Sweet woodruff, herb walter, wood musk, master of the woods. *Colors:* Flowers white; leaves pale green. *Fragrance:* Pleasant, tart, hay-scented. Drying increases the scent. *Bloom Time*: April–late May. *Origin:* Europe

Habitat: Damp woods. **Earth** (soil type): Moist, well-drained, limy, humusy soil. **Water** (moisture needs): High. This plant likes to keep its feet wet. **Fire** (sun/shade requirements): Partial shade to shade. **Air** (climate): US Climate Zones 4–8.

Tip and Warnings: An excellent ground cover. Good in the **Fire** Garden. For best results plant woodruff on a Sunday. This is the traditional herb that goes into May wine.

Magic: Woodruff is reported to bring wealth, justice, and encouragement. As incense, it produces a sense of equilibrium and represents victory, especially for athletes. It also signals change. *This herb is traditionally burned during Beltaine and during divination ceremonies. Rites involving woodruff are most powerful in the spring. Clothe yourself in orange.*

WORMWOOD (*Artemisia absinthium*) This is the herb of **Ill-omen.**

Horticulture

Description: A hardy perennial with woody base, tall erect stems and small, rayless flowers. All parts covered with a silvery down. Height 2–4 feet. *Name Lore:* The name "wormwood" possibly refers to the fact that it at one time was used to kill intestinal worms. A competing theory suggests that the name is related to the Teutontic *wer* ("man") and *wod* or ("courage"). (The word "vermouth" is related.) This plant may be the "bitter gall" of the Bible. *Other Names:* Absinthe, old woman, green ginger. *Similar and Related Species:* Sagebrush, *A. tridentate*, is native to the American plains. *Colors:* Flowers greenish-yellow; leaves are silver green or grayish. All parts of the plants are covered in a silvery down. *Fragrance:* Leaves are aromatic with a bitter piney or citrus scent. *Bloom Time*: July–August. *Origin:* Mediterranean region.

Habitat: Rocky waste places, hillsides, roadsides. **Earth** (soil type): Well-drained. It can handle very poor, dry soil. **Water** (moisture needs): Drought tolerant. **Fire** (sun/shade requirements): Full sun. **Air** (climate): US Climate Zones 4–8.

Tips and Warning: Wormwood was an important plant in every medieval herb garden. For best results, plant on a Sunday. Because of their silvery color, other kinds of artemisia are useful for separating colors. However, wormwood must be kept away from other garden plants. The absinthin it contains, which will wash off leaves into the soil, is toxic to other plants. Wormwood is an ingredient of the notorious drink absinthe (It's what Van Gogh was drinking when he cut off his ear.) It is now illegal to sell drinks containing wormwood. It is a fairly dangerous substance; taken over a long time, absinthe is habit forming and causes neurological damage. Wormwood is listed unsafe by the USFDA. Although some people use wormwood for incense, it really is poisonous and should never be used indoors. Its famously repellent scent banishes insects and almost anything else.

Magic: This is a plant of ill-omen. "He has filled me with bitterness, he has made me drunken with wormwood." Lamentations 3:15. It was formerly used as an aphrodisiac. If you burn the leaves and stems in a graveyard you will summon evil spirits. Otherwise, you may call up spirits in general, not necessarily evil ones. Supposedly this is the plant that grew in the path left by the serpent in the Garden of Eden. *It is used in love magic, purification and divination ceremonies. Those born under the sign of Cancer have good luck with wormwood. Invoke Diana.*

YARROW *(Achillea millefolium)* This is the herb of **Divination**.

Horticulture

Description: Creeping perennial herb with erect, downy stems and finely dissected, hairy, thin fernlike leaves. Flowers grow in flat-topped clusters at the top of the stems. Over 200 species. Height up to 2.5 feet, many smaller. Yarrow is a member of the daisy family. ***Name Lore:*** *Millefolium* means "thousand leaves," and *Achillea* refers to Achilles. Achilles is said to have used the plant to stanch his men's bleeding wounds. The Old English word for this plant, *gaerwe*, and means "healer." ***Other Names:*** Milfoil, arrowroot, nosebleed, devil's nettle, seven year's love, sanguinary, devil's plaything, bloodwort, woundwort, stanchweed, staunchgrass. One common variety, *A. ptamica* is often called sneezewort. (It was once used as snuff.) ***Colors:*** Basal leaves dark green, stem leaves gray-green. Blooms whitish or pinkish florets for the wild variety. The cultivated variety comes in many colors, including golden yellow. The frequently cultivated *A. millefolium* "Fire King" is a wonderful red, but it can be invasive. ***Fragrance:*** Strong, semi-sweet, pleasantly aromatic leaves when crushed. ***Bloom Time***: May–September. Peak bloom is in spring, but if the flowers are picked off, it will continue to produce flowers occasionally until frost. ***Origin:*** Originally Asia and Europe, now cultivated all over the world. There are also a few Native American species.

Habitat: Old fields, dry banks, and roadsides. Can also be found in marshy places. **Earth** (soil type): Tolerant of many soil types, including poor soil, but does not like to stay wet. **Water** (moisture needs): Low. Drought resistant, but can also tolerate humidity. **Fire** (sun/shade requirements): Full sun. **Air** (climate) US zones 2-9. A few rather dislike the heat, although most common cultivars can handle it.

Tips and Warnings: Plant yarrow on Friday for the most efficacious results. It is a wonderful choice for a moon garden. Yarrow was a critical component of every medieval herb garden; it is a superior garden plant, and rumored to be strengthening to its neighbors. Yarrow can be used as a border plant or ground cover, and is a positive lifesaver for a barren area. The plant divides easily, which is a good thing, since it needs to be divided every year or so. In the West, it is traditional to pick and burn yarrow on St. John's Eve. In China it was picked on the fifth day of the fifth month – around the time of the Summer Solstice. Yarrow is attractive to beneficial wasps. Yarrow should be taken only in moderation. It can cause skin irritation if used excessively or over long periods.

Magic: Yarrow has actually been found in a Neanderthal grave, attesting to the ancient powers of this plant. The Chinese used yarrow stalks in consulting their great book of divination, the *I Ching*, which was even known as the Yarrow Stalk Oracle. Some say the devil uses yarrow to cast his spells. In some western traditions, it is unlucky to bring it into the house, but planting yarrow near the doorstep will keep out the devil himself. The Celts, like the Chinese, used yarrow for divination purposes, especially love-divination. It was employed to divine the thoughts of others, to forecast the weather, to avert evil spells, and to banish evil spirits. Carried with nettle, it dispels fear.

Some say that putting a piece of yarrow in the bed or beneath the pillow will make you have prophetic dreams, especially about your true love. In other traditions, yarrow is said to provide protection to sleepers when placed beneath a pillow. In a similar way, nine yarrow stalks bound together with copper wire and tied with a green ribbon can be used as a marriage charm. Yarrow draws fairies. It can be used in purification, protection, and divination rituals. Yarrow can also be used in an ointment at a handfasting or wedding rite, since it supposedly binds a couple together for seven years, which for some people is long enough. *Rites with yarrow are most efficacious when Venus is visible. Clothe yourself in yellow. Yarrow may be carried as an amulet. Leos have good luck with yarrow.*

YEW *(Taxus* species) This is the herb of **Death.**

Horticulture

Description: The evergreen, resinous, coniferous yew comes in both tree and shrub and varieties. It has peeling bark. Male and female flowers are on separate trees. Most Yews are extremely long-lived, some having achieved an age of 1000 years. Unlike other conifers, the yew has no cones. Seeds are naked, mainly on separate plants, usually developing from bud base. There are twenty species worldwide, about four native to the United States. Many are poisonous. One of the most magical is the English Yew (*Taxus baccata*). Height 80 feet. *Name Lore:* The tree's Latin name, *Taxus*, means bow. *Other Names:* Chinwood. *Colors:* Berries red. Bark is red-brown. Needles dark green above and light green below. "Flowers" small and yellow but produce enormous amounts of golden pollen. *Fragrance:* Slightly but penetratingly aromatic. Some varieties (like the Florida Yew or "stinking cedar") have an unpleasant odor. *Bloom Time*: March–April. *Origin:* Temperate climates all over the northern hemisphere.

Habitat: Woods, cliffs, and scrub. **Earth** (soil type): Limy, chalky. **Water** (moisture needs): Average **Fire** (sun/shade requirements): Shade tolerant. **Air** (climate): US Climate Zones 5–8

Tips and Warnings: The yew should be planted on Saturday. It is considered very dangerous to cut down a yew. Scott Cunningham recommends a yew, if planted, be placed in the southwest corner. Nearly all parts of the plant, especially the seeds, are poisonous. It is said that no fewer than three British kings were killed by a bow made of yew; on the other hand, Robin Hood was married beneath a yew tree.

Magic: The yew is considered one of the five magical trees of Ireland (the others were an oak and three ash trees) and some Native American tribes regarded yew as the greatest of trees. This is probably because it continues to grow even in extreme old age and often with a hollow trunk. It is an herb of consolation, but more ancient associations connect the yew with death. To fall asleep under a yew tree might mean the sleeper will never awaken. The yew has been used to commune with spirits of the dead and with times gone by, and is said to keep evil spirits away from the beloved deceased. The Celts used sticks of yew for divination, in much the same way the Chinese used yarrow stalks. Yew was also used to dowse for lost objects and to confer invisibility and psychic ability.

Yew can also conjure up fairies and spirits. Fairies are fond of yew trees, and one story tells about the time, they tried to dress it up, first with needles of gold and then with needles of crystal. Both times the experiment failed (The golden needles were stolen and the crystal ones eaten by goats); so the fairies allowed the yew tree to resume its natural and beautiful dark habit. It is a paradoxical plant, symbolic of both practical day-to-day activities and of the final mysteries of death and immortality. In the Victorian language of flowers, the yew is a symbol of resurrection and was used in churches on Palm Sunday and Easter to represent this. Yew is used in death passage rites. *Rites involving yew are most effective when performed at midwinter, Lughnasa. Invoke Hecate, goddess of witches, and Banbha, one of the last great warrior queens and goddess of death. Capricorns seem to have the best luck with it. Choose a time to perform the rite when Saturn is visible. Wear pale clothing. Yew may be carried as an amulet. This tree has strong associations with death and destruction, and should be used with extreme care.*

List of Magical Plant Attributes

1. Acacia: Victory over Death

2. Adder's Tongue: Serpent Deities

3. Agrimony: Unconscious

4. Alder: Unity

5. Alfalfa: Plenty

6. Allspice: Vitality

7. Almond: Duality

8. Aloe: Healing

9. Amaranth: Paradise

10. Anemone: Forsakenness

11. Angelica: General Protection

12. Anise: Handfastings (Weddings)

13. Apple: Desire

14. Arbor Vitae: Cleansing (See also Cedar)

15. Asafetida: Exorcism

16. Ash: Axis Mundi (The World Tree)

17. Asphodel: The Underworld

18. Aster: Mabon

19. Bachelor's Buttons: Release from a Painful Past

20. Bamboo: Flexibility

21. Basil: Reconciliation

22. Bay Laurel: Oracle

23. Beech: Ancient Knowledge

24. Belladonna: Silence

25. Benzoin: Purification

26. Bergamot: Material Success

27. Betony: Home Protection

28.   Birch: Feminine Spirit

29.   Bittersweet: Expulsion

30.   Blackberry: Lughnasa

31.   Black Hellebore: Frenzy

32.   Blackthorn: Darkness

33.   Blessed Thistle: The Mother Goddess

34.   Borage: Courage

35.   Box: Eternity

36.   Bracken Fern: Invisibility

37.   Broom: Wind and Storm

38.   Bryony: Protection Against Lightening

39.   Buckeye: Gamblers

40.   Buckthorn: Elven Wishes

41.   Burdock: Animal Magic

42.   Calendula: Proof Against Demons

43.   Camphor: Release from a Love Affair

44.   Caraway: Attachment

45.   Catnip: Cat Magic

46.   Cedar: Cleansing

47.   Celandine: Escape

48.   Centaury: Chiron, the Centaur

49.   Chamomile: Comfort

50.   Cherry: Youth

51.   Chervil: Communication with Departed Spirits

52.   Chickweed: Bird Magic

53.   Chicory: Overcoming Obstacles

54.   Cinnamon: Energy

55.   Clover: Good Luck

56.   Coltsfoot: Horse Magic

57.   Columbine: Proof Against Envy

58.   Comfrey: Safe Travel

59.   Coriander: Physical Love

60.   Cumin: Domestic Harmony

61. Cypress: Eternal Life
62. Daffodil: Ostara
63. Daisy: Love Divination
64. Damiana: Sexual Attachment
65. Dandelion: Prevision
66. Dill: Discernment
67. Dittany: Spiritual Manifestation
68. Dogwood: Dog Magic
69. Dragon's Blood: Empowerment
70. Echinacea: Strength
71. Elder: Cursing and Blessing
72. Elecampane: Psychic Powers
73. Elm: Shadows
74. Evening Primrose: Hunting Magic
75. Eyebright: Cheerfulness
76. Fennel: Persuasion
77. Fig: Enlightenment
78. Figwort: Health
79. Fir: Winter
80. Flax: Beauty
81. Forget-Me-Not: Remembrance
82. Foxglove: Fairy Folk
83. Frankincense: Consecration
84. Fumitory: Samhain
85. Garlic: Defense Against Vampires
86. German Chamomile: Comfort
87. Ginger: Success
88. Ginseng: Fertility
89. Grape: Celebration
90. Hawthorn: Beltaine
91. Hazel: Insight
92. Heal-all: Bewitchment Protection
93. Heather: Imbolc
94. Hemp: Visions

95.   Henbane: The Damned
96.   Holly: Yule
97.   Hollyhock: Prosperity
98.   Honeysuckle: Balance
99.   Horehound: Spell-Breaking
100.   Houseleek: Safety
101.   Hyacinth: Relaxation
102.   Hydrangea: Spinsterhood
103.   Hyssop: Purification
104.   Iris: Spring
105.   Ivy: Ecstasy
106.   Jasmine: Moon
107.   Juniper: Proof against Witches
108.   Larkspur: Leadership
109.   Lavender: Refreshment
110.   Lemon Balm: Compassion
111.   Lenten Rose: Mental Clarity
112.   Lilac: Recollection of Past Lives
113.   Lily: Purity of Heart
114.   Linden: Soothsaying
115.   Lotus: Spiritual Truth.
116.   Lovage: Legal Victory
117.   Lupin or Lupine: Wolf Magic
118.   Male Fern: Rainbringer
119.   Mandrake: Fertility
120.   Marigold (Tagetes): Proof Against Minor Demons
121.   Marjoram: Joy
122.   Meadowsweet: Summer
123.   Mistletoe: Druids
124.   Monkshood: Astral Projection
125.   Moonwort: Unlocking
126.   Mugwort: Clairvoyance
127.   Mullein: Light in Darkness
128.   Myrrh: Sacrifice

129.   Myrtle: Creativity

130.   Nettle: Banishment

131.   Oak: Masculine Spirit

132.   Olive: Peace

133.   Oregano: Proof Against Satanic Influence

134.   Parsley: Dark Forces

135.   Pennyroyal: Calming

136.   Peony: Honor

137.   Peppermint: Change

138.   Periwinkle: Wizards and Sorcerers

139.   Pine: Dispelling Negativity.

140.   Pomegranate: Sexuality

141.   Poplar: Sympathy

142.   Poppy: Dreams

143.   Potentilla: Power

144.   Primrose: Inner Beauty

145.   Purslane: Night Protection

146.   Rose: Romance

147.   Rosemary: Self-Confidence

148.   Rowan: Empowerment

149.   Rue: Witches

150.   Saffron: Luxury

151.   Sage: Wisdom.

152.   St. John's Wort: Litha (Midsummer)

153.   Sandalwood: Spirituality

154.   Southernwood: Seduction

155.   Sunflower: Sun

156.   Tansy: Repulsion

157.   Thistle: Autumn

158.   Thyme: Resolve

159.   Valerian: Transformation

160.   Vervain: Enchantment

161.   Violet: Immortal Love

162.   Walnut: Secret Treasure

The Gardener's Year

"There are no finalities in nature. Everything is streaming."
(Ralph Waldo Emerson, *Journals*)

The true gardener welcomes the regular tasks that connect her to the earth and its fruits. If ever there was labor of love, garden work provides it. Just as a garden is never "done," neither are you. "To the attentive eye, each moment of the year has its own beauty, and in the same field, it beholds, every hour, a picture which was never seen before and which shall never be seen again" (Ralph Waldo Emerson, *Journals*).

And while it used to be simple to list plants in the order of bloom, today's many cultivars give gardeners a choice, to some extent; you can command your own bloom schedule.   Pore over those plant catalogs carefully. If you want daffodils from early March until mid-May, you can have them by ordering the right varieties.

Early Spring:

Do: Clean up the remnants of winter, which may include nipping back on such hardy weeds as chickweed, which however magical it may be, is still a nuisance. Clean out the remains of leaves and sticks and McDonald's wrappers that have unaccountably blossomed in the garden. Fertilize bulbs. If you are starting tender plants from seed, you'll need to do it indoors, using a sterile growing medium. (Seedlings are susceptible to many diseases.) Grow as directed, making sure the seedling have enough light and are not over-fertilized. Turn the compost pile! Take soil tests if needed.

Enjoy: March/April is the season for spring-flowering bulbs, the first plants that appear after the winter snows. Rock gardens are in their glory. Even the casual gardener cannot tire of the rhythmic procession of snowdrops, crocus, and Siberian squills. Then come the daffodils, those spring giants who trumpet their yellow way into the consciousness of even the most nature-dead soul. The perennials are beginning to green up as well. Other magical early flowers include anemones, primroses, violets, periwinkle and hellebore.

Mid and Late Spring:

Do: Lightly fertilize perennials; prune forsythias and lilacs after flowering, divide perennials, prepare beds, cut off dying flowers of spring bulbs, but leave the foliage; fertilize roses; divide crowded summer and fall-blooming plants. Plant out bare-rooted roses and hardy annuals and perennials. Stake delphinium and lilies if needed. Remove spent flowers, but don't cut back on the foliage.

Enjoy: Flax, forget-me-nots, crested iris, alliums, iris, yarrow, anemone, dianthus, potentilla, violets, peonies, phlox, bachelor's buttons.

Early Summer:

Do: Set out tender plants (after last frost); weed, mulch.

Enjoy: Astilbe, larkspur, lilies, poppies, thyme, catnip.

Summer:

Do: Weed; deadhead; water; control bugs; stake later blooming tall plants; divide and replant daylilies and lilies, poppies, irises, and primroses. Re-blooming roses should be fertilized in late summer to encourage fall bloom; order new bulbs for fall planting. In warmer areas you can plant new bulbs.

Enjoy: Hollyhocks, astilbes, phlox, dahlia, yarrow, cranesbill, roses, geranium, monkshood, some species of phlox and lily, hibiscus, monarda, lobelia, centaury, veronica.

Early Fall:

Do: Plant new bulbs; fertilize old bulbs. Don't throw away those raked leaves. Use them for winter mulch!

Enjoy: Asters, chrysanthemum, aconitum.

Late Fall:

Do: Over-winter tender plants; clean up. Prune appropriate plants.

Early Winter:

"The leafless trees become spires of flame in the sunset, with the blue east for their background, and the stars of the dead calices of flowers, and every withered stem and stubble rimed with frost, contribute something to the mute music." (Emerson *"Nature"*)

Do: Mulch.

Enjoy: If you want blooms all year round, and live in a cold climate, think about bringing your garden indoors for the winter. In milder climates, you can enjoy lupine, dianthus, some varieties of poppy, phlox, pansies, primroses, and calendula.

Late winter:

Do: Prune appropriate plants. Check out the garden for signs of plant heaving and replace soil around exposed roots.

Enjoy: Pore over seed catalogs and dream of spring. It's coming!

Divination or Fortune-telling with Magic Plants

One special kind of herbal magic is that of divination or fortune telling. The art of fortune-telling with herbs goes by the general technical name *botanomancy*. However, botanomancy has several sub-varieties including: *phyllomancy* (telling fortunes by means of reading the veins in leaves); *phyllorhodomancy* (reading rose petal and leaves); *causinomancy* (burning herbs for divination purposes), which may include *capnomancy* (reading the smoke patterns produced by burning herbs). Using laurel wood or leaves for this purposes is specifically known as *daphnomancy*, although the inventors of the process, the Babylonians, used cedar. The name comes from Daphne, a Greek nymph who was turned into a laurel tree.

The Druids used oak branches and mistletoe in special kind of tree-divination called *dendromancy*. (Although *dendro-* is a prefix meaning "tree" in general, the word is usually reserved for using oak or mistletoe for this purpose.)

In general, when the material burns quickly, it is considered a good omen. It is also considered a good sign when the smoke rises quickly to heaven; having it hang around the altar is not favorable.

Crithomancy is using grain (usually barley) and flour for divination. The paste of cakes is offered up as a sacrifice, and then closely examined for the sought-for answers.

Sortelege is divination using pebbles or nuts. *Augury* uses the movements of birds and animals. *Geomancy* uses sand or earth.

Nor should we forget *tasseography*, which is the art of reading tealeaves. This is a complex specialty in itself, and is traditionally done with the classic tea plant *Camellia spp.* Two common traditions associated with tea: bubbles forming on the top mean money is coming; a floating piece of tea stem suggests the arrival of a visitor (soft stems signify a woman, hard stems a man). In addition, there are a number of precautions to be taken with tea to avoid bad luck: always stir it clockwise, don't allow two persons to pour out of the same teapot, and add sugar before milk.

Glossary

Ahura Mazda: The good, wise god of Zoroastrians, the lord of the light.

Aine: Celtic goddess, queen of the fairies.

Alternate: Leave arranged successively on opposite sides of the stem.

Anaphrodisiac: Reduces sexual desire.

Anesthetic: Dulls pain.

Annual: Plant that completes its life cycle year – from germination to death – within one.

Anther: Terminal part of the stamens in a flower; contains pollen grains.

Aphrodisiac: Causes sexual arousal.

Aromatic: Agreeable, distinctive, stimulating fragrance. Usually describes the fragrance of parts other than the flower.

Axil: Usually, the angle between the leaf and stem.

Balder: The beautiful god of light and vegetation in Norse myth, killed by mistletoe.

Basal: At the base of the stem.

Bast: Egyptian cat goddess.

Belenos: Celtic god in charge of cattle and sheep.

Beltaine (Beltane): May Day celebration. Ultimate spring festival when sexual and reproductive powers are at their height. It is not entirely a benign month, however, and in ancient times, sacrifices (sometimes human) were performed to ensure the fertility of the year.

Biennial: A plant that completes its life cycle with two years, growing in the first year and flowering and fruiting in the second year.

Blodewedd, also Blodeuweth: Celtic goddess of spring.

Bract: Small leaf or scale like structure from the axil of which a flower cluster may arise.

Bran: Celtic (especially Welsh) deity.

Brighid also Bride: Ancient Irish sun and river goddess, associated with spring. Daughter of Dagda.

Brigantia: Ancient English sun and river goddess. Sometimes known as "The High One." Associated with spring.

Cachet: Crushed or powdered herbs (usually unpleasant tasting) put into a capsule for easy swallowing.

Calyx: The outer whorl of the parts of a flower, either in one piece or divided into sepals.

Candlemas: See Imbolc.

Capsule: A dry fruit with one or more seeds.

Cardea: Italian goddess of childbirth.

Cerealia: Feast honoring Ceres and celebrated in mid-June.

Christmas: See Yule.

Cordate: Heart-shaped, usually referring to leaves.

Cultivar: A variety of plant that was produced by natural species and maintained by cultivation.

Cybele: Mother goddess.

Dagda: Celtic deity of complete knowledge, father of the gods.

Deciduous: Said of tree or shrub that loses its leaves in the winter.

Drupe: Fleshy fruit with one or more seed encapsulated by a stony layer.

Etain: Celtic sun goddess.

Fall Equinox: September 22 or 23. Celebration of grains, breads, and cakes, as we welcome the fall. In contemporary times, this is not the rather ominous holiday it once was. Most people have been sweltering all summer, and welcome the return of crisp weather, and the opening of schools. For many people it signals a beginning rather than an end. Indeed, in the ancient Middle East, the fall festivals coincided with the New Year, as in Rosh Hashanah, rather than having the year begin in spring as in the Celtic tradition. The rule seems to be that where winter is a true hardship, the New Year begins in spring. Where it is not (or where it is a welcome respite), the New Year begins in autumn.

Family: Group of related genera.

Faunus: Greek/Roman god of meadows, shepherds and prophecy. Leader of the fauns, who look like humans except for their tails, pointed ears, horns and cloven feet.

Flora: Roman goddess of gardens and flowers.

Floralia: Festival celebrated April 28 till the beginning of May.

Floret: Small flower in a flower head.

Freya: Norse goddess of love.

Friga (also Frigg, Frigga): Scandinavian goddess of the sky. She knows the future of humankind but will not reveal it.

Fruit: Ripe seeds and their surrounding structures.

Gaea: Greek goddess of the earth, marriage, death, and afterlife. She is the first-born child of Chaos.

Glabrous: Smooth, not hairy.

Green Corn Ceremony: Native American feast occurring in July, marking a new year. A bonfire, partly fueled with young years of corn is lit. It is the time when all debts and grievances are forgiven, and a new start is available for everyone.

Guan-Yin also Kuan-Yin: Chinese goddess of mercy.

Gwydon: Celtic god of arts, magic, and civilization.

Halloween: See Samhain.

Handfasting: Marriage

Hathor: Egyptian goddess of the sky, love, and joy.

Hecate: Greek goddess of magic and death. Goddess of witches. Associated with the Underworld.

Helios: Greek sun god.

Herne: Ancient British hunter-god,

Hex: A witch's spell.

Hexagram: Six-sided figure formed of two interlocking triangles.

Hyacinthus: Spring flower god worshipped in ancient Greece. Also called Narcissus, Antheus, or Adonis.

Hybrid: A plant produced by the cross fertilization of two different species.

Imbolc (Candlemas): A feast of purification, falling 40 days after Christmas, on February 2. Biblical law proclaimed that women had to be purified 40 days after the birth of a son. However, February 1 was holy long before this. Februus was a Roman god who presided over purifications, particularly those associated with death. The entire month of February was sacred to him. In Roman times Lupercalia also occurred during February. Christians renamed February 2, Candlemas, or the Purification of the Virgin Mary. (The Council of Trullus tried to stamp out the whole festival, opining that the Virgin Mary was unpolluted and so needed no purification.) Today, of course, in the US the same day is Groundhog Day, and is still a celebration of the light. On this day, by age-old custom, the gardener look for hints about the upcoming growing season. It was decided (on what principle I am unable to determine) that if Imbolc (or Candlemas or Groundhog Day) were sunny, winter – would continue for a further period. If it is showery, spring is on the way.

Irene: Greek goddess of peace.

Iris: Greek goddess of the rainbow.

Ishtar: Babylonian/Assyrian goddess of love, fertility, spring, and the earth.

Isis: Egyptian goddess of women, the sister and wife of Osiris.

Lakshmi: Hindu goddess of beauty and wealth.

Lanceolate: Said of narrow leaves that taper.

Latex: Milky fluid exuded from some plants.

Laxative: An agent promoting evacuation of the bowels.

Leaflet: A subdivision of a compound leaf.

Litha: Midsummer or Summer Solstice. Some older calendars considered them to be the same day, in fact, and sometimes it is unclear which day is meant when the old records refer to "Midsummer," which, one would think would be later in the year, if by "midsummer" one means the "the middle of summer." However, summer for the Celts comprised different months than it does for us. Luckily, there is plenty of magic to go around for both days.

Lugh: Celtic god of arts and crafts.

Lughnasa: This Celtic feast, occurring August 1, is an early harvest festival. Blackberry pies are traditional. It is a joyful time, but tinged with the consciousness that fall and winter are coming.

Mabon: Fall Equinox.

Méan Earraigh: Spring Equinox.

Michael: Powerful warrior archangel.

Mithras: Persian god of war, justice, and order, heavenly light, and discipline.

Nectar: sugary liquid produced by many plants.

Nix: German fresh water spirits, with human bodies and the tails of fish. They can assume other shapes and even become invisible.

Nut: Dry, one seeded fruit.

Ogma: Irish warrior credited with the Ogham Tree Alphabet.

Olwen: Celtic goddess, daughter of Yspaddaden Pencawr, or Giant Hawthorn.

Opposite: Growing in pairs at the same level on opposite sides of the stem, usually referring to leaves.

Ostara: Spring Equinox. The name of the festival is derived from the Germanic goddess Ostara, otherwise given as variously given as Eostra, Eostrae, Eostre, Eástre and Austra. A word derived from her name is "estrus" meaning heat in animals.

Ovate: Egg shaped.

Persephone: Queen of the Underworld and wife of Hades.

Petiole: Leaf stalk.

Pinnate: Leaf with three or more pairs of leaflets arranged in two opposite rows along a common stalk.

Potion: Herbal tea or brew.

Poultice: Herbs mixed with hot water or made into a warm paste and spread on a cloth or towel, and then applied to an inflamed or painful body part.

Prajapati: Hindu god of life and creation.

Ra: Egyptian Sun god.

Rammon: Middle Eastern god.

Sachet: Cloth bag filled with herbs.

Talisman: Magical object usually consisting of magical symbols, letters, or characters, either written on parchment or engraved on metal. They are carried or worn to protect the owner from danger.

Tincture: A liquid produced by soaking ground-up plant materials (leaves, roots, etc) in ethyl alcohol or in apple cider vinegar to produce a scented liquid.

St. John's Day: June 24, the feast day of John Baptist, the oldest saint's day in the calendar of the Catholic Church. Also called Midsummer. Traditionally, Midsummer's Eve is the time to light a bonfire of powerful magical protection. Herbs that may be included in the bonfire include chamomile, fennel, figwort, hawthorn, mugwort, male fern, and St. John's wort. Other plants that have special powers on Midsummer's Eve or Day include elder, dogwood, dandelion, chicory, cherry, hemp, larkspur, mistletoe, stonecrop, and violet. There are literally hundreds of spells and magical rites that gain singular power on this day. Here's just one example – an old marriage divination ceremony. At midnight on Midsummer's Eve, walk backwards into the garden and pick the reddest rose in full bloom. (If you have hybrid teas rather than old English roses for which the ceremony was intended, a Chrysler Imperial or Mr. Lincoln will work just fine. Wrap the rose in a clean white cloth and keep it hidden. Bring it out on Yule and place it on your bosom. The man who takes it away (what's left of it) will be your husband.

St. Swithin's Day (July 15): If it rains on St. Swithin's Day, it will rain for the rest of the summer. If it doesn't, it won't. This is, personally, my favorite holiday.

Samhain, (Halloween): A cluster of varying religious traditions surrounds this ancient holiday. For the Celts it was Samhain, coming at the very end of harvest time, and marking the beginning of the dark days of winter. It is sacred to the departed spirits. In one Celtic tradition the New Year commences at midnight on October 31. It is a time to light bonfires, and in ancient times people jumped through the flames for good luck. During this night, also, the spirits of the dead are allowed to wander freely. Fairies and other little people also make free this night. More ominously, demons and evil spirits may also be abroad. The old custom of Trick or Treat is meant to placate these spirits, as well as those who masquerade in their costumes – partly to get some free candy, but also to blend in with the spirits so as not to be harassed by them. In the Christian tradition, it is the feast of All Hallows Eve. November 1 is All Saints Day, and November 2 is All Souls' Day. In some traditions, the parade of souls continues for three nights: October 31, November 1, and November 2. A comparable celebration in Mexico is *El dia de los Luertos*, "the Day of the Dead." A flower associated with this remembrance is the marigold (*Tagetes*), the *cempasuchil* or "flower of the dead." The strong-smelling yellow and orange blooms are strung into garlands and strewn upon the earth, marking a trail from the home to the cemetery. The coxcomb (*Celosia*), an ornamental strain of grain amaranth is also used during this time. Originally, the locals used the native amaranth (*Amaranthus retroflexus*) to make a seedcake, in which the seeds represented the gods. However, the Catholic Church found the accompanying ceremony disconcertingly like the consecration of bread at the mass, and encouraged the use of the less offensive celosia instead. Carnations and gladioli are also popular flowers during this time.

Sekmet: Egyptian lion-headed goddess of war, retribution, and the destructive power of the sun.

Somnos: Roman god of sleep.

Tammuz: Babylonian sun god.

Taranis, also Tannus: The Celtic god of thunderstorms.

Thanatos: Greek god of death.

Thoth: Egyptian god of time and learning.

Walpurgisnacht: May Eve – so called in Germany.

Wassailing: A ceremony in which carolers sing to the apple trees, blessing them and pouring libations on the roots.

Yantra: In Hindu or Buddhist thought, a diagram or graphic design used to aid meditation and focus the mind.

Yggdrasil: The Norse world-tree.

Yule (December 25): In some places, Winter Solstice and Yule are celebrated as one holiday, but they can also be separated. For the ancient Romans, the entire month of December was held sacred both to Saturn and to Sol, the sun god. The Yule log (preferably oak, ash, or beech) should be a gift from a friend or else a log from your own land. Buying a Yule log is extremely bad luck. A libation of hard cider or ale is poured on the log, which is adorned with greenery before it is burned. Corn or wheat flour can be sprinkled on the log also, as an offering to the harvest spirits. The log should be allowed to smolder until Twelfth Night (January 5). The ashes should be preserved to mix with the topsoil for next year's garden. Retain a sprig of Christmas holly all the following year for good luck. On Twelfth Night wassailing apple trees will banish evil spirits.

A Note on Incense

Most magical plants can be burned as incense. The individual incenses have their own magical significance, but most function under one of the following broad categories:

Invocative – To attract spirits

Exorcistic – To drive away spirits

Somnolent – To bring drowsiness and sleep

Illuminative – To help the practitioner meditate or enter a state of psychic awareness

The same herb, depending on the quantity, mode of preparation or length of time burned, may have all these attributes. In general, sweet-smelling herbs draw good spirits and exorcize bad, and vice versa, but there are exceptions.

Resources

Bell, C. Ritchie and Anne H. Lindsey. *Fall Color and Woodland Harvests.* Chapel Hill, NC: Laurel Hill Press, 1990.

Boland, Maureen and Bridget. *Old Wives' Lore for Gardeners.* New York: Farrar, Strauss, and Giroux, 1976.

Bricknell, Christopher, ed. *Royal Horticultural Society A – Z Encyclopedia of Garden Plants.* London: Dorling Kindersley, 1996.

Bunney, Sarah, ed. *The Illustrated Book of Herbs: Their Medicinal and Culinary Uses.* New York: Gallery Books, 1984.

Culpeper, Nicholas. *Complete Herbal.* Ware, Hertfordshire: Wordsworth, 1995 reprint.

Cox, Jeff and Marilyn Cox: *The Perennial Garden: Color Harmonies through the Seasons.* Emmaus, PA: Rodale Press, 1985.

Crawford, E.A. *The Lunar Garden: Planting by the Moon Phases.* New York: Cynthia Parzych Publishing, 1989.

Cunningham, Scott. *Magical Herbalism.* St. Paul: Llewellyn Publications, 2002.

DeWolf et al: *Taylor's Guide to Bulbs.* Boston: Houghton Mifflin Company, 1986.

Don, Montagu. *The Sensuous Garden.* New York: Simon and Schuster. 1997.

Duke, James A. *Herbs of the Bible.* Loveland, CO: Interweave Press, 1999.

Dunwich, Gerina.
Herbal Magick. Franklin Lakes NJ: New Page Books, 2002.
Wicca Garden. New York: Citadel Press, 1996.

Eberhard, Wolfram. *A Dictionary of Chinese Symbols.* London and New York: Routledge, 1986.

Essential Gardening Encyclopedia. San Francisco: Fog City Press, 2003.

Gardening for Fragrance. Brooklyn Botanic Garden Record, 1989.

Greer, John Michael. *Natural Magic: Potions and Powers from the Magical Garden.* St. Paul: Llewellyn, 2000.

Grieve, Mrs. M. *A Modern Herbal.* Harmondsworth, Middlesex: Penguin Books, 1984 reprint.

Griffin, Judy. *Mother Nature's Herbal.* New York: Gramercy Books. 1997.

Grimassai, Raven. *Italian Witchcraft: The Old Religion of Southern Europe.* St. Paul: Llewellyn, 2003.

Halpin, Anne. *Year-Round Flower Garden.* Upper Saddle River, NJ: Creative Homeowner, no date.

Harper, Pamela J. *Designing with Perennials.* New York: Sterling Publishing, 2001.

Hopman, Ellen Evert. *A Druid's Herbal for the Sacred Year.* Rochester, VT: Destiny Books, 1995.

Houdret, Jessica. *Practical Herb Garden.* London: Hermes House, 2003.

Knopf, Jim, et al. *A Guide to Natural Gardening.* San Francisco: Fog City Press, 1997.

Little, Elbert. *The Audubon Society Field Guide to North American Trees (Eastern Region).* New York: Alfred A. Knopf, 1980.

Lunardi, Contanza. *Simon and Schuster's Guide to Shrubs and Vines and Other Small Ornamentals.* New York: Simon and Schuster, 1987.

Macunovich, Janet. *Easy Garden Design.* Pownal, VT: Storey Communications, 1992.

Martin, Laura C. *Wildflower Folklore.* Chaclotte, NC: East Woods Press, 1984.

Moore, Abd al-Hayy. *Zen Rock Gardening.* Philadelphia. Running Press. 1992.

Morrison, Dorothy. *Bud, Blossom, and Leaf: The Magical Herb Gardener's Handbook.* St. Paul: Llewellyn, 2001.

Moura, Ann. *Green Witchcraft: Folk Magic, Fairy Lore, and Herb Craft.* St Paul: Llewellyn, 2003.

Niering, William A. *The Audubon Society Field Guide to North American Wildflowers (Eastern Region).* New York: Alfred A. Knopf, 1979.

Paterson, Jacqueline Memory. *Tree Wisdom: The Definitive Guidebook.* London: Thorsons, 1996.

Phillips, Roger. *Trees in Britain, Europe and North America.* London: Pan Books, 1978.

Reader's Digest Encyclopaedia of Garden Plants and Flowers. London: Readers Digest Assocation, 1985.

Rose, Francis. *The Wildflower Key, British Isles – Europe*. London: Frederick Warne, 1981.

Shafer, Violet. *Herbcraft*. San Francisco: Yerba Buena Press, 1971.

Sinnes, A. Cort. *How to Select and Care for Shrubs and Hedges*. San Ramon, CA: Ortho Books. No date.

Swenson, Allan A. *Herbs of the Bible and How to Grow Them*. New York: Citadel. 2003.

Swerdlow, Joel L. *Nature's Medicine: Plants that Heal*. Washington D.C. National Geographic.

Treasury of Gardening. Lincolnwood, Illinois: Publications International, LTD.

Vitale, Alice Thomas. *Leaves in Myth, Magic, and Medicine*. New York: Stewart, Tabori, and Chang, 1997.

Wells, Diana: *100 Flowers and How They Got Their Names*. Chapel Hill, NC: Algonquin Books, 1997.

Wylundt's Book of Incense. York Beach, ME: Weiser, 1996.

Conclusion

Saint Francis was at work in his garden, hoeing. A visitor, who apparently thought that Francis should have his mind on higher things, indignantly asked him what he would do if he discovered the world would end the following day. Without a pause in his work, the good Saint responded, "I'd keep hoeing." Care for the earth until the end of time.

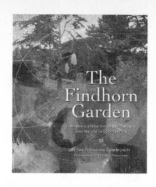

The Findhorn Garden

Pioneering a New Vision for Humanity and Nature in Cooperation

by The Findhorn Community

208 pp pbk

ISBN 1-84409-018-3

Over 40 years ago, on windswept and barren sand dunes in the far north east of Scotland, a miracle was occurring. The most wonderful plants, flowers, trees and organic vegetables were growing to enormous sizes in a small plot around a thirty-foot caravan trailer inhabited by three adults and three children living on £8 a week unemployment benefit. Guidance by God and absolute faith in the art of manifestation led them to this apparently unlikely place to create a magnetic centre which, they were told, would draw people from all over the world. Their discovery of how to contact and cooperate with nature spirits and devas made the seemingly impossible possible. The Findhorn phenomenon had begun.

Today, that same caravan stands in tribute to the pioneering faith of its former residents, amid a thriving village housing hundreds of people from all over the world; alongside an organisation recognised internationally as a leading centre for spiritual learning, and surrounded by innovative and ecological businesses. The garden has expanded and spawned a huge organic farming initiative feeding hundreds of people.

The Findhorn Community is a living demonstration of what can come about when man co-operates with nature and the beings of higher worlds; when people are united by a common goal based on social, spiritual and ecological values. The Findhorn garden is where it all started and this book explores the relationships with angelic realms and devas which first gained the community international recognition, while also looking at the wider work of the community and its huge impact upon all who visit.

About Findhorn Press...

Findhorn Press was born in 1971 when the demand for the guidance of Eileen Caddy (one of the founders of the world famous Findhorn community) was so great that it was decided to publish it as a bound book: God Spoke to Me *was launched and is still in print today! This was followed by many other books by Eileen Caddy, as well as several meditations tapes. Her latest title is the new (2002) expanded version of her autobiography,* Flight Into Freedom and Beyond.

In 1994 Findhorn Press was purchased by Thierry and Karin Bogliolo, two long-term community members, and it has been run and developed as an independent publishing house since then. Its main office is still on the Findhorn campus but thanks to high speed internet connections several of its employees live in other parts of the world.

Findhorn Press has grown tremendously since it became independent, and publishes works by Diana Cooper, Martin Brofman, James F. Twyman, Marko Pogacnik, Darren Main, John Stowe, Jack Temple, David Lawson, Judy Hall and many others. While many of our authors are living or have lived in the Findhorn community, the others share the spiritual vision which is congruent with its core principles and practices.

Findhorn Press strives to bring healing and hope into our world. We seek to inspire and educate and inform our readers in every corner of the Earth — many of our books are published in several languages. Thank you for joining us on our journey into a positive and heart-centered future.

www.findhornpress.com

For further information about the Findhorn Foundation and the Findhorn Community,
please contact:

Findhorn Foundation
The Visitors Centre
The Park, Findhorn IV36 3TZ, Scotland, UK
tel 01309 690311
enquiries@findhorn.org
www.findhorn.org

for a complete Findhorn Press catalogue, please contact:

Findhorn Press
305a The Park, Findhorn
Forres IV36 3TE
Scotland, UK
tel 01309 690582
fax 01309 690036
info@findhornpress.com
www.findhornpress.com